**Apartheid
and social research**

Apartheid
and social research

Edited and introduced
by John Rex

The Unesco Press

The authors are responsible for the choice and the presentation of the facts contained in this book and for the opinions expressed therein, which are not necessarily those of Unesco and do not commit the Organization.

The designations employed and the presentation of material throughout this publication do not imply the expression of any opinion whatsoever on the part of Unesco concerning the legal status of any country, territory, city or area or of its authorities, or concerning the delimitation of its frontiers or boundaries.

Published in 1981 by the United Nations Educational, Scientific and Cultural Organization
7 place de Fontenoy, 75700 Paris
Printed by Imprimeries Réunies, Lausanne

ISBN 92-3-101898-1

© Unesco 1981
Printed in Switzerland

Preface

This book, *Apartheid and Social Research,* was commissioned by Unesco as part of its contribution to International Anti-Apartheid Year. It differs, however, from other Unesco projects on apartheid in that the study forms part of Unesco's collaboration with international non-governmental social science organizations. As such, the book reflects not only the situation of the social sciences under the apartheid regime in South Africa but also the preoccupations of the international social science community.

The study was undertaken for Unesco by the Research Committee for Ethnic Minorities of the International Sociological Association, of which Professor John Rex, himself born in South Africa, is chairman. All the chapters are by South African social scientists, most of them still working within the republic. It is not surprising, therefore, that there should be some overlapping. We have decided not to edit this out, since, while the elimination of some repetition may indeed produce a more elegant manuscript, no article treats the available material in exactly the same way and it is precisely the accumulation of 'evidence' that permits the reader to assess the effects of apartheid in the social sciences. These effects are not confined only to the text. The ratio of Black writers to White writers is in itself symptomatic of a situation in which there are relatively few Black trained social scientists. The fact that one chapter is signed 'Anonymous' indicates the practical effect of political repression within the republic on the publication of academic work. If most of the book is on access to training and access to research, it is because the whole question of theory becomes secondary in a situation where the main problem is maintaining some research under conditions of sharp conflict and within the restrictions of White supremacy kept in place by draconian legislation and by force.

Some of the information in this book, while new, will not be surprising to those familiar with the workings of apartheid. It will come as no shock to many to find that Blacks are unequally represented as social scientists, that they are more than that—they are often simply absent both in terms of power and in terms of numbers. The trek abroad of South African social scientists is also well known by the world social science community. It is not unexpected that bannings should affect social scientists, that researchers should be harassed by the South African police, that research notes could be confiscated, etc. These facts, suspected, take on however a new significance when they are related as they are in this book, by those who have for years lived with them. The book therefore is a witness to the all-pervading nature of the system of apartheid, even where, as in most of the chapters, the writers are in no sense militant opponents of the present South Africa and in no way whatsoever linked to the liberation movements.

The book is also of interest to social scientists who are interested in the problems of the social sciences *per se*. For it is in South Africa that issues, often muted in more 'free' societies, are seen at their sharpest.

Social scientists are, everywhere, engaged in finding funding for their research, or for research in general. This has been the case particularly in recent years when there has been, in many countries, a cut-back on resource allocations to university research. South African social scientists, like their counterparts in other parts of the world need funds if they are to pursue research. Funding comes, as in most other countries, principally from the government, and from major business enterprises; in the case of South Africa from mining interests. It is not at all surprising that this research is predominantly geared, directly or indirectly, towards implementing the policies of the government and of the private sector. 'Policy-oriented social sciences' may not necessarily mean implementing the obvious aspects of apartheid. It may 'only' mean designing effective criteria for the 'scientific' selection of African labour in line with modern management techniques. An anthropologist may be called upon, not to create apartheid institutions, but only to do research into 'tribal' culture or into 'tribal' boundaries. At this level the 'problem' is relatively simple: in the final analysis he who pays the piper calls the tune—but it is not without implications for the question of 'objective' science. This is particularly so in the social sciences where the links between pure and applied, between science and technology, are not as well elaborated as in the natural sciences.

It becomes obvious, however, even in the comparison of slant between White writers and Black writers within this volume, that the question is much more complex. Trained in the *same* sciences, the ranking given to the *same* facts are quite different, and the salience given to the racial factor is not the same. Moreover, as if to emphasize the problem, an analysis of what is researched in the republic illustrates that the questions asked, the choices in the 'free' selection of research topics, follow closely the evolution of and the social conflicts within, South African society. The effects of apartheid turn out to be not simply the direct results of discrimination or of repressions, but to be also indirectly articulated through informal selection, through the production and reproduction of a certain knowledge. Obviously this is of interest beyond the borders of the republic.

John Rex who introduces the volume and who is its editor underlines the issues apartheid presents to the social scientist and places the question within the broader context of the social responsibility of the social scientist.

While Unesco has sponsored this volume, it must be emphasized that the Secretariat does not necessarily share the opinions of the writers. Indeed, it is important that each writer speaks from his own viewpoint if the debate that is needed is to proceed.

Contents

1. **Introduction**   John Rex   11

2. **Social research in a divided society:
   the case of South Africa**
   David Welsh   27

3. **Constraints on, and functions of, research
   in sociology and psychology in contemporary South Africa**
   Michael Savage   45

4. **Anthropological research in contemporary
   South Africa**   Michael Whisson   67

5. **Servants of apartheid?—A survey of social research
   into industry in South Africa**   E. Webster   85

6. **The vocation of a sociologist in South Africa**
   Heribert Adam   115

7. **Social research and the Black academic
   in South Africa**   Anonymous   129

8. **The Black universities in South Africa**
   Marcus Malusi Balintulo   141

9. **The Black Consciousness movement
   and social research**   Nyameko Pityana   161

10. **Structural and cultural factors in a liberated
    South Africa**   John Rex   185

1 Introduction

John Rex
Director, Social Science Research
Council Research Unit on
Ethnic Relations, University of
Aston in Birmingham (United Kingdom)

It is probably true to say that when the present study was commissioned, both those who commissioned it and those who were to carry it out saw the task as a relatively simple and unambiguous one. Apartheid was nearly universally agreed to be an evil form of racial despotism and, in common with other types of despotism, was thought to preclude the possibility of social research; itself thought of as a wholly desirable process through which truth could be revealed and justice achieved.

It hardly needs recalling here that racial segregation and White racial supremacy have been of the essence of the political and social structure of the Union of South Africa since its inception in 1910. The Union was only achieved after the British Government of the day had agreed to accept the Boer Republic of the Transvaal and the Orange Free State and, for that matter, the British Colony of Natal into union with the Cape without requiring them to accept even the qualified franchise for non-Whites which existed in the Cape. Black and Coloured voters in the Union could therefore only act as a pressure group, whereas the two-thirds majority of both Parliamentary houses required to amend the Constitution was easily obtainable by the White voters.

The history of the Union is a history of the use of White legislative power progressively to deprive Blacks, Coloureds and Indians of rights which they enjoyed in the economic, residential, industrial and political spheres. Thus:
1. The Native Land Act divided up the land so that the Black population (about four-fifths of the total) were confined to one-fifth of the land.
2. The Native Urban Areas Act required that all Africans (Black Bantu) were to have passes and to reside only in scheduled areas, called locations, in the towns.
3. The Mines and Works Act made it illegal to employ Blacks in skilled jobs in the mines and public works and the accompanying Industrial Conciliation Act made it possible for Industrial Councils of White employers and unions to reserve skilled work for Whites.

4. General Smuts' South African Party was able to merge with the more moderate Nationalists under General Hertzog only after agreeing to collaborate in removing African voters from the common roll and replacing them with three White representatives who would speak for them in an Assembly of 163.

The election of the Nationalist Government on an explicit programme of apartheid in 1948 was not so much the result of a desire to institute a new social system as of fear on the part of the electorate that Smuts, emancipated by the war from his alliance with Hertzog, would undermine existing patterns of segregation, basically because he wished to placate the demand of the mine-owners and other employers for cheaper unskilled labour.

The first Nationalist Governments of Malan and Strijdom, however, did have a legislative programme which went beyond that of the United Party. On the one hand they sought to extend urban residential and national and local political segregation to the Cape Coloured and Indian populations and, on the other, they set out to suppress all organizations (especially African organizations) which, by their teaching and activity, threatened the status quo.

So far as segregation went, the Nationalist Governments of the 1950s were primarily concerned with removing those few African property-owners who had acquired property in White areas before the Urban Areas Act, with rationalizing and systematizing the procedures for the control of urban migration and with creating Coloured and Indian urban areas. The main effort of these governments, however, was devoted to dealing with subversion (meaning, for them, the undermining of White racial supremacy) either through political activity or through the development of education.

Civil disobedience, which was the weapon used to resist the government by the African National Congress in the early 1950s, was ruthlessly dealt with by the application of criminal sanctions of a draconian sort and, to deal more generally with opposition, the Suppression of Communism Act was introduced wherein any proposal to change the constitution by other than Parliamentary means or by any which might further the objects of communism was defined as 'communism'. Many hundreds of individuals, including a minority of Whites, were imprisoned or banned under the Act and as the need to root out resistance increased in the 1960s, many legal safeguards against imprisonment without trial were eliminated. Increasingly, the apartheid state had the appearance of a police state.

If what European sociologists call the 'repressive state apparatus' was strengthened, however, attention was also given to the 'ideological state apparatus'. Most notably this involved the separation of African education from the ordinary educational system and from missionary control and placing it under a special Department of Bantu Education. This department, it was made clear, would see to it that African children were not educated to aspire to equality with Whites. According to the doctrine of Christian National Education each national group should have its own special education including, in the case of the Afrikaner ruling group,

Afrikaner history and Afrikaner biology, but, in the case of the 'Bantu', the Afrikaners would exercise trusteeship. The emphasis in Bantu education, designed as it was to perpetuate inferiority, was on primary education, but, since even a helot nation needed some professional servicing, the idea of Bantu secondary and higher education had to be conceded and provision had to be made to ensure that this education was kept separate and segregated from the subversive and universalist ideas around which university education particularly was built. The main theme of educational policy thus became the administration of an increasingly recalcitrant secondary and higher education sector for Africans to ensure that education did not mean subversion.

We shall return to the question of Bantu education as we explore the meaning of 'social research'. Here we see that a special meaning attaches to the very term 'education' itself as a part of the policy of apartheid. Before we turn to this second term, however, we must note that, from the accession to power of Dr Hendrik Verwoerd as Prime Minister, the meaning of 'apartheid' itself underwent significant development and was to continue developing.

The emphasis of the Malan and Strijdom Governments had been much more upon the maintenance of White supremacy than it had been upon racial and ethnic segregation. Malan did, however, decide to appoint a commission, the Tomlinson Commission, to investigate how far such segregation was possible within a modern state. This commission concluded that if South Africa incorporated what were then called Bechuanaland, Basutoland and Swaziland and also invested heavily in the rural African reserves in South Africa itself it might be able to achieve a situation in which there were in the country all-Black areas on the one hand and White areas whose defining characteristic was that not more than 50 per cent of the population were Black.

In emphasizing what he regarded as the positive aspects of apartheid, Verwoerd attempted to follow through this logic and Dr Vorster, who succeeded him, promising to 'carry on along the road on which Hendrik Verwoerd fell', eventually produced the full 'homelands' policy. This policy involved giving a degree of political independence to what had previously been only rural reserves, but regarding African populations in the White areas as migrants only, with no claim to political rights there because of their citizenship in their 'homelands'.

The policy of establishing Bantustans was claimed by the government as a significant advance beyond the policy of White supremacy pursued by its predecessors. Its critics refused to accept that the independence accorded to the 'homelands' or Bantustans could have any serious reality given their economic dependence on South Africa. None the less, the emergence of new African spokesmen in these territories was a new factor in the situation.

Paralleling the Black-homelands policy, though not contiguous with it, was the development of segregated education.

As Marcus Malusi Balintulo shows in his contribution to this volume, the purpose of the new Black universities was primarily a means of policing

African thought. But, as in the case of the homelands, the new universities gave rise to unintended consequences. Breaking the link with White radicalism which the African militants had previously had did not force them into subservience. Rather it fostered that Black Consciousness to which, in different ways, both Heribert Adam and Nyameko Pityana refer as a new factor affecting both politics and education.

This development of the so-called positive aspects of apartheid in regional terms, however, was not the only form of change in the policy. Indeed they could be said simply to involve its extension to its logical limits. In the view of some, a more fundamental change and one which possibly constituted a contradiction within the apartheid policy was the move towards recognition of African trade unions. As Webster points out, the recommendations of the Wiehahn Commission and still more their amendment in practice by the government, suggest that no fundamental change in the power situation in industry was envisaged. Yet there does seem to have been some new concept involved here, for instead of looking on all African workers as being, in principle, migrants, the Wiehahn Commission was groping its way towards acceptance of the idea of a permanent African urban work-force or proletariat, an idea which Rheinallt Jones had been preaching to the Chamber of Mines as early as 1950. Industry was increasingly demanding the right to use semi-skilled and even skilled African labour and the government, while not wanting to abandon racial domination, was compelled, as Adam has suggested elsewhere, to modernize it by permitting this new extension of the exploitation of African labour.

If we ask what apartheid is as a sociological form rather than as an ideological concept, its essence, of course, lies in the squeezing of a partially independent 'reserve' economy which, while it served to reproduce the labour supply, could not of itself support its population. The adult male population of the 'reserves' could then be exploited as compound labour in the mines for nine months of the year and the migrating surplus of families could be policed and controlled in the locations set up under the Urban Areas Act. The reserve, the compound and location were thus, as I have pointed out elsewhere, the essential institutions of labour exploitation and, of course, of apartheid. What seemed to be happening in the late 1970s was the recognition of a new sector of the labour market involving the incorporation of workers into the economy and the polity in a new way.

Parallel to this development was the beginning of the recognition that Africans in urban townships would need to be directly incorporated into the polity through some sort of urban councils, independent of the 'homelands'. This had not gone very far by the end of the decade, but the very attempt to re-establish control after the Soweto riots of 1976 had to involve some de facto recognition of urban African power.

The government in the late 1970s was also being forced, by the pressure of world opinion, to make further adjustments in the outward appearance of apartheid, by allowing Black guests in some high-class hotels, by modifying its policy on segregated sport and by even considering modifying its 'immorality' laws which made sexual relations and marriage between the races illegal. Its capacity to do this was limited by the ideological commitment of its supporters to apartheid for its own sake, independently of any political and economic advantages which it might bring. None the less, such moves were indicative of the desire of the government to modernize apartheid and make it more acceptable not only to its own industrialists but to the outside world.

Changes of this kind have led some academics to the view that apartheid has now fundamentally changed its nature. Thus Professor N. J. Rhoodie of the Institute for Plural Societies, replying to an inquiry in connection with the production of this volume, writes:

> Afrikaner sophisticates in the academic sphere do not use this concept any more. Apartheid represents a phase in South African history and we are rapidly moving out of this phase—hence the fluidity in current socio-political thinking. It is naïve to conceive of 'apartheid' as a static immutable system, some sort of permanent condition existing within fixed and precisely determined parameters. I certainly hold no brief for the caricature normally conceptualized as 'apartheid', but I can support a policy aimed at creating a plural democracy based on federalist/confederalist/conservationalist principles.

The fact that Professor Rhoodie's institute is now said to have been financed by the Department of Information does not lessen the importance of this remark. Nor does the fact that, as we have seen, the newer forms of apartheid are by no means democratic. It still remains a fact that the system has adapted to new conditions and, in analysing the implications of apartheid for social research, we have to take account of the newer as well as the older form.

In suggesting that apartheid as a political system has a malign effect on social research, it is necessary to point out in the first place that there is not and probably never has been a country in which the quest for truth on social matters has been uninterruptedly and fully pursued and the findings of researchers always applied. Not only is it the case that all countries interfere with social science to some extent, but in those instances in which there is intellectual freedom, social scientists have no reason or motivation to concern themselves with major issues of social justice. As Heribert Adam points out, quoting Pierre Van den Berghe, 'The Switzerlands of this world cannot produce Dostoevskis and Solzhenitsyns' and in the peaceful democratic societies, social scientists are often employed in justifying the regime or in ensuring its smooth functioning.

Harry Lever has suggested that part of the failure of social research in South Africa is also due not to any government interference and oppression, but simply to a lack of energy and will on the part of sociologists. There is certainly some truth in this. But, in so far as Lever is claiming that there should be no government interference with research in politically sensitive areas, he overstates his case. A purely fact-finding, positivist type of research design may well be acceptable to governments and the feeling on the part of sociologists that they have a large sphere of operation may only mean that they have fitted themselves into the professional niche which the system has assigned to them.

Adam is surely more correct in claiming that the strength of sociology in and about South Africa arises from the very fact of oppression. An oppressive system produces political intellectuals motivated to oppose it and that motivation is a valuable resource for sociology, even if its inquiries are subsequently hampered by ideologists, politicians and policemen. South Africa in fact has been highly productive of sociologists and of sociological inquiry, even if the vocation of the sociologist leads him into conflict with the powers that be. The problem of the suppression of social research arises not only because the government is oppressive, but because the aspirations of sociologists are higher.

Aspirations alone, however, do not produce research evidence. There may be many obstacles in the way of the conduct of research itself. The concept of social science which prevails in the researcher's milieu, the way in which the problem is formulated, the conditions attached to the provision of research resources, access to data and informants, the possibility of publishing one's results and the possibility of influencing political change are all variable elements in the social science situation and it is at each of these points that the character of a political regime may affect the freedom of research.

Karl Mannheim has made sociologists at least aware of the importance of the less recognized obstacles to research which take the form of self-deception or a 'lie in the soul'. We shall return to this notion later. Immediately we should notice that, while there may be widespread agreement to resist the more immediate limitations on the researcher's freedom, only those who have been forced by their circumstances to bring wider situations into question will begin to point to the falsehood which arises from the concepts of social science used or the ways in which theoretical problems are formulated.

A related but not exactly coincidental point here is the fact that, while the implementation of apartheid may have created a tyranny and that tyranny itself may have created obstacles to social research, it is possible that some researchers will object to those limitations which result from the tyranny, without being aware that they are constrained by the notion of racial supremacy itself, independently of the enforcement functions of the tyranny. Thus there will be many White researchers who, while they object to living in a police state, do not question White power. Black Consciousness as a political movement raises these more fundamental questions.

It would be unfair to contributors to this volume, like Welsh, Savage and Whisson, to suggest that they fall into this category of those who are unaware of the 'lie in the soul' of the researcher. All of them indeed make reference to the difficulties of the researcher extracting himself from the ideological standpoints of his society and having dangerous thoughts. None the less, as practical academics in universities their main emphasis is upon the availability of resources to academics to do research.

It is clear that on this level the resources made available to academics by the Human Sciences Research Council and by pre-existing bodies have been infinitesimal when compared with the amount spent on research on the natural sciences or on agriculture. Moreover, although the council claims that it is not in business to serve a 'dogma superimposed from above as an instrument of national policy' it seems clear that, in the structure of its committees, as well as in the kinds of research it encourages it shows biases and blindnesses, which result in it directing resources to research which is at least not disadvantageous to the government. It is not the case that there is massive evidence of research projects being rejected on overtly political grounds, but it does seem to be true that academics are discouraged from seeking support for projects which might be thought to be subversive.

Capitalist industry in South Africa is an alternative source of funding and Whisson claims that, while this is not plentiful, it 'appears to be distributed without strings attached and has been used not infrequently to sponsor projects critical of the migrant labour system'. Webster points out, however, that industry does finance a very large amount of research of which academics take little notice. This research is carried out as part of the very industrial operation itself. Thus in the 1930s:

> The applications of scientific principles in the management of Black mineworkers proceeded with the help of industrial psychologists . . . The first task was to develop a series of simple repetitive tests to assist in the placement of new recruits into the categories of semi-skilled, unskilled and 'boss-boys' . . . The second was to introduce more systematic methods of acclimatizing a mineworker . . . For three hours per day for eight days recruits undergo 'stepping exercises' . . . At the end they are reclassified according to their pulse-rate during stepping into three categories—those able to perform strenuous, less strenuous and light work respectively.

Thus it would seem that, if the mine-owners sponsored research, as distinct from responding to grant applications, they did so in the interest of increasing labour exploitation. None the less, in more recent times, as Webster goes on to point out, there have been more significant and widely conceived projects. It should be remembered here, that, given the conflict of interest between industry and government, research in the interest of capitalist power is not necessarily research in the service of apartheid. Webster's claim is that apartheid *compounds* the limitations which capitalism places on research—not that its own restrictions follow from those created by industry.

In fact there is little doubt that a researcher from one of the European countries would find the restrictions placed on social science by South African industry severely limiting, unless he was able to work within areas (such as the substitution of a more permanent and urbanized labour force for a migrant one) which was in industry's interest. Even more severe, however, are the restrictions imposed by apartheid itself and by the tyranny to which it gives rise and these occur primarily at the point of access to data sources, to people and to places.

It is clear that, from the point of view of the present South African Government, the main concern is that a researcher at large in the Black areas, whether in the urban locations or the reserves, is difficult to distinguish from a political agitator. At best, he is unlikely to give the impression in his dealings with Africans that he supports apartheid (his very presence in the Black areas being a deviant act) but at worst he might actually give legitimacy in his questioning to banned institutions. Thus Monica Wilson and Archie Mafeje might have consciously excluded all reference to the African National Congress from their questions and Pierre van den Berghe might simply have failed to behave as a member of the superior race and hence seemed to White South Africans only an innocent abroad, yet both research projects might have been thought to be subversive of normal Black-White relations. Still more was this likely to be the case if, as Whisson suggests, the researcher felt that he could not talk openly and honestly to his informants *unless* he was willing to discuss the African National Congress.

The most important controls exercised over researchers seeking direct contact with Africans are the necessity of obtaining permission before entering a Black area, the fact that some political informants as well as the researcher might be banned persons and the possible seizure of research notes, questionnaires and tapes. To say this is not necessarily to claim that there are a large number of cases of permission to enter a 'reserve' or location being refused. What does seem to be the case is that anyone who does enter Black areas is likely to be watched at every point by the police and harrassed if at any stage he appears to be supporting 'subversion'. Informants may be arrested, data seized and the researchers themselves detained or removed from the area.

Quite central to the control of research as it is to the control of political activity is the banning of persons under the Suppression of Communism Act. A banned person cannot hope to undertake research, since the kind of social contact which he seeks with informants will almost certainly involve his going outside the area to which he is confined and having social intercourse of a kind which could be interpreted as holding a meeting. Thus many academics in South Africa today are excluded altogether from the research process. But even if the researcher is not banned, his potential informants may be and will either not be able to meet him or, if they are, to give information only within limits or under pressures of a kind which make that information highly dubious.

Access to data of a written kind is less hedged about with restrictions, but even here the attempt to control the dissemination of dangerous ideas affects research. Librarians know that it is dangerous to make the writings of the African National Congress available and will not be helpful to the researcher who wishes to use them. Occasionally, moreover, a researcher may stumble upon a state secret which a government in an increasingly oppressive state might wish to keep from public knowledge. This will be especially true of military secrets but might also affect non-military areas.

The ubiquitous effects of the Suppression of Communism Act also affect the publication of results. Publishers and authors may be prosecuted for quoting the African National Congress or for publishing material which is thought to further the objectives of communism. There is also an impressive list of academic works which may not be imported or possessed. Over and above this, moreover, it is possible that those who express dangerous and critical ideas may be imprisoned or otherwise punished, as was the case with Dr Barend Van Niekerk who made allegations of racial bias against the judiciary.

All that we have said so far, however, refers to the kind of interference with academic freedom we would expect under any tyranny, except in so far as it is facilitated by the check which is possible on entry into segregated areas. This does not, however, touch what may be the heart of the problem of social research in South Africa, namely the elimination at an earlier stage of the very questions which might lead to answers embarrassing to those who seek to maintain White supremacy.

The simplest way in which this is done is by not addressing questions of race relations at all but joining in academic and intellectual debates which are concerned with other matters. Thus in recent years there has been a considerable growth in theoretical sociology in South Africa concerned, for example, with discussing the ideas of Talcott Parsons or with non-political types of sociology such as small-group analysis on which the distinguished American Professor of Sociology in the University of Cape Town is an expert. On the other hand, there has been growing interest in such areas as political and urban sociology with a considerable increase in the level of sophistication of the methods of survey design and analysis. Such research gives South African social science continued respect in the eyes of the world without its existence being threatened through the opening up of dangerous areas.

More fundamental in its effect on social science thinking, however, is the restriction which comes not from looking in the wrong direction, but rather from a simple inability to see. It is this set of questions to which the papers by an anonymous author on the Black academic, by Balintulo and by Pityana are directed, as is to some extent that by Heribert Adam.

The first point to notice here is that the normal structuring of academic debate is affected by the way in which Black academics are excluded from the mainstream of African life or at least from playing a major part in it. Balintulo shows that only two possibilities have been envisaged in the provision of university education for Blacks. The first was the creation of a university college with the specific intention of bringing Blacks into touch with White liberal ideas and thus excluding 'Zionism'. The other was the separation of African higher education from that provided for Europeans so that African students should not be exposed to the limited kind of subversion which might come from White liberal ideas. Parallel to this, our anonymous contributor argues that, while the Afrikaans universities excluded the Black academic from research altogether, the English-speaking universities used him in a subordinate role to collect data on projects conceived by his White masters.

Pityana's chapter on the Black Consciousness movement deals mainly with its political aspects, but its implications for social research are enormous. Already in his chapter, Adam recognizes that an entirely new approach to problems might emerge when Black nationalism displaces Afrikaner nationalism and White liberalism in setting the themes of social research. Pityana's article gives us some idea as to where this new approach might lead. Essentially the Black Consciousness movement amongst students showed that whereas for Whites, even liberal Whites, the problem was one of exposing the more outrageous *consequences* of White supremacy and promoting *discussion* about them, for the new generation of South African Black students it was the nature of *the system itself* which was at stake and its discussion was a life-and-death matter.

Karl Mannheim, whose important writings on the sociology of knowledge have been too readily displaced in academic debate by the more relativistic works of Kuhn and Feyerabend, suggests that in a potentially revolutionary social situation there will be two kinds of social science, that which is ideological and sees many institutions as necessary because they serve the status quo, and that which is utopian seeing these same institutions as doomed because they stand in the way of change.

Mannheim's concepts of 'ideology' and 'utopian' thinking, however, suggest that it is misleading and unrealistic. Myrdal, who wrote explicitly about race relations, suggested something more: he urged social scientists to make their value-standpoints explicit and when they said that something was necessary it was important to say in relation to what ends or goals it was necessary. But he did not regard such statements as unrealistic. They referred to sequences of change which could be brought about.

What this suggests is that in a situation of social conflict one may envisage four types of social science and ideology (Fig. 1).

	Maintaining status quo	Promoting revolutionary change
Unrealistic	Ideology	Utopianism
Realistic	Social science in the service of repression	Social science in the service of change

Fig. 1

This figure is of some importance in relation to Adam's chapter. Adam suggests that, instead of being above the struggle, social science in South Africa must take a committed point of view. He then suggests that there are four such alternatives: that of Afrikaner nationalism; that of African nationalism; that of liberalism; and that of Marxism. Against these he opposes his own realistic social science, which does not substitute moral confessions for practical research on what can be done. How do those alternatives relate to those in our figure?

It would seem that Afrikaner nationalism was concerned with maintaining the status quo through expunging any values which threaten the unity of the Volk and the supremacy of the Afrikaners. That is to say it is a kind of ideology. Black Consciousness is the opposite of this. It is concerned with producing a new 'psychic glue', with decolonizing the minds of Blacks. It is, in a very special sense, utopian. Liberal and Marxist analyses are thought of as more realistic and both in the service of social change, with one emphasizing prejudice as the source of racial institutions and envisaging change through the logic of industrial capitalism and the other seeing racialism as following from the needs of capitalism and capable of being changed by working-class revolution. Additionally, liberal writers have veered towards utopianism through their substitution of moral confessions for serious research. Both liberalism and Marxism, however, tend towards utopianism through their overemphasis upon prejudice and capitalism as the source of racialism and their wish-fulfilling belief as to how it is to be changed. Adam's own pragmatic realism is offered as an alternative to both of these.

This argument for pragmatic realism, however, is unnecessarily tied up with a notion of immediately practical changes. It includes some indication of preference for a continuation of investment and for accepting the Bantustans as better bases for a programme of change than that provided by the more catastrophic solutions. Like Leo Kuper, who has always abhorred the possibility of violence and sought evolutionary solutions in what is possibly a revolutionary situation, Adam has opted here for exploring certain more limited scenarios of change. He does not consider whether there might not be at least equal justification for the social scientists considering what means are necessary for the overthrow of the existing system and whether these means could not realistically be made available in the near future.

This brings us to the point where we must note that there is a missing chapter in this book. We have accounts of the search by social scientists for the freedom to work within an essentially reformist framework, publishing their results however shocking and seeking to persuade the powers that be to remove scandals and we have contributions suggesting that African social scientists might pose different research problems and perceive their situation differently. What we do not have is a realistic sociology of revolution. This surely is something which has to be considered as legitimate a task for social science as the pragmatic reformist sociology which Adam advocates.

The pragmatic type of sociology begins by assuming incremental change in areas where such change is considered permissible without any alteration of the power balance preceding the proposed change. Thus the present South African Government would actually agree to building up the strength of the Bantustans and would not stand in the way of increased overseas investment, even if it were true (as has not been proven) that such developments ultimately undermined the system as a whole. Adam's strategy is either to support the new legal forces against the regime or merely to hope that the regime itself would adapt to new circumstances.

It is, however, not entirely realistic to suggest that the only changes which can be expected to occur over the next twenty years will be those approved by the government. Crucial variable elements in the situation are South Africa's role in the world economy, the position of the external forces of liberation, and the possibility of an internal breakdown of law and order.

The possibilities which will arise in the sphere of economic pressure have been discussed by R. W. Johnson in his book *How Long Will South Africa Survive?* Johnson's work is interesting in that he does not believe that pressure from guerrilla armies will be an important factor in bringing about change. Crucial to his analysis are the supply of oil and the price of gold. On the first of these South Africa is precariously placed, but, on the second, for the moment, because of the rise in the gold price during the world depression, the regime appears secure. But, whatever the present de facto state of affairs, these two factors and others like them are capable of being affected by diplomatic activity within a changing world balance of power.

Johnson notwithstanding, the most important feature of South Africa's situation in the larger world is the collapse of the colonial and racist regimes to the north. Guerrilla activity in Mozambique and Angola eventually produced a situation which the Portuguese army could not contain and generals of that army ultimately established in Portugal a government which conceded independence to the two territories. Both territories now had socialist governments and Angola had the support of substantial Cuban forces. As against this Mozambique found itself still deeply dependent upon South Africa both through migrant labour and through other economic ties.

The new situation was sufficiently flexible for the United States and the United Kingdom to become concerned, in their own interest, about the spread of communism across southern Africa and this in turn increased the need to negotiate with the Rhodesian guerrillas based in Zambia and Mozambique. In due course a majority rule constitution was negotiated and the new African-ruled state of Zimbabwe came into being. Similarly the former League of Nations Trust Territory of South-West Africa moved towards becoming an African-ruled state to be called Namibia.

In all of these changes, South African military involvement was limited and it seemed that the regime thought it unwise to extend its lines of communication by becoming involved in a prolonged military engagement to the north. No doubt the South African Government would be willing to take any necessary military action against guerrillas based in Zimbabwe, and Zimbabwe, like Mozambique, Zambia and Botswana, would be too preoccupied by its own problems of economic survival to allow itself to be the base for a liberation army for some years to come. Nevertheless, the situation is a fluid one and the availability of military aid from the socialist countries does not leave the guerrillas or Zimbabwe totally at the mercy of South Africa.

This brief excursion into possible scenarios of political conflict in southern Africa is not itself social science. But it offers a very different approach to the problem for social science from that adopted by the

Afrikaner nationalists, who envisage only limited change through the devolution of power to the Bantustans or from that of the more liberal English academics who work within the framework set by government sources of finance and the Suppression of Communism Act. It does not involve a retreat into either grand theory or abstracted empiricism, the two ways in which, as C. Wright Mills saw, sociologists usually retreat from the difficult world of politics. It is not simply a practical technique for the decolonization of the mind through consciousness-raising. And finally, while severely practical, it considers many of the accepted institutional forms as changeable in a way which Adam's pragmatic realism does not.

Perhaps a word should be said here in qualification of the uniqueness which we are claiming for a new sociology of liberation. It is by no means intended to deny the relevance either of the consciousness-raising of the Black Consciousness movement or, in certain circumstances, of Adam's pragmatic realism. The decolonization of the mind is preached by Black Consciousness in the internal movement as the essential precondition of the new social sciences of liberation taking hold there as well as among the external forces of liberation. It has an important and complementary role to play. As to Adam's pragmatic realism, it will always be important as a safeguard against utopianism and moral posturing. What is necessary is that there should be a continuous dialogue between pragmatic realism and the sociology of liberation so that it does not become simply defeatist.

The problem of looking at institutions from the point of view of the contributions which they make to, or the obstacles which they place in the way of, liberation is however not quite as simple as it at first seems. Liberation from what and for what end?

The obvious answer to the question is liberation from White supremacy and for the achievement of democracy. For many of those in the liberation movement, however, this is an insufficient goal. South African society is an expression of capitalist imperialism and, according to the Marxist analysis it is its capitalism and not solely its racism which must be overthrown. More than this, the Marxists argue, racism can be defeated only in so far as capitalism itself is overthrown.

It is this argument which produced, from the late 1960s onwards, the debate about South African history and historiography. There is no point in trying to resolve that debate here. In fact, it cannot be that easily resolved. What we have are two models of South African society: one which sees its racist structures as an archaic legacy at odds with the modernizing force of capitalism and the other which starts from the capitalist mode of production as the prime mover and looks at all institutions from the nationalist state to the traditional economics of the 'reserves' in terms of their contribution to facilitating the operation of the capitalist mode of production. What is not always made clear in the debate, however, is that such models are hypothetical only and that their validity or otherwise rests upon the degree to which they have explanatory purchase on historical political events.

The testing of theory, however, occurs not solely through observation and research, but through practice, through political action and its subsequent assessment in reflection. At this point the work of the scholar and the politician are difficult to disentangle. It must be said, however, that on this point social scientists have remained strangely academic and detached. The liberals have limited themselves to assessing the impact of the modernizing forces of capitalism and the Marxists to the struggles of the working class against capitalism. There is, as yet, little in the way of social science which begins from the goals of the African liberation movement and treats the distinction between Marxist and liberal as of secondary significance only. The Marxist excuses himself from looking closely at African politics on the ground that its leadership is *petit bourgeois,* while the responsible liberal sees such movements as irresponsible and troublesome. The significance of the Black Consciousness movement may in the long run be seen to lie in the fact that it does choose this new starting-point. From its point of view there is nothing sacred about capitalism or its opposite. It is quite possible that as the forces of political liberation gather strength it will become apparent that capitalism as an economic system cannot accommodate them. But the proof of the point will lie in the political struggle itself not in theoretical academic dogmas.

Webster's chapter in this volume is of some relevance here. He describes a process in the relations between capitalism and social science and apartheid and social science in which the goals of capitalism and the goals of apartheid are at odds. Apartheid compounds the effects of capitalism, adding new restrictions to legitimate social science and possible social change. Capitalism has to live within this political framework for the moment. If, however, the framework itself were destroyed capitalism might pursue social change along lines which have been, as Webster suggests, aborted by apartheid. It would still remain to be seen whether it could accommodate Black Nationalism or the social science of liberation.

To some extent all of these problems will become academic, however, in a situation in which, not the internal revolution but the external forces of liberation are the means through which change will be brought about. Highly relevant therefore, *as social science,* will be the understanding of the means of social change which is gained in experience by the guerrilla armies. This will not be simply an understanding of military techniques, though it will amongst other things be that. It will involve the whole complex sociology of the establishment of a state within a state, of the setting up in microcosm of a new social order and of relating that new order to the existing modern economy with its more complex structural problems. It is this set of problems which already faces the Government of Mozambique. Increasingly they will face the political leaders of Zimbabwe, Namibia and Zambia.

Finally, supplementing the social science of liberation will be the social science of reconstruction. Liberation must at some stage mean majority rule and that must mean that both the system of racial hierarchy and domination and the system of labour exploitation which goes with it will come to an end. At this stage the question will arise of what is to be done with the various ethnic minorities and their cultures as well as with the prevailing pattern of industrial organization. It is already clear that the liberation movement is not committed to an inverted form of racism. It may therefore have to devote an important part of its intellectual resources to the development of appropriate cultural and educational policies for a multi-ethnic society while not allowing the preservation of minority rights to be used as a cover for subverting the new social system. I have dealt with some of these problems in a brief final chapter.

It is obvious that, in this introduction, we have gone well beyond present conceptions either of the social science of the status quo, or of a practical science of reform as seen by academics. Our claim is that the social science of liberation and the social science of reconstruction are part of the total contribution of social science to the future of southern Africa. The most interesting thing that this volume has revealed is that all of its contributors in one way or another realize this. The authors of the first four chapters all point out that while even present social science is restricted by a fearful apartheid government, that government has as yet hardly been challenged by social science perspectives based on Black Nationalism. Adam, in his reflection on the relative courage of South African social scientists, also sees them as moving in this direction. And, clearly, the Black contributors, by expressing their resentment at an academic tradition, which, even in its more liberal forms, excludes them, are already bursting the bonds which it has tried to set for their thinking. No doubt the South African Government will continue to do what it can to restrict social science within its present limits. The community of social scientists, however, is not subject to the control of that government and will continue to develop a social scientific understanding of apartheid and not merely a social science conducted within the restrictive framework of apartheid.

Bibliography

ADAM, Heribert. *Modernizing Racial Domination.* Berkeley, University of California Press, 1971.
FEYERABEND, Paul. Against Method: Outline of an Anarchistic Theory of Knowledge. *Minnesota Studies in the Philosophy of Science,* Vol. 4. University of Minnesota Press.
JOHNSON, R. W. *How Long Will South Africa Survive.* Macmillan, 1977.
KUHN, Thomas. *The Structure of Scientific Revolution.* Chicago, 1970.
KUPER, Leo; SMITH, M. G. *Pluralism in Africa.* Berkeley, University of California Press, 1969.
LEVER, Henry. Some Problems on Race Relations Research in South Africa. *Social Dynamics* (Cape Town), Vol. 1, No. 1, 1975.
MANNHEIM, Karl. *Ideology and Utopia.* London, Routledge & Kegan Paul, 1960.
MILLS, C. Wright. *The Sociological Imagination.* New York, Oxford University Press, 1959.
MYRDAL, G. *Value in Social Theory.* London, Routledge & Kegan Paul, 1958.
Report of the Commission for the Socio-Economic Development of the Bantu areas within the Union of South Africa. Pretoria, 1955. (U.G. 61).

REX, John. The Compound, the Reserve, and the Location—the Essential Institutions of South African Labour Exploitation. *South African Labour Bulletin,* Vol. 1, No. 4, April 1971, p. 401.

WRIGHT, Harrison M. *The Burden of the Present: Liberal-Radical Controversy over Southern African History.* London, Rex Collings, 1977.

2 Social research in a divided society: the case of South Africa*

David Welsh
University of Cape Town

The focus of this chapter is on the problems which scholars encounter in conducting research in the more controversial or sensitive areas of South African society. Of course, different perspectives and differing locations in the social structure will shape individuals' views of what is and what is not controversial or sensitive. What appears to one scholar as an ordinary commonplace observation may appear to another as highly contentious, even an insult to the ethnic group to which he belongs. The segmentation of the wider society is reflected in the South African scholarly community itself, if indeed one can talk of a single such community.

Social research in South African universities, at least on any sizeable scale, is a comparatively recent phenomenon. The major emphasis in research has traditionally been in the physical and natural sciences. Writing in 1932 an American observer, Robert Herndon Fife, explained this emphasis in terms of South Africa's 'newness' as a country which made conditions difficult for maintaining European standards of life. Research was viewed in instrumental or utilitarian terms which meant that universities allocated much the greater proportion of their funds and energies to the physical and natural sciences, whose 'pay-off' in these terms is greater than those of the humanities or social sciences (Fife, 1932).

Substantially the same analysis holds good today. In 1971, a total of approximately R45 million was spent on research and development, of which about R29 million was spent by the state and the remainder by industry. Of this a little over 1 per cent was allocated to the social sciences.

Official reports published in 1938, 1939, and 1940 showed conclusively that university institutions were conducting only limited research, in all fields. They were under-staffed, starved of funds for research, and handicapped by inadequate libraries. Although there were varying degrees of emphasis on its centrality in a university's role, the universities and university colleges were favourably disposed to the sponsoring of research.

* This chapter first appeared as an article in *Social Dynamics* (Cape Town), Vol. 1, No. 1, 1975.

The constraints, however, forced them to remain substantially in the high-school mould as primarily teaching and examining institutions.

The major source of research funds was the state. A Research Grant Board established in 1918 provided paltry sums for university research. The National Bureau of Educational and Social Research was established in 1929 to serve all those state departments which dealt with educational and social welfare: by 1939 the government was spending about £6,000 a year on the bureau, compared with £200,000 a year on agricultural research. To be sure, these limited funds were augmented by generous grants from the Carnegie Corporation of New York, which funded the first major sociological investigation into the poor-White problem.

In 1937 the bureau invited applications for research grants from funds given by the Carnegie Corporation. The response from the universities, however, was largely disappointing. In attempting to ascertain why this was so the bureau elicited from the universities an acknowledgement that insufficient research work was being conducted in the educational and social fields. Apart from the general constraining factors cited above the universities singled out further handicaps that were peculiar to educational and social research. First, these areas were relatively new as fields of scholarly investigation; secondly, there was a shortage of trained investigators who could train others in the techniques of social research; thirdly, there was a serious deficiency of public statistics relating to such issues as unemployment, housing, income distribution and, especially, the vital and social statistics of the African and Coloured populations.

Significantly, nearly all the universities stressed the need for research into the problems arising out of the racial issue. One of the projects funded was a study of the origins and incidence of miscegenation in South Africa during the seventeenth and eighteenth centuries. A more controversial topic in the South African context can hardly be imagined! It appears, however, never to have emerged as a published study.

Politicians, university administrators and academics themselves expressed whole-hearted support for the idea that scholars involve themselves in research into the pressing political, racial and social problems of the day. In an address to the South African Association for the Advancement of Science in 1921, a zoologist, Professor J. E. Duerden (1922), urged that scientific studies be made of South Africa's diverse peoples:

> Much of the study calls for that personal detachment and freedom which we hold to be one of the prerogatives of the man of science. Though it may not be usual to regard these problems as subjects of scientific inquiry [there is] urgent need for the methods which science can apply, and . . . it is fitting that questions of this nature should receive the attention of the Association. We do not encroach upon the stormy preserves of the politician. We assist by the elaboration of facts and principles for him to apply in practice, among the varied and often divergent interests of the whole population; and at the same time may help in the building-up of correct ideals for the public.

In his presidential address to the association in the same year C. T. Loram (a prominent figure in African education) endorsed these sentiments, and suggested a list of highly contentious topics in the field of race relations for scholarly investigation. According to Loram 'those engaged in the administration of Native Affairs want your help. Our neglect of a scientific treatment of the Native question has not only become a reproach but is now a positive danger' (Loram, 1922).

In 1929, a young Stellenbosch academic, Dr H. F. Verwoerd, expressed a strong plea for a closer connection between the activities of the state and those of the universities. He cited examples of fields such as the administration of the railways and gaols, where scholars and students could become practically involved in research to the mutual benefit of themselves and the state. In this way the state would get

> honest and enlightened investigation, which was at present almost impossible, owing to the fact of the political party, in power for the time being, fearing that the discoveries of defective or antiquated methods, could be used as a weapon by the other political party.

Verwoerd urged that the universities be accorded greater liberty to discuss the big problems that faced South Africa. Intellectuals, he said, should be encouraged to approach these problems on the basis of their knowledge and mental outlook.

It was partly with a view to the 'solution' of the racial problem that a School of African Life and Languages (the forerunner of the present School of African Studies) was established at the University of Cape Town in 1921. In 1919 an official committee recommended to the government that it should immediately establish

> a school of such strength as will show a real and adequate interest on the part of South Africa in problems whose solution is necessary for the future safe development of a country in which White and Black are to live side by side.

The government accepted the recommendation and allocated a sum of £3,000 for the purpose in 1920-21. This amount was slashed by half even before the school was established and seriously jeopardized its early expansion. If the official view was that scientific studies of changing African societies and of race relations were highly desirable, official practice showed a disinclination to pay overmuch regard to the research findings of academics. The Native Economic Commission (1930-1932) grappled with some of the thorniest issues facing South Africa, but it did not include among its members a single academic who was professionally concerned with African affairs. The commission noted the interest which the universities showed in 'the Scientific study of the Natives' and recommended that greater encouragement be given to such work.

General Smuts repeated this call in a speech at the University of Cape Town in 1938 when he urged the universities to tackle South Africa's most fundamental problem: 'as world peace is today the greatest of all human interests, we in South Africa could at least make a beginning by stabilising racial and social peace within our own borders and this University should even be in the fore-front of that noble cause' (*The Star*, 8 March, 1938).

But what did the academics achieve? The experiences of W. M. Macmillan, the historian, suggest that conclusions that ran counter to official predispositions were coolly, even hostilely, received. In his pioneering historical works Macmillan did much to undermine the orthodox White view of South African history. As a pamphleteer and as author of *Complex South Africa* (Macmillan, 1930) he brought a keenly critical focus to bear upon contemporary problems. For these activities Macmillan incurred the Hertzog government's hostility to his conclusions and recommendations in the field of official policy.

A leading social anthropologist, Isaac Schapera, acidly criticized policy-makers in 1939 for ignoring academic findings. The practical use of anthropology was obvious but 'in few other countries with similar problems has the influence of the anthropologist been so small'. The anthropologist himself was partly to blame 'but the Government and the public at large cannot be absolved from indifference and even wilful neglect' (Schapera, 1939).

The truth was that White South Africans of both linguistic groups were highly sensitive to criticism of their way of life and the racial policies associated with it. This sensitivity applied not only to academic investigators but to creative writers as well if their writings probed into the basis of White attitudes. In his introduction to the Hogarth edition of William Plomer's novel, *Turbott Wolfe,* Laurens van der Post gives a vivid description of White South African reaction to the novel which had explored the theme of sexual attraction across the colour line. It caused an 'intellectual riot'. It reminded van der Post of the way in which baboons reacted to seeing their reflections in a mirror—'they looked frantically behind the mirror but always from the front there was an authentic baboon-person staring back at them. They could never accept reality and finally they would smash the mirror to pieces'.

In his autobiography Plomer says that *Turbott Wolfe* 'had particularly stung the Whites in that part of their psychological being where guilt and fear and self-deception in regard to the Natives . . . had been wrapped away from the light of reason'. Similar sensitivity to sharply critical writing about South African attitudes led to the early demise of the journal *Voorslag* with which Roy Campbell, Plomer and van der Post were associated.

Field-work in African communities in this inter-war period was not especially difficult. In conducting the research for her classic study *Reaction to Conquest* in 1931-33, Monica Hunter found African and official informants in Pondoland co-operative. By using personal contacts she was able to move around easily. In the urban part of the research (in East London) her work was facilitated by a meeting with the trade-union leader Kadalie, who used his influence to facilitate her access to the African community. Possibly because of this contact she was subject to a measure of police surveillance. There were more difficulties in obtaining information about conditions on White-owned farms, especially those of the poorer farmers. There was resistance to probing of labour conditions, but, again, use of personal contacts overcame some of the problems.

E. G. Malherbe encountered problems, however, in conducting research in the late 1930s into the extent of bilingualism among Whites. He wrote (Malherbe, 1939): 'Social thinking in South Africa is at the present time so shot-through with racial and political suspicion and prejudice, that it becomes very difficult to conduct scientific investigations of an objective nature into social and cultural phenomena . . .' His research required an investigation of the home background. His probings evoked bitter comment from a church magazine which considered his research a violation of parental sovereignty because he asked children, without the parents' knowledge, a variety of questions about household affairs. He was, moreover, attacked in Parliament because the questions would allegedly heighten ethnic consciousness among the young respondents. Another member attacked the survey as 'an attempt to collect ammunition' in order to carry out the policy of bilingual education, i.e. teaching Afrikaans- and English-speaking children in the same classrooms in both languages. Bilingual education was a hotly contested political issue. The study, when it was published, evoked much heated controversy which might have daunted a scholar less sturdy than Malherbe (Malherbe, 1946).

A consideration of the problems arising out of the climate for social research was the subject of a large conference held in Durban in 1954 (University of Natal, 1954). Much attention was paid to the problems caused by racial polarization and by the possible reluctance of government agencies to foster research that questioned, even if only by implication, the fundamental postulates of policies. Research workers reported that difficulties were being encountered in the African reserves; permits were being refused and resistance to research was emanating from the people themselves. Two of the civil servants present, Dr P. A. W. Cook of the Native Affairs Department and Dr P. J. Olckers, Director of Public Service Training, expressed willingness to co-operate and explicitly welcomed research by academics. Cook said that research on race relations had never been the monopoly of his department and it was prepared to assist individuals and teams from universities to conduct research.

The African academics at the conference pointed out some of the reasons behind African suspicions of research. Z. K. Matthews said that Africans in urban and rural areas would co-operate with investigators provided they were convinced that their motives were genuine and that they were not subtle conveyors of propaganda. Selby Ngcobo outlined in detail the difficulties: a researcher would be watched from both sides of the colour line; if he were seen often in company with or was too friendly towards White officials African suspicions would be aroused; conversely a too-friendly relationship with Black officials would evoke the suspicions of the White officials. The officials expected research activities not to disturb the existing system of discipline and control, while the Africans who constituted the subject of the research expected or hoped that it would contribute to an amelioration of their position. Ngcobo, drawing upon his experience as research assistant in the Economics Department of the University of Natal, said that educated Africans, African trade-unionists and leaders of other organizations tended to draw distinctions between research conducted by independent scholars and that undertaken by various governmental bodies:

> Just as they doubted the impartiality of the latter so they were sceptical of the value to them of the former; they often argued that the powers-that-be would either ignore any findings in their favour or only make use of those facts which were in line with their policy.

A second line of criticism from Africans was that some of the research had been conceived in purely instrumental terms and was aimed at making Africans slot more easily into the limited range of occupational roles that were open to them.

The issues that were raised at this conference cover fairly fully the range of problems experienced by academic social researchers in South Africa. It is a society with an oligarchical social and political structure. (I ignore for present purposes the extent to which the policy of separate development may imply a future dismantling of the existing hierarchical structure.) The dominant White group has created for itself a social charter, justifying that dominance. Many of the elements of the social charter concern the group's history, its beliefs about its own characteristics and those of the groups it dominates. Academic research into one or all of the elements of the charter could, in the nature of things, have explosive results by demonstrating the mythical or false bases of beliefs. The government, naturally, has a strong vested interest in perpetuating the charter as a means of legitimating its authority. It follows that in so far as the government is a major pump primer of research or allocator of research funds its interest will be primarily in fostering research of a 'problem-solving' or utilitarian nature; it will be less interested in or, perhaps, even hostile to, research that examines the dominant group's sacred cows (in whatever fields they may graze).

A further factor, related to what I have said, is the growing authoritarianism of the state. The range of permissible views and opinions has been contracted by laws that place untrammelled powers in the hand of the executive. Over a wide area of political, economic and social life increasing powers of official discretion have been established. Now, free scientific inquiry has what Reinhard Bendix has called 'an inherent radicalism' (Bendix, 1970, p. 95). It is the social sciences primarily that provide the challenge to authority in all spheres, because their focus is upon human affairs and the problems of social interaction. The more authoritarian the society the more likely it is that free inquiry in the social sciences will be circumscribed. Louis Wirth (1936, p. xvii) has written:

> That there is an area of 'dangerous thought' in every society is . . . scarcely debatable. While we recognize that what it is dangerous to think about may differ from country to country and from epoch to epoch, on the whole subjects marked with the danger signal are those which the society or the controlling elements in it believe to be so vital and hence so sacred that they will not tolerate their profanation by discussion. But what is not so easily recognized is the fact that thought, even in the absence of official censorship, is disturbing,

and, under certain conditions, dangerous and subversive. For thought is a catalytic agent that is capable of unsettling routines, disorganizing habits, breaking up habits, undermining faiths, and generating scepticism.

Of course, it should not be inferred that the state is the only agency that shapes the climate for research. While its importance in this respect is undoubted, religious groups, group loyalties and pro- and anti-scientific *Weltanschauungen* can all contribute to resistance of free inquiry (Hobson, 1936, p. 39). All of these factors operate in South Africa and reinforce the areas of 'dangerous thought' with an *extra patina*. But the decisive factor is the structural position of the dominant group as a numerical minority, which perceives itself as being in danger of losing its grip on society. Its authoritarianism flows from this, and decisively affects the conditions for social research.

In 1965 Dr S. Biesheuvel noted that there was a discernible trend to expect the scientist, especially the social scientist 'to operate within the framework of government policy, not to question but to provide support'. He decided that it was 'only one step to the production of acceptable information'. He alluded also to an increasing tendency for the research function of the universities to be taken over by the state, by state-sponsored organizations or by large industrial laboratories (Biesheuvel, 1965, p. 13).

In quantitative terms, the amount of social research conducted by universities and by autonomous bodies exceeds the amount conducted by state-sponsored bodies such as the Human Sciences Research Council (HSRC) or the National Institute for Personnel Research. The former body was created by statute in 1968 and is governed by a Council appointed by the Minister of National Education. It contains under its umbrella ten research institutes which actually conduct or promote research in the respective divisions; and it disburses also research and publication grants and bursaries to individual scholars or to academic departments (a total of R325,000 was disbursed on research grants in 1970-71).

According to its first annual report (1969-70), the HSRC's attitude is that:

> social sciences research is not a dogma super-imposed from above as an instrument of national policy; and the aim of the HSRC is to encourage and stimulate research in the social sciences by free and independent scholars whose labours, it is hoped, will lead to the fuller satisfaction of the needs and aspirations of the various peoples in our country.

It is also stipulated that the members of the Council, who are appointed for two-year periods, must have distinguished themselves in the field of human sciences or possess special qualifications in respect of some or other aspect of the council's activities.

The recommendations for the funding of research projects emanate from a series of advisory committees in the different broad fields of the social sciences. Most of these committees (whose memberships are detailed in the council's third annual report, 1971-72) are numerically dominated by Afrikaans-speaking academics from conservative institutions. There is a handful of liberally minded English-speaking academics. No Blacks serve on any of the committees, and nor, indeed, are the Black universities represented. (This presumably follows from the council's operating under the aegis of the Ministry for National Education which is concerned with White education only.)

From a review of the annual reports and publications of the HSRC it is clear that its own research workers 'operate within the framework of government policy' and provide useful information for policy-makers. What is less clear are the considerations that govern its allocative function. It is believed by some scholars, mostly in the English-medium universities, that the HSRC accords preferential treatment to those research projects that do not impinge upon controversial areas. It is not possible to confirm or deny the validity of this feeling because the projects and scholars who are refused research grants are not listed in the council's annual reports. Those who make this assertion, however, do so emphatically and cite examples of refusals of support. It is alleged also that some scholars, having regard to this belief about the HSRC, simply do not apply to it for funds in the first place.

The allegations cited in the preceding paragraph do not rest on hard evidence; indeed it is mostly of the hearsay variety. It should also be noted that the allegations are vigorously denied by HSRC. As indicated above, the internal activities of the HSRC are confidential, and, as a semi-autonomous body, it is not obliged to provide details about its decisions to Parliament.

A major area of government control of social research is the requirement that scholars wishing to conduct research in the African reserves or 'homelands' first obtain a permit from the Department of Bantu Administration and Development. It is not possible to say precisely how many scholars are granted or refused permits. The minister declined to answer a parliamentary question seeking to elicit this information on grounds that records of the categories of applicants' occupations were not kept. What is known is that a significant number of applications from academics have been refused. It is also true that the processing of applications can take as long as six months or even longer.

Officially the department's attitude is to treat each application on its merits. It appears that South African citizens tend to receive preferential treatment over foreigners who, it seems, are automatically viewed with greater suspicion. This is not to say, however, that no foreigner is granted a permit. Once granted, the permit may be withdrawn at any time, without reasons being given. It stipulates also that permit-holders may not lodge with Africans—which means that a social anthropologist cannot live in a hut in a village. Mostly, it appears that the permits do not allow persons to be in a reserve at night-time. This means that important after-dark ritual activities cannot be observed at firsthand. A further departmental requirement is that permit-holders must show the drafts of their writings to the department prior to publication. It is clear that this may lend itself to a form of pre-publication censorship either by officials or by the investigator himself, as he may well think that his future applications may be jeopardized if the department takes a poor view of his findings. One academic told me that he had a permit which he could not afford to have withdrawn as he was in the middle of a large project: he applied self-censorship in his other writings and in what he said.

Most, but not all, of the applicants who have been refused permits are from the English-medium universities. Permits have also been refused on occasion to members of the South African Institute of Race Relations, which is a liberal though highly respected and sober organization. The situation in regard to permits is viewed so seriously in the English-medium universities that two departments of social anthropology have now abandoned hope of conducting research (either by staff or by graduate students) in the reserves.

Permits were also required from local authorities to conduct research in urban African townships. Far fewer problems about getting permits have been encountered with local authorities than with the central government. It is feared, however, that the takeover of urban African administration by administration boards under the aegis of the central government will lead to the same problems as encountered in other areas. As far as I know, only one permit has been refused to a student by a local authority. In this case the proposed study was a survey of African political attitudes. Local authorities tend to be reluctant to allow research workers into the townships after dark, out of concern for their physical safety. Nor can a social anthropologist live with the community he is studying, as he would do in normal field-work conditions. As with the central government, permits issued by the local authority can be withdrawn at any time without reasons having to be given.

To a greater or lesser extent, the social investigator, as in every country, will be dependent in each case on the co-operation of the authorities for statistical and other information about the subject being investigated. Such co-operation can have an important bearing on the quality and richness of the material assembled by the scholar. It is evident that the political complexion of the scholar has a bearing on the amenability of officials. It is unlikely that a radical opponent of official policies would be granted a permit to enter a reserve in the first place, but assuming he were, and his views were known, it is unlikely that officials would be as frank and co-operative with him as they might well be with a scholar who accepted the basic framework of the policy. Of course much depends upon the individual officials and scholars concerned, but social scientists, critical of official policies, and especially those from the universities with liberal traditions, believe that they receive differential treatment from government departments.

Bureaucracies tend by nature to be secretive; in South Africa the tensions of society and growing authoritarianism give an added dimension to this fundamental predisposition. Opposition members of Parliament report that over the past twelve years it has become steadily more difficult to extract information from the executive by way of parliamentary questions. In some cases the requested information is refused on the ground that 'it is not in the public interest' that it be made known; in other cases a minister will plead that the business of his officials does not permit the time to be expended in gathering information, or that the information is not kept, or that it is not filed according to the categories required by the questioner. More and more questions relating to Bantu affairs have been refused answers on grounds that the desired information is kept by the 'homelands' government. To some extent an analogous situation applies in respect of Coloured affairs.

Similar problems are encountered in connection with the official census. At the 1954 Durban conference on social research several participants complained about the inadequacy of official statistics. E. G. Malherbe explained that the permissible questions on census forms were determined by the Statistical Council and 'obviously this body tended to be conservative in its views'. The conference passed a resolution emphasizing 'that the Census of the Union of South Africa asks fewer questions and thus makes less total data available than any other member of the British Commonwealth of Nations'.

A major objection to the census today is the incredible length of time taken for the data to be published. There are also curious breaks in continuity (i.e. data furnished in previous censuses not being furnished again) which in one case, at least, appears to be because the trend revealed was politically embarassing. A further serious problem about census-taking has been the resistance of Blacks. 'The enumerators ... are often regarded as agents of the administration, even detectives. They are to be avoided or confused as much as possible particularly by the many who are illegally within the urban area.' Such attitudes can seriously hinder the research worker whose questions may lead subjects to suppose that he is a census official. In one case the result was the boycott of a study.

Resistance to investigation has increased with the growing polarization of the society. The more authoritarian the political system becomes the more nervous subjects are about imparting information. Difficulties are encountered especially by scholars investigating 'total' (i.e. multiracial) communities. Concerning his study of Port Nolloth, Martin West (1971, p. 117) reported that his close contact with Black people in the town prevented his doing any serious work among the Whites:

> Whites were suspicious of my presence in the town (some believing me to have political motives) and disapproved strongly of my relationship with non-whites. It was therefore impossible to establish any rapport with the white population as a whole, and most information was gained from casual meetings and observations, particularly in the hotel and bar.

Similar problems were encountered by Pierre L. Van den Berghe, an American sociologist who studied race relations in Natal in the early 1960s. He made no secret of his value orientations and determined that even in a highly colour-conscious society he would remain 'colour-blind'. He reported (Van den Berghe, 1967, pp. 189-90):

On both sides of the colour bar, attempts were made to explain or rather reinterpret my unconventional behavior in terms of existing roles. For whites I was a Communist agitator, or more frequently an odd foreigner who had not yet learned how to 'handle the Natives'. Amusement at my social 'ineptness' was a more common reaction than anger or even annoyance. Often, whites predicted that I would soon become converted to their way of thinking and acting. It was probably on the part of westernized Indians that my role was most readily accepted at face value, and that initial suspicion, amusement, or hostility was most completely absent. Politically militant and educated Africans often tried to fit me into the role either of a police informer or an agent provocateur, or of a missionary-type 'do-gooder' or paternalist. Traditional or older Africans, on the other hand, whether through caution or through inability to shed suddenly the force of habit, often continued to behave in the submissive manner that most whites expected. Needless to say, this imbalance in the relationship made for much awkwardness.

In as politically tense a society as South Africa it is not surprising that the outsider investigating a community is often assumed to be engaged in political activity—by a process analogous to that of witchcraft. In his study of a Cape Coloured reserve, W. P. Carstens found his informants generally co-operative, but in one locality his field-work was blighted when a White church official accused him of subversive political activity within a few hours of his arrival. In other areas he found that barriers were occasionally raised when he was eliciting information about those aspects of religious belief which would not be acceptable to the missionary (Carstens, 1966, p. x).

Several cases have occurred where security police have tailed research workers and subsequently questioned informants. This is naturally intimidating both to the investigator and to the investigated, the former fearing that the information he has obtained could land his informants in trouble, and the latter fearing that their information could be prised out of the investigator. Gwendolen M. Carter and her associates reported several incidents involving security-police surveillance and interference, including 'a mysterious disappearance and reappearance in a police station of a briefcase in a locked hotel room'. In another episode an African opposition member of the Transkei Legislative Assembly was rudely ejected from a hotel room by the manager on grounds that the hotel was for Whites only and subsequently questioned by the security-police. Two members of Professor Carter's team were searched by the security police on leaving the country (Carter et al., 1967. pp. xiii-xiv).

Anthropological studies of Black communities in recent years have tended to mute or avoid altogether examination of political attitudes and activities. They are largely absent in Philip Mayer's study of Xhosa in East London. He reports that (Mayer, 1961, p. 297):

In a present-day South African town the role of a White newcomer closely questioning Black informants about their private affairs can never be a grateful one, and . . . he may risk being given incomplete or misleading information because of his colour.

In their study of Langa, Monica Wilson and Archie Mafeje (1963, pp. 11-12), elected not to investigate political organizations or trade unions. They say:

> Questions were not asked about them early in the investigation because that would have aroused suspicion, and during the course of the study the two main political organizations, the African National Congress and the Pan African Congress, were banned. Furthermore, two cases occurred in which journalists were imprisoned for refusing to reveal to the police their sources of information on political matters.

It can, in other words, be dangerous for the informant and for the investigator personally to be in possession of 'hot' material. As far as I am aware, however, no scholar has been detained by the authorities for interrogation about information obtained in the course of his investigations. But the very existence of such a possibility is probably a deterrent to embarking in the first place upon investigations that may uncover explosive material.

It should not be inferred from the cases cited above that all investigation into political attitudes has become impossible. In Henry Lever's study of the South African voter the refusal rate among respondents was only about 2 per cent, even though many searching questions probing political attitudes were asked. Other studies of voting behaviour have also been made, and opinion polls on highly contentious issues are regularly published in the press. Nearly all of the latter are undertaken by reputable survey organizations. Furthermore, studies have been made of African political attitudes.

Several social scientists have encountered resistance from the groups being investigated on the ground that such investigation highlights their difference. Thus Hilda Kuper found some Indians who felt their position in the country was 'so insecure that some of them expressed anxiety at a book which discussed their way of life as being in any way different from that of White South African's'. A similar reaction was encountered by an African field-worker investigating African community life in Johannesburg. Apart from the suspicion that the field-worker was an informer or a municipal official, there was ambivalence among some educated respondents who felt that any attempt to study Africans was a means of providing justification for separate development which aims at giving Africans no contact with the broad stream of world culture. According to the leader of this project, refusal rates were as high as 50 to 60 per cent.

An unknown factor in research into sensitive areas is the 'lie factor'. Several scholars report that they were given deliberately misleading information, or that they strongly suspected that it was misleading. For example, with the rigorous application of urban influx controls it has become increasingly difficult to extract reliable information from Africans about their job histories, length of sojourn in the urban area, rural land rights, and related questions. This is especially so where the data required is directly related to the right to remain within the prescribed urban area.

The rise of Black consciousness—itself an index of racial polarization—is also making its effect felt upon academic research. African organizations that were willing to be studied only two years ago have become much more 'secretive' and resistant to probing. The new mood marks a rejection of all things White, including social research. As the racial line is more firmly drawn the different categories of Whites are lumped together as representing a cohesive bloc; and heightened racial pride increasingly takes on the form of resentment that any non-Black should take an interest in, or have any empathy with, Black society.

So far much of the discussion has focused upon the problem of Whites conducting (or sponsoring) research into Black communities.

It is also apparent 'however' that the tensions of society and the high degree of group conflict make social research within the White groups difficult in some respects as well. Two interestingly parallel case-studies may be cited as examples. Dr C. J. Alant's sociological study of the way in which members of the Nederduitse Gereformeerde Kerk relate to the Church ran into serious difficulties because of objections by elements within the Church to the questionnaire which respondents were asked to complete. Particular objection was made to two questions: 'It is a sin to vote for a political party which does not specifically maintain the Afrikaans language and traditions', and 'It is a sin for a White to marry a non-White even if this were not against the law of the land'. The objections were aired in the press and the publicity adversely affected the return of completed questionnaires.

The second case is J. Polley's investigation of a large Protestant church's response to separate development. The survey sought to examine the question at all levels within the Church. The proposed project encountered hostility from the university department to which Polley was attached, presumably because it was 'too controversial'. He then transferred to another department which took a more kindly view of the project. But then he encountered resistance from elements within the Church itself. Synods refused to allow the questionnaire to be distributed on the ostensible ground that this would interfere with synod business. Polley was then forced to send out the questionnaires by post and involve himself in substantial costs that could have been avoided if the official channels of the Church had been made available to him.

In both of these cases, it seems clear that the Churches concerned did not want the hard and steady light of academic investigation to shine upon their inner essence. In both cases, the investigations could have produced embarrassing findings, such as that rank and file members, clergy or other office-holders did not share fully the official views of the Church on highly charged issues. Both bodies, therefore, proved resistant to probing.

Conclusion

This chapter has sought to isolate the problems which social research encounters in South Africa. Much evidence could be cited to show, however, that these problems are by no means unique to South Africa. Nor do the findings alter my view that South Africa's complexity makes it one of the most interesting societies in the world and a richly rewarding laboratory for social research. There are ways around most, if not all, of the problems; but the investigator's ingenuity and resourcefulness may often be taxed to the limit. Social research, it seems to me, is the art of the impossible: it can be done even in the most hostile of environments.

Scholarly environments, however, reflect the polarities of the wider society, and the environments themselves shape the research interests of the various social science departments to a significant degree. Each is part of a 'social circle' in Znaniecki's sense, and its members tend to address themselves to that circle and not to the wider society (Znaniecki, 1968, p. 14). The pressures of the social circle shape the values which the investigator brings to his research, they influence his choice of topic, his handling and interpretation of data: Mannheim's 'socially unattached intelligentsia' is an unknown species in South Africa.

Several observers have noted a tendency for social scientists to shy away from the especially contentious areas of their respective disciplines. I. D. MacCrone said in 1952 that psychological research into human relations in South Africa was dragging its feet and that many South African psychologists were turning to the study of the behaviour of rats rather than of men: 'They appear to be afraid of what research into human relations may bring to light.' Similarly in sociology S. Pauw noted in 1964 and H. Pollak in 1968 that the discipline had substantially avoided the study of race relations (Pauw, 1964, p. 1097; Pollak, 1968, p. 249). In economics relatively little attention has been paid to issues such as income distribution, labour relations and trade unions. Political science as a discipline in South Africa has hardly got off the ground; of the little research done by its practitioners much has been historical in nature. It appears that political scientists have been daunted by 'the range of problems which seethe under their noses'. In every discipline, of course, there are exceptions, but then they are the exceptions that prove the rule.

Much the same analysis could be made of disciplines like law and education which in some respects impinge directly upon the social sciences. An analysis of academic legal research shows that only a tiny minority of its practitioners have ventured into the thorny thickets prevailing in areas such as security legislation, the enforcement of civil rights, or the analysis of judicial behaviour. Similarly, academic educationists seem generally to have muted their asking of what might be considered the fundamental questions concerning education and society in South Africa.

The analysis presented in the above two paragraphs is, in its very nature, impressionistic. I put forward the hypothesis in the most tentative of terms, recognizing fully that stock needs to be taken of the position in each discipline by its practitioners.

Of course, university administrators, bureaucrats, politicians and the dispensers of research funds unanimously disclaim any hostility to research into sensitive topics that may produce findings unpalatable to authority (in whatever sphere). Openly to manifest such hostility would be tantamount to acknowledging that one beats one's wife. There is, however, an awareness of the possible clash between the claims for the autonomy of science and those of society (or of its constituent segments) which may deem that some areas are taboo and would be desecrated by secular, rationalist investigation.

A former rector of Stellenbosch University, Professor H. B. Thom, alluded to this possibility in the following terms:

> The universities are there to serve the nation, but that does not imply that they are there merely to accept what are popular traditions and views held by the community or the nation. It does imply, however, that universities cannot revolt against historical patterns which have been accepted by the community. At present, there is a pattern which has been evolved in this country and has been accepted by the people and the universities must show respect for this pattern.

Thom accepted, however, that universities existed also to show the way and that there would be times when they would have to speak their mind even if this meant contradicting traditions or popular beliefs. Elsewhere Thom reaffirmed the right of scholars to publish unpopular findings, provided it was done responsibly and through the appropriate vehicle—a learned journal. He cited the case of some Stellenbosch professors who were seriously concerned that certain honestly reached conclusions would be incorrectly interpreted and that this could lead to unnecessary division and strife. They consulted the then Prime Minister, J. G. Strijdom, who listened to their problems and then commented:

> You are university people. It is your task to give guidance. Do not worry if you are sometimes ahead of the people. You are honest and upright, and as long as this is the case, our people won't take it amiss (The *Argus*, 1 1967).

This may have been reassuring to the professors concerned, but it is surely an indication of the magnitude of the problem if scholars feel obliged to seek reassurance from no less than the Prime Minister himself. Furthermore, one wonders what the reaction would have been had the professors told him what their honestly reached findings pointed starkly to one conclusion: that existing policies were untenable and ought forthwith to be abandoned.

It is of relevance to the conclusion of this chapter to ask what topics in the South African context are taboo. Taboos can be enforced by a variety of sanctions both formal (in extreme cases by prosecution) and informal. Pressure can be exerted by the state, by the scholar's university or by the community at large, or a combination of all of these.

So far as is known, only one scholar, Dr B. Van Niekerk, has been prosecuted for publishing his research findings. This case, which is described in detail in another chapter, resulted in an acquittal on a technicality. The issue of the scholar's right to explore judicial behaviour in the context of racial attitudes widely held in the society was not settled, although the presiding judge gave every indication that were he to pronounce on the issue he would have found for the protection of judges from such analysis.

In view of this finding and in view of other intimations from judges that they resent academic criticism, it must be concluded that the judiciary is substantially a taboo area. This does not, of course, imply that criticism of individual judgements (providing no *mala fides* were imputed to the judge) is forbidden, but analyses purporting to demonstrate 'executive-mindedness' among judges, or racial selectivity in the distribution of punishment, or the political factor in judicial appointments would undoubtedly rank as taboo.

It is also clear that legislation such as the Prisons Act and the Defence Act has created a further area of taboo for the press. Although the strength of this has not been tested by academics (a further pointer to lacunae in social and political research) it is highly probable that it would be considerable, especially if the investigator came from an institution whose ethos was generally critical of official policies. The taboo would apply even more strongly in the field of security.

The Suppression of Communism Act creates a further taboo area. Read in conjunction with the Unlawful Organizations Act of 1960 it makes historical, political or social research into banned organizations, such as the African National Congress, practically impossible. For one thing, the documents produced by or pertaining to such bodies are mostly not available, and even where they are it would be an offence to cite them. In 1965, it was reported that a graduate student at Pretoria University had written a master's thesis on the African National Congress which was passed *cum laude* by his department. The thesis, however, contained numerous quotations from persons restricted under the Suppression of Communism Act. The university decided to allow the candidate to present his thesis, but nobody apart from his two examiners would be permitted to see the work, pending permission from the Department of Justice to allow it to be published (*Sunday Chronicle,* 25 July 1965).

Much of the material presented in this chapter has illustrated, by implication, the growth of secretiveness in South African society. Fragmentation has hardened group loyalties and institutional loyalties within groups. Such a process breeds secretiveness because in a situation of acute inter-group tension, groups or institutions within groups are likely to fear that probings by members of other groups (or by indiscreet or disloyal members of the group itself) will reveal dark secrets or show some of their most tenaciously held beliefs to be myths or shibboleths. The crucial point here is that such findings can then be exploited by the enemy. And herein lies the major source of resistance to social research.

References

BENDIX, R. 1970. *Embattled Reason—Essays in Social Knowledge.* New York, Oxford University Press.

BIESHEUVEL, S. 1965. *The Changing Function of the Universities.* Durban, University of Natal.

CARSTENS, W. P. 1966. *The Social Structure of a Cape Coloured Reserve.* Cape Town, Oxford University Press.

CARTER, Gwendolen M.; KARIS, Thomas; STULTZ, Newwll M. 1967. *South Africa's Transkei.* London, Heinemann.

DUERDEN, J. E. 1922. Social Anthropology in South Africa: Problems of Race and Nationality. *South African Journal of Science,* Vol. 18, No. 8, p. 30.

FIFE, R. H. 1932. *Report on Tendencies in Education in East and South Africa.* New York, Carnegie Corporation.

HOBSON, J. A. 1936. *Freedom and the Social Sciences.* London, Constable.

LORAM, J. A. 1922. The Claim of the Native Question upon Scientists. *South African Journal of Science,* Vol. 18, pp. 99-109.

MACMILLAN, W. M. 1930. *Complex South Africa.* London, Faber & Faber.

MALHERBE, E. G. 1939. *Educational and Social Research in South Africa.* Pretoria, South African Council for Educational and Social Research.

——. 1946. *The Bilingual School.* London, Longmans, Green.

MAYER, P. 1961. *Townsmen or Tribesmen.* Cape Town, Oxford University Press.

PAUW, S. 1964. South Africa. In: Joseph S. Roucek (ed.), *Contemporary Sociology,* pp. 1095-9. London, Peter Owen.

POLLAK, H. 1968. *Sociology Post Graduates of South African Universities.* Durban, Joint University Committee on Sociology and Social Work.

UNIVERSITY OF NATAL. 1954. *Research Needs and Priorities in the Social Sciences.* Durban. (Mimeo.)

VAN DEN BERGHE, Pierre L. 1967. Research in South Africa—The Story of my Experiences with Tyranny. In: Gideon Sjoberg (ed.), *Ethics, Politics and Social Research,* pp. 183-97. Cambridge, Mass., Schenkman.

WEST, Martin E. 1971. *Divided Community.* Cape Town, A. A. Balkema.

WILSON, Monica; MAFEJE, Archie. 1963. *Langa.* Cape Town, Oxford University Press.

WIRTH, Louis. 1936. Introduction. In: Karl Mannheim, *Ideology and Utopia.* London, Routledge & Kegan Paul.

ZNANIECKI, Florian. 1968. *The Social Role of the Man of Knowledge.* New York, Harper Torchbooks.

3 Constraints on, and functions of, research in sociology and psychology in contemporary South Africa

Michael Savage
University of Cape Town

Introduction

Social research is never conducted in a political vacuum: the structure, tensions, and values of a society condition and are reflected in the type of social research that is produced within it. In South Africa, an authoritarian political system and a deeply divided social structure have interacted with one another to create a climate which is inhospitable and even menacing to free-ranging social inquiry. A growing battery of informal and legal restraints have emerged to circumscribe freedom of inquiry and are ensuring that certain topics remain 'off-limits' to all but the boldest or most foolhardy researcher. The restraints that the society has placed on academic research and analysis are severe and frequently make it easier for free-ranging analysis and research into South African society to occur outside the country, where access to books and periodicals is not limited by censorship and where open debate from all viewpoints is possible. Yet in what follows it will not be claimed that severe internal restraints *alone* are responsible for the apparent reluctance on the part of most researchers to take on the analysis, in their writing and teaching, of many of the most socially relevant and historically significant questions about South African society. Social scientists, like other members of this society, are limited and restricted by the norms, values and socially determined perceptions of the South African social structure, with the result that such questions often do not even occur to them. Too few of them are able, or have been trained, to stand 'outside' their own linguistic or ethnic setting to examine the causes of the development and underdevelopment of their society, its inner tendencies and the forces within it that may lead to its transformation. In short, constraints on social research in South Africa spring both from the authoritarian nature of the society and from the 'trained incapacity and professional psychosis' of many social scientists working within South Africa.[1]

The purpose of this chapter is to consider some of these themes and to consider particularly the place of sociological research, with some reference to psychological research, in the contemporary South African setting. It should be noted at the outset that the inherited academic division of labour that has been drawn between different social science 'disciplines' is regarded as being largely unimportant, except in limiting the vision of individual writers. The constraints facing psychological or sociological research hardly differ from those facing economic, historical or political research: limitations that hinder free inquiry in the field of agricultural economics also hinder the work of sociologists concerned with farm labour, and constraints placed on the study of jurisprudence similarly limit criminological research. It will be necessary to march freely across disciplinary boundaries to examine these restraints for no social science discipline is unaffected by restraints placed on the liberty of one of them. It is both artificial and dangerously misleading to consider the impediments to research faced only by single disciplines and such a focus encourages a fragmented and myopic view of the climate conditioning social research in South Africa.

In what follows the limitations to freedom of inquiry in the social sciences deriving from their place and organization in South African society will first be examined; then specific agencies which exert pressure on or control social research will be considered and, finally, the cumulative impact of these restraints and the function of sociological and psychological research will be discussed.

Social research and social structure

The majority of social research within South Africa occurs within its sixteen universities. In quantitative terms, such research far exceeds the amount of research produced by state-sponsored bodies, such as the Human Sciences Research Council or the National Institute for Personnel Research, or by autonomous research institutes. South African universities through their training of sociologists and psychologists and through their support of research workers profoundly influence the quality and type of social research that is produced.

The South African university system mirrors the deep cleavages and inequalities of the society and is moulded around its pattern of racial and ethnic segregation. There is little doubt that these universities have helped to harden and even legitimate these cleavages.[2] Afrikaans-language universities, through the values they espouse, and through their practical activities, have contributed to the shaping and implementation of apartheid. Black universities, established despite resistance to segregated education and generally manned by graduates of Afrikaans universities, have come to be one of the rallying points of African nationalism and of Black resistance to White domination. Finally English-speaking universities have come to occupy an uneasy middle position. Not only do universities reflect the ethnic and colour divisions of the society; they reflect its inequalities. White South Africa has some 230 university students per 10,000 of the population (a figure only exceeded by the United

States); the African population has 4.4 students per 10,000 of its population at universities.[3] In terms of capital expenditure on universities some R36.7 million was spent directly on White universities and some R8.7 million on Black universities in the financial year 1976/7.[4]

Against this background it is not surprising both that the type of training of social researchers reflects the divisions in the society and differs according to the university setting in which it takes place and that the White population provides all but a few of the trained sociologists and psychologists. In short, the socialization and allocation functions that are carried out by any university, in South Africa are given an extremely racial twist.[5]

Turning first to the syllabuses of university courses in sociology, the teaching of research techniques and methodology has a very high priority with some three-quarters of all universities teaching in this politically neutral area over the whole three years of a first degree.[6] In contrast, the teaching of theory appears to be de-emphasized and a conservative brand of it dominates most syllabuses. In Afrikaans-language and Black universities theory courses are structural-functional, consensus-orientated and American in their general approach. One commentator has noted that this dominant framework

> fits the White South African mind well, emphasising order, equilibrium, gradual evolutionary change—all watchwords of White South African politics. Two consequences flow from this: theory is predominantly contemporary but the more recent theoretical debates are also ignored. Sociology before Parsons is restricted to Durkheim, Weber and occasionally Comte; sociology after Parsons seems not to exist.[7]

In addition, syllabuses are characterized by offering several courses in applied sociology, which have a heavy meliorist emphasis, being focused on social problems encountered by people in the adjustment to industrial capitalism—poverty, housing, migrancy and so forth. This emphasis not only reflects the expectations of the largest single group of sociology students—those training for a career in social work—but helps narrow the intellectual climate by stressing an approach which to use Peterson's terms focuses on 'the engineering of solutions rather than the clinical examination of problems in their larger context'.[8] While research methods, conservative theory and applied sociology dominate university sociology syllabuses, there are some universities in which bold and innovative efforts to teach Marxism and to call into question the nature of the South African political economy are taking place. However these efforts are both small in number and hampered by the political harassment of the university staff who teach them, as well as by the system of censorship which excludes the use of many key works necessary for the adequate teaching of such courses. Not surprisingly a 1973 questionnaire survey of final-year sociology students found that Afrikaner students were least critical of their curriculum and Black students most critical, levelling most of their criticism at courses in theory and research methods.[9]

What is apparent is that within the teaching of sociology, the debate on the critical issues facing South Africa is too often blunted, or even avoided and that the particularly contentious, or sensitive, areas of the society are often only marginally examined, where they are examined at all. This can be illustrated in various fields. In sociology there is no single South African university that offers a distinct year-long course devoted to the study of race and ethnic relations; instead this important field is subsumed as one among other component parts of a variety of courses in the social sciences. Similarly, in the teaching of industrial sociology the overwhelming emphasis is on training students to become 'servants of power' and offering managerial insights into the problems of industrial organization. In political sociology, as in political science, it is the exception rather than the rule that any detailed or empirical analysis of the South African political system is presented in the classroom. Similarly such sociologically (and economically) important but sensitive topics as income and wealth distribution, trade unions and labour organizations and patterns of corporate ownership and control are all but avoided; in part because so little research has been conducted in these areas. It should be emphasized that the avoidance and near-avoidance of such sensitive areas in sociology finds support in the organization of syllabuses in other subjects. In psychology, no deep study of the psychology of racism and of the stresses that it inflicts on individuals is offered by any South African university. In English there is only a minuscule amount of critical analysis and rigorous scholarship concerned with local literature and a compulsory acquaintance with the writing of Black South Africans is rarely insisted upon. In history, only one university runs a distinct year-long course in African history. In law, no university departments travel far in their teaching in the complex areas of the analysis of contemporary judicial decision-making nor do they seriously examine current security legislation. In medicine, little emphasis is given to community and preventive medicine, nor to the relationship between the existing political and health structures of South Africa.

This list could be lengthend to indicate that it is more usual than not for controversy and vigorous and deep-probing analysis and debate of South Africa's problems to be blunted in the classroom. One reflection of this is found in students' ignorance about the basic operations of their society. In a social-awareness questionnaire administered at two English-language universities to large classes of first-year sociology students in 1975, 88 per cent of these students were unable to identify to the nearest 3 million the number of Africans in South Africa and most grossly overestimated the number of Jews in the population, half wrongly believed that without official permission it is not permissible for a White to entertain an African to dinner and half wrongly believed that the country has an official religion, namely Protestantism.[10]

The bias of syllabuses and the 'self-restraints' reflected within them are reinforced by a variety of political pressures. Censorship prevents a wide range of important published works from being used, bannings have silenced critical and outspoken teachers as well as research workers, and specific legislation either prevents or limits free discussion in the classroom of such topics as disinvestment, conscientious objection, Marxism, African nationalism, judicial behaviour and drug usage. Less formal pressures have also been brought to bear on students and teachers: people within the university have been employed by the security police to spy on their colleagues, classroom discussions on sensitive issues have been complained about to university and public authorities and political pressures have been brought to bear to influence both appointments and promotion of staff.

It is against this background that the training of social research workers takes place and it is not surprising that it profoundly influences the bulk of sociological and psychological research work produced in South Africa. The type of training of sociological research workers in South Africa acts as a major constraint on their ability to grapple with fundamentally important questions about the nature of South African society. Pollak has argued that

> despite the commendable amount of sociological research undertaken by South African sociologists it can scarcely be claimed that much of it is of a fundamental nature. . . . In relation to their numbers and volume of their research, sociologists in South Africa have not made substantial contributions to the analysis of economic, political and social aspects of inter-group relations, nor on the attitudes regarding the different races on policies and practices in the field of race relations in South Africa.[11]

Her comments are borne out by the recently published *Bibliography of South African Sociology*, which provides a relatively comprehensive list of all sociological writings up to 1975.[12] The largest section of this bibliography is that dealing with 'Race and Ethnic Group Relations' but an examination of it reveals that many of the items cited are not by sociologists, and those that are provide only muted and tangential comments on race relations. An over-concentration on the study of White social attitudes is evident together with a corresponding de-emphasis on those of Blacks, and on structural studies of racism. The next largest section in the bibliography is devoted to 'Social Problems' with most of the items cited being written from a social welfare perspective and not containing clinical analyses of the relationship between the South African social structure and the 'social problem' being investigated. The third largest section lists research undertaken within the general field of industrial sociology and most of these writings having a 'problem-solving' orientation. Few of them touch upon an examination of capitalism and its ideology in South Africa.

Many of these emphases are accounted for by the small number of trained Black research workers, who could bring to an examination of research problems (and also to the choice of problems for research) radically different experiences and perspectives from those of the White researcher. The dearth of Black research workers, which is mirrored in the enrolment of a mere twenty-three postgraduate students in sociology in Black universities in 1978, forms a crippling handicap to the development of social research dealing with the crucial social and political issues confronting southern Africa. The cognitive conservatism of most research and its failure to deal with fundamentally important issues is, in great measure, a direct result of the numerical domination by the Whites of the research process. The few Black social researchers who have operated within South Africa—such as Fatima Meer, Archie Mafeje, Noel Manganyi, Nimrod Mkele—have made some of the most important contributions to South African social science. However, their criticisms and probings of the society have generally not been welcomed and some, such as Meer, have been banned, others have been severely harassed and many have left the country, having found it impossible to operate as scholars within it. It is doubtful whether the position of the Black researcher in the research process will change in the near future, as many politically aware Blacks refuse to enrol in segregated universities and those that do, and are students of the social sciences, are exposed to teachers who predominantly are graduates of Afrikaans-language universities and reflect in their teaching the biases of their own training. Above all the political climate remains overtly hostile to any Black probing into the operations of South African society.

Apart from the universities, the other major institution directly affecting social research is the Human Sciences Research Council (HSRC). The HSRC, which was founded in 1969, is the major state agency for funding and conducting research and contains ten research units including the Institute for Sociological, Demographic and Criminological Research. The bulk of its finance is derived from a direct government subsidy, which in 1976/77 amounted to R4.3 million, a figure which should be contrasted to the R30 million government subsidy granted to its sister organization, the Council for Scientific and Industrial Research.[13] The HSRC in 1976/77 employed some 214 full-time research workers and some 80 per cent of its research money is spent on supporting its own research. The organization is governed by a Council of ten members, all White, who are appointed by the Minister of National Education who is in charge of White education. The attitude of the HSRC to social research is set out in its first annual report, which stated:

> In the Republic, however, social sciences research is not a dogma superimposed from above as an instrument of national policy; and the aim of the HSRC is to encourage and stimulate research in the social sciences by free and independent scholars whose labours, it is hoped, will lead to a fuller satisfaction of the needs and aspirations of the various peoples in our country.[14]

It is difficult to assess whether over the years of its existence the HSRC has fostered the growth of 'free and independent' scholars. On the one hand, the organization has supported independent research into some sensitive areas and provided grants to some cognitively radical social scientists. On the other, the HSRC is seen as being a conservative government agency operating within the confines of government policy. No Blacks serve on any one of its eleven controlling committees, which are all dominated by academics drawn from conservative Afrikaans-language institutions. Its publications too are marked by a deep conservatism and at times an overt commitment to apartheid. One indication of this is found in the April 1978 *Newsletter* of the HSRC reporting on the initiation of HSRC research into mentally gifted schoolchildren. After a preamble the newsletter states:

> ... an exceptional intellect can only be utilised to the optimal benefit of society if its possessor has learnt to deal with people, *is guided by a Christian National philosophy of life,* has a balanced outlook as regards his sense of values and is endowed with wisdom that is based on moral and ethical grounds [emphasis added].[15]

Such a statement from the HSRC indicates that those not holding to the government created and approved 'Christian National' philosophy, that is opponents of the government and non-Christians, cannot contribute to 'the optimal benefit of society'. An examination of HSRC publications shows that few of them deal with important or sensitive issues and the majority of them are pedestrian documents concerned with such topics as the adaptation of Czechoslovakian immigrants into Pretoria, church attendance, the use of tobacco and alcohol in the South African population and worker absenteeism. As Welsh points out, it is clear that its own research workers operate within the framework of government policy, but what cannot be demonstrated is whether, in allocating research money to those working outside of the HSRC, it systematically favours research projects that do not impinge upon controversial areas.[16] Until recently, the HSRC refused scholars permission to publish any 'interim' report on research undertaken with HSRC funds unless they had obtained the council's permission to do so, and scholars had to submit a final research report 'acceptable' to the HSRC. This position has led the HSRC to cable a political scientist at a conference refusing her permission to deliver her prepared paper. The 'acceptability' ruling for final reports has also led to uniquely South African situations: for HSRC readers have been known to recommend that research reports not be accepted as they have quoted from banned publications or set the policy of apartheid in a bad light.[17]

The other major agency controlling non-university research is the National Institute of Personnel Research (NIPR) whose chief emphasis is on research into industrial psychology. In this broad area it has undertaken a considerable amount of research for the Defence Force, State Departments and for private industry. The work of the NIPR is marked by a high standard of technical competence and by a problem-solving orientation. Inevitably reflected in this work are many of the tensions of a divided society, particularly as found in the workplace. NIPR research reports, while detailing with many of these tensions, attempt generally to steer clear of potentially controversial comment on them and instead emphasize the empirical and technical details of the research. The organization has not always managed to avoid political controversy. At one stage the Defence Force broke off its relationship with the NIPR for reasons never made public. One of its research projects involved testing the I.Q. levels of a sample of members of different population groups. The result of this research revealed the Afrikaner group in the sample to have the lowest average I.Q. Considerable pressure was said to have been put on the director of the NIPR not to allow the results of this research project to be published. The director refused to interfere with the publication of this research and later a critique of the project was published by one member of the NIPR staff.

In addition to sociological and social research being conducted by university departments and state-funded institutions, there are a range of autonomous institutions which conduct research (such as the South African Institute of Race Relations and the Africa Institute) as well as a considerable number of research institutes attached to universities.[18] Many of these research bodies have produced important and fundamental research into sensitive and controversial areas and, as discussed later, have been attacked for doing so. Recently the Department of Information 'scandal' involving the use of millions of rands of public funds for secret projects to buy publicity favourable to apartheid has revealed that some of the secret projects involved the financing of three university research institutes—the Institute for the Study of Plural Societies at the University of Pretoria, the Institute for Strategic Studies also at the University of Pretoria and the Centre for International Politics at the University of Potchefstroom. Of these three institutes the Institute for the Study of Plural Societies has been particularly active. It was headed by a sociologist, Professor Nic Rhoodie, and claimed independence while secretly receiving R100,000 a year to do research and organize conferences. To hide its true nature top South African business men, such as Iscor's Dr T. Muller and Volkskas Bank's Dr Jan Hurter, became ghost donors to the institute with the Department of Information paying for their contributions. The institute has run conferences both in South Africa and New York which sociologists such as Talcott Parsons and Heribert Adam have attended. The 'secret' financing gives rise to the possibility that other secret money is being used to consciously subvert 'free and independent' sociological research.

This section, with its emphasis on the institutional setting in which sociological and psychological research occurs, has attempted to sketch out the power of institutional conservatism in influencing the research process. Who it is who is selected to be trained as a social researcher, the biases and emphases in what they are taught and the organizational framework of social research are as significant in shaping social research in South Africa as the direct constraints placed on research by the state and by community agencies.

Agencies of restraint

A large number of differing groups and agencies directly restrain freedom of social inquiry, and particularly inquiry into the 'sensitive' areas of South African society. Laws prevent Whites from going into urban Black townships or African rural areas without official permits; access to mine compounds, which are 'private property', requires permission as does entry to White farms. Bans prevent access to key informants and restrict mobility for interviews. Censorship has meant that a large range of essential literature is unavailable to South African sociologists and psychologists. Research workers have been harassed by police, some scholars have been prosecuted for publishing their work or possessing the published work of others. Community groups and voluntary organizations have placed pressure on researchers and prevented them from gaining access to important material. This partial list of constraints is best probed by first considering some illustrations of the pressures by the state that individual social researchers have encountered during their work.

One of the clearest illustrations of pressure being brought to bear on a researcher occurred in 1970 when a scholar was prosecuted for having published his research findings. Barend Van Niekerk, a law professor, published two articles in the *South African Law Journal* in which he gave an overview of the situation in South Africa as regards capital punishment.[19] In these articles he included the results of a questionnaire that he had distributed to all practising advocates about their views and experiences concerning the death penalty. The questionnaire contained two questions about possible racial discrimination in the administration of justice. The one question being: 'Do you consider, for whatever reason, that a non-European tried on a capital charge stands a better chance of being sentenced to death than a European?' The other question asked: 'If your answer was 'Yes' [to the previous question] do you think the differentiation shown to the different races as regards the death penalty is conscious and deliberate?' In his published articles Van Niekerk reproduced these two questions and commented:

> Whatever conclusion one may draw from the results of these two questions, the fact which emerges undeniably is that a considerable number of replying advocates, almost 50 per cent in fact, believe that justice as regards capital punishment is meted out on a differential basis to the different races, and that 41 per cent who so believe are also of the opinion that such differentiation is 'conscious and deliberate'.[20]

Van Niekerk was then charged with contempt of court for bringing the South African judiciary into contempt, violating their dignity and respect and casting suspicion on the administration of justice. During his trial, no attempt was made to question or dispute the accuracy of his reported results; central to the charge and judgement was the mere posing of the two questions. He was acquitted on the technicality that there was an absence of *mens rea*, or intent to commit crime, but in giving judgement the presiding judge indicated that in his view contempt had been committed. Consequently, the trial clearly indicated the perils that any future scholars might face if they were to investigate closely judicial behaviour and the social factor in sentencing policy. Van Niekerk later wrote that as long as the judgement in his case stands there will be

> no further attempt in South Africa to devote scholarly attention to the racial factor in our administration of justice. Neither is there much likelihood (and this is more important as far as the newspapers are concerned) of robust

comment about the possible influence of social factors in the administration of justice. It needs little argument to conclude that if the mere reporting of the results of an enquiry could lead to a prosecution . . . there will be few people willing to take chances as regards the publication of more robust comments and criticism.[21]

In the years that have elapsed since this case, no scholarly research or published article in South Africa, directly or indirectly, has dealt with questions of judicial behaviour and the administration of justice. The practical effect of the Van Niekerk case has been to warn researchers that investigations into race and racial attitudes in the administration of justice, into judicial behaviour and sentencing policy are essentially 'off-limits' and are topics on which any researcher writes at his peril. As a consequence, as Dugard has commented: 'Most academic lawyers have therefore sought safety in the quiet waters of private and commercial law—like the jurists of Imperial Rome and authoritarian Holland before them.'[22] Yet it is not only lawyers that this prosecution has affected—the sociologist interested in criminology, in the issues of racial discrimination and the appointments and behaviour of judicial officers is also affected by the implications of this judgement, as are research workers who may be concerned with examining aspects of the psychology of racism in public life.

Some of the warnings embodied in the Van Niekerk case were underlined the following year when Van Niekerk was again charged with contempt of court, for having in a public speech criticized judges in their approach to the Terrorism Act. This time he was convicted. In 1975 also he was charged and convicted for having defamed the Minister of Justice in a newspaper interview by implying that racial discrimination played a part in a government decision to recommend clemency for a convicted White murderer but not to recommend it for a Black murderer convicted of having taken part in the same crime.

Prior to the Van Niekerk case another area, the examination of the administration of prisons, had essentially been declared 'off-limits' to critical scrutiny. In 1968 the *Rand Daily Mail* editor and Benjamin Pogrund, one of the paper's journalists had been prosecuted for publishing a series of articles on prison conditions. The Prisons Act of 1959 makes it an offence to publish 'any false information concerning the behaviour or experience in prison of any prisoner or concerning the administration of any prison . . . without taking reasonable steps to verify such information'. The onus of proof is on the accused and those charged in the *Rand Daily Mail* case were found guilty. The practical effect of the Act and of this prosecution is that it is now impossible either to publish any adverse information about the administration of prisons or any probing analyses of conditions within them without immediately running the risk of prosecution. Since this prosecution, critical scrutiny of the prison system has ceased and no sociologist nor psychologist to my knowledge has entered this potential minefield.[23]

A more recent case poses equally severe threats to social scientists. In 1978, a graduate student in psychology at Rhodes University undertook a study of the use of drugs among the students at the university. One report of this study appeared in the student newspaper and the report was subsequently picked up first by a conservative Afrikaans newspaper and then by the national press. As newspaper reports of the study spread countrywide they became more lurid and filled out with comment (some of the comments revealing South African White prejudices, for instance a warden of a women's residence at the university was quoted as saying that 'women students using drugs were easily identifiable by their abnormal interest in natives. They became over affectionate and flung their arms round natives'.) One morning at 2 a.m. the student, who had conducted the study, was woken by police and taken for questioning. Police seized his research notes together with tape-recordings of interviews that he had made during his study. At the police station, the student was told that he would be held for fourteen days for questioning, as is provided for under the Drugs Act, and that the period of detention would be renewed until such time as he identified his informants and the voices on the tape. The student identified these informants and was released. Subsequently several persons were arrested and charged under the Drugs Act. Such a case clearly raises difficult ethical issues for social scientists: chief of these being should social scientists working within South Africa undertake research on issues where it is likely that police may attempt to discover the identity of their informants? This case, together with other incidents where police have seized research material, or imprisoned journalists for refusing to reveal their sources of information, point to the danger that social scientists face in collecting information on such socially sensitive topics as Black political activities, prison conditions and individual deviant behaviour.

The dilemma facing social scientists, of being damned as ineffective if they do not do research into sensitive areas, or being considered foolhardy if by doing it they unwittingly expose their informants, or themselves, to harassment, is a peculiar one demanding peculiar solutions. One Grahamstown sociologist, engaged in a survey of Black workers, destroyed her sampling list after police had acted against the student studying drug usage and thus effectively prevented herself from further interviewing any of her informants or later carrying out a follow-up study. Other sociologists, such as Pierre Van den Berghe, report that they have adopted different solutions by publicly deceiving people as to the true nature of their research in the hope that this would shelter them and their informants from unwelcome attention.[24]

A comparable incident took place at the University of Cape Town during 1977, when an American graduate student was employed by a university research unit to investigate Black South Africans' subjective experiences at work. As a foreigner, it was thought that Black South Africans would talk to him more freely and easily about their perceptions of their work than they would to a White South African. A part of his research involved the tape-recording of a series of interviews with Black workers. It is probable that one topic emerging in these interviews concerned political organizations. After completing many interviews the researcher left the country hurriedly and very shortly afterwards police seized his tape-recordings. Subsequently the police were approached for the return of these tapes, as they were to form the basis of a forthcoming publication. After some months the tapes were returned to the research unit by the police and it was then discovered that they had been wiped clean, and important and irreplaceable research material due for publication had been lost.

The experience of sociological research material falling into the hands of the police is not unusual. Several South African research workers have been 'raided' by security police and had publications which are important for their research confiscated and files temporarily removed from them. In 1977, a graduate sociology student writing a thesis on the Black Consciousness movement was stopped at a police road-block and, when it was discovered that he had research notes on this movement, was detained for questioning at the local police station. After some hours he was released but police held his notes for several weeks, returning them to him a few days before his thesis was due to be submitted. Visiting social research workers also have had their material fall into police hands. Professor Gwendolen Carter and her associates experienced the mysterious disappearance of a briefcase from their locked hotel rooms and its reappearance in a police station, and some of her assistants were searched by the security police on leaving the country.[25] Although I have been unable to verify the accuracy of this, it was reported to me that a visiting researcher managed to obtain on loan a copy of the Hoek Report, a secret document prepared for the ultraconservative Afrikaner Orde examining the power and workings of the giant Anglo-American Corporation. Within hours the researcher was visited by security police, the document taken and the person requested to leave the country immediately.[26]

These selected practical illustrations of interference by the state and its officials are given to provide a backdrop against which to examine briefly the web of legislation and government policy circumscribing the research process. The impact of such legislation and policy on research cannot usually be so directly observed, particularly as it often prevents actual research being carried out in the first place.

The network of legislation and policy that denies researchers access to people, places, publications, documents and information on public affairs is vast. Mathews in an important recent book *The Darker Reaches of Government* states:

> Denial of access to information is carried to its logical extreme by the relevant laws in South Africa. These laws are so negative in terms of both number and impact that it is impossible to conceive of anything on the positive side. This is true even at the level of local government where provisions requiring council meetings to be open are subject to the uncontrolled discretion of councils to resolve themselves into closed committee sessions. Local government documents other than council minutes may not be inspected unless permission is given. . . .[27]

At the national level, four aspects of government restraint on access to information particularly affect sociological research: censorship, restrictions governing access to places, bannings of individuals and a variety of legislation regulating the gathering and reporting of specific information.

Turning first to censorship, an estimated minimum of some 18,000 published works are banned, including many sociological classics, most writings on Marxism, on African nationalism, a large range of works on South African society, political movements and all writings of South Africans who are banned or listed under the Internal Security Act. Among banned books are those such as J. Dollard, *Caste and Class in a Southern Town*; André Beteille, *Social Inequality*; C. Wright Mills, *The Marxists*; I. M. Zeitlin, *Marxism Re-examined*; H. J. and R. E. Simons, *Class and Colour in South Africa*; Leo Kuper, *Passive Resistance in South Africa*; A. Sachs, *Justice in South Africa*; together with most analyses of southern African Black writers such as G. Mbeki, *The Peasants Revolt*; E. Mondlane, *The Struggle for Mozambique*. The complex thicket of censorship legislation has been ably commented upon by a limited number of South African writers to indicate the near impossibility of serious South African scholars keeping abreast of social science—and other—scholarly writing.[28] Monica Wilson has commented that 'a scholar must holiday abroad if he is to keep up to date with history, literature or even theology written by black South Africans'.[29]

The scale of censorship has been stepped up with the Publications Act of 1974, which has encouraged the Publications Control Board to focus its attention on 'political' material and enabled it to prohibit the possession of banned works (a 'right' that formerly rested with the government). During the first year of its operations 191 publications were banned on political grounds and of these it was prohibited to possess 20. In 1977 however 317 works of a total of 1,160 were banned on political grounds and it was prohibited to possess 282 of these; in 1978 some 1,178 works were banned and of these it was prohibited to possess 437.[30] This trend is reflected in increasing actions against the press. Since 1976 the important Black newspaper serving Soweto, *The World,* has been banned, as have been issues of other Black newspapers *The Voice* and *The Nation* and an escalating number of issues of student newspapers. A clear trend of increasing political censorship is occurring and to a growing extent 'political and artistic expression alike are at the mercy of an Afrikaner elite which controls both the legislative and executive branches of government'.[31]

To a limited extent, libraries are able to hold banned material of 'a non-communistic nature' but:

> Hardly a library in South Africa has ever held it a duty to preserve the ephemeral pamphlets, leaflets and unpublished documents which an author needs in order to reconstruct the course taken from time to time by the ANC. ... Since 1960 to harbour records and publications of an unlawful organisation has been virtually a criminal enterprise. To walk into even a university library and ask for such things is to see the librarian shudder—and in some centres you would be fortunate if he did not telephone the police before you left the library.[32]

Accompanying overt censorship are two equally important other forms of censorship: conscious self-censorship and unconscious self-censorship. Overt censorship has created a climate promoting these latter forms of censorship, which have come to assume increasing importance. Conscious self-censorship led the publishers of *The Oxford History of South Africa* to excise Leo Kuper's chapter on African nationalism, which quoted many banned people and publications, from the South African edition of the book. In its place fifty-three pages were left blank. The publishers feared that if they included the chapter, the whole book would be banned and that the Oxford University Press might be prosecuted. Kuper accused the publishers of acting in 'the self-appointed role of surrogate censor' and of committing 'an act of political regression'. [33] After some years the publishers were informed that the book would not be banned in its uncensored version and the full version of it became available (despite the then head of the Bureau of State Security launching an attack on the 'communistic nature' of the book). [34] This episode starkly brings out the existence of self-censorship and several social scientists I have spoken to admit to having engaged in this practice. Most recently, the editors of a book of sociological readings said that they had omitted selected readings by authors who were banned, for fear of having their book proscribed. The testimony to the power of ideological control ultimately lies in the field of unconscious self-censorship: much of what could be termed the sociological imagination originates from the subconscious and ideas formulated there may be unconsciously suppressed by self-protective mechanisms. One writer commented in an interview that his

> imagination is interfered with because one is continually aware of what society expects and approves. . . . When I was writing in the United States for an overseas market I could feel my process of imagination was incredibly freer. I find this kind of suppression of thought very frightening. [35]

Another major area of legislation restraining sociological research is that governing access to places. Whisson, in Chapter 4, sets out the limitations placed on anthropological research workers wishing to enter 'Black' areas and such limitations equally affect sociological and psychological research. One illustration of these restrictions occurred recently when a sociologist was given permission to interview in a Black urban area but had to first submit for approval his questionnaire to officials at a Bantu Affairs Administration Board. They returned his form, having deleted some important questions. The general effect of having to obtain permission to enter 'Black' areas, as Hammond-Tooke points out, has been

> to force the research worker to 'play it safe' either by selecting as politically neutral a topic as possible or by failing to push his interaction with the people or questioning as far as he should (less his permit be withdrawn). This uncertainty also affects publication of results. There is a danger that if a report is published which criticises government policy, either implicitly or explicitly, further fieldwork facilities will be withheld. [36]

Because of the permit system there are also limitations placed on methods of inquiry, as, for instance, it is generally not possible for White researchers to live in the houses of Africans or to enter African townships at night. Blacking has remarked that

> One result of this situation is the growth of a division of labour in South African anthropology: the Blacks collect the data and the Whites write it up. In this way White anthropologists continue to be the only experts on the Blacks. [37]

As significant are the restrictions governing access to South Africa itself. Cotter and Karis have documented the large range of noted Africanist scholars who have been refused visas to enter South Africa and suggest that in particular visas are refused to scholars who the government considers might take a hostile stance to apartheid or probe too deeply into contentious or sensitive areas in the society. [38]

Legislation banning individuals also affects free inquiry. Since the introduction of bannings in 1950, some 1,358 banning orders have been issued and some 367 people who have been banned have left the country. [39] As of October 1978, 146 people in South Africa were living under 3- or 5-year bans, amongst these are several staff and students of universities, together with many Black unionists, Black political leaders and community workers. Although relatively few of those banned have been involved in social research, they have tended to be people concerned with research into such sensitive topics as wages and working conditions and political organizations. Not only has their silencing affected important research work but the system of banning has restricted access to key informants and their writings, and there can be little doubt that the system has discouraged others from entering into research into contentious fields. A vast range of other legislation either directly or tangentially shapes the research process in South Africa, which cannot be fully commented upon here. [40] Indications of the far-reaching nature of this legislation are found in legislative measures prohibiting any person from furnishing information about any business enterprise in response to 'any order, direction or letter of request issued or emanating from outside of the Republic'. Similar prohibitions about obtaining information on the affairs of business men and companies are contained in the Wage Act, the Shops and Offices Act and the Industrial Conciliation Act, and these prohibitions have been used to deny trade unions the official adjudications of complaints they have made on behalf of their members. [41] Inquiry into police behaviour is also limited by the 1979 Police Act Amendment which makes it an offence to publish 'any untrue matter' about the police 'without having reasonable grounds ... for believing that the statement is true'. The penalty for such an offence is a fine up to R10,000 and/or imprisonment for five years. A simple denial by the police of the accuracy of any report would probably succeed in preventing publication of such things as alleged malpractices or discrimination by the police. Similar legislative measures essentially ensure that sociologists and psychologists face a significant danger of prosecution if they publish hard-hitting analyses of the military or state security forces and their behaviour.

Such legislation reaches down to the level of publication of opinion polls. In 1978, legislation was passed which prohibits the publication of these polls during election periods. During the Parliamentary debate on this measure it was claimed that opinion polls have 'a preconceived malicious intention of influencing voters' and were conducted by 'so-called learned professors' who were 'agents' of the opposition. No evidence was presented of polls influencing any electoral outcome and outside of Parliament it was suspected that this prohibition was not unrelated to a growing attraction to the habit of executing messengers bearing unwelcome news.

The growing power of the state to control access to information and its publication has led to many of the basic and important aspects of South African society being shrouded in secrecy and not being able to be exposed to public scrutiny. Where social scientists do attempt to probe into areas which are considered sensitive, they often have to face attacks for doing so.

In 1975, a political scientist at a well-known university embarked upon a study of public policy-making. He interviewed the then Prime Minister, several members of the Cabinet and senior public servants. His research was aimed at understanding policy-making by studying the process of how decisions were reached in such areas as the compilation of the budget, the control of the then Department of Information, and the decision to invade Angola. Having completed the interviews for his study, the political scientist himself was interviewed by a journalist on his preliminary findings, and a report of this interview appeared in the local press. It is then believed that the head of the political scientist's university department heard that the Prime Minister was annoyed at the appearance of this report. As the Prime Minister could decree any description of the workings of the Cabinet to fall under the Official Secrets Act, it is thought that the head of the department wrote apologizing for the appearance of the article on behalf of the department and the university, and in return received letters from both the Prime Minister and members of the Cabinet thanking him.

The political scientist then wrote the following letter to the Prime Minister

> Dear Mr Prime Minister,
> The Head of my Department has informed me that he has received a letter from you in which you expressed annoyance at my use of information obtained during an interview I had with you.
> In my original letter to you requesting an interview I stated that I was writing a chapter on public policy and desired to have a view from the top. At no stage was confidentiality discussed and I assumed that the interview would be on the record.
> If it was your intention that the discussion be off the record, I would appreciate it if you would communicate this directly to me.

In reply he received a letter from the Prime Minister's Private Secretary

> Dear . . .,
> I have been instructed by the Honourable the Prime Minister to acknowledge receipt of your letter dated. . . .
> It is clear from your letter under reply that you do not appreciate or pretend to appreciate the gravity of what you have done and under such circumstances correspondence with you will serve no purpose whatsoever.

The political scientist then wrote up his research which was published as a chapter in a book but all quotes and all case-studies were deleted by the publisher who considered that their publication might be thought to be a violation of the Official Secrets Act. Even a footnote thanking Cabinet members for their help was replaced with a note of thanks to senior people active in public life.

A similar episode occurred when the director of a university research institute of criminology wrote a biting analysis of the security laws. His article was given wide publicity and he informally heard that the then Minister of Justice was no longer willing to give him assistance on any matter. The institute at which he worked helped edit an academic journal and after this incident it appeared that some members of the editorial board who were state officials were distancing themselves from the journal. Other public pressures have been more overtly expressed. In 1978, social scientists published a report of a survey on employment of Black workers living at the Crossroads squatter camp. The report was immediately attacked in a press statement by the chairman of the local administration board who called it 'irresponsible and provocative', adding that it was 'entirely unreliable' as 'would be the case with every survey on Crossroads carried out by any private organisation'. [42] A similar attack was launched in Parliament on another sociologist, who had written to the local press a series of letters regarding this squatter camp. He was accused in the House 'of encouraging the people of Crossroads to break the law and defy authority. The result is inspired defiance of national policy'. It was also suggested that his influence and meddling may have stirred up hate for Whites, which is an actionable offence.

Another instance of unpalatable arguments leading to a government attack on their author occurred when a prominent Afrikaner business man, Dr A. D. Wassenaar published his book *Assault on Private Enterprise*. In it he proposed the novel argument that 'government intervention in the economy had grown to a point when one must ask whether South Africa could not be considered a communist state with an Afrikaans economic dictatorship'. [43] In an unprecedented move a government M.P. introduced a parliamentary motion that 'This house is of the opinion that the Republic's present economic system . . . is based on the principles of free enterprise.' The purpose of the motion appeared to be to enable the Prime Minister to launch a bitter attack on Dr Wassenaar. This attack was widely reported in the press and it would be surprising if Afrikaner academics failed to understand the lesson behind it: criticism of government policy could lead to public denunciation by their elders and potential exclusion from the centres of power.

It is not only from state and government officials that attacks and restrictions on sociological research and academic argument take place. There are community pressures also resisting free inquiry and research. Some of these pressures emanate from a Black community resistant to 'White research' upon them and adopting strategies to short-circuit it, [44] but at present most of the pressures derive from within the White community. This is scarcely surprising for, as has been pointed out by several authors, typically efforts to constrain free inquiry come from those who have a vested interest in the status quo and who fear that free inquiry may stimulate dissension and unrest.

Several episodes of White community antipathy to research have been reported. Van der Merwe, who directed a nationwide study of White elites, reports on a senior civil servant who withdrew his questionnaire after having completed it, and who then launched an active campaign against the study:

> One of his major objections was that, even though we promise individual anonymity we might reveal group characteristics. When asked to explain he said it would be highly undesirable and embarassing to the government if our findings would report liberal and anti-government attitudes among senior civil servants. We were unable to give the assurance that such findings would be concealed. [45]

Religious groups in the White community appear to be particularly prone to exerting influence on free research. Welsh in Chapter 2 reports on two episodes where religious groups have hampered open inquiry and several reports have reached me of university theological faculties exerting pressure on more forthright teachers and departments in Afrikaans universities and of hindering free-ranging sociological research into groups on campus.

Community pressure has also been exerted from, or on, financial supporters of academic work in the social sciences. In 1978, a National Party M.P., Mr Kent Durr publicly argued that 'business men should prevent their grants to universities being used by socialist thinkers'. [46] Another instance involved the planned use of a historic photograph on the cover of an annual report of a research institute at the University of Cape Town. The photograph was of three important student leaders—the President of the Afrikaans Studentebond (Mr Johann Fick), the President of the National Union of South African Students (Mr Neville Curtis) and the President of the South African Students' Organization (Mr Steve Biko). These leaders had been brought together for the first time to attend a conference some years back on the role of students in society. Staff of the institute had placed the photograph of this historic meeting on the cover of the report and some issues of the report had been printed before the chairman of the institute's major donor agency objected on the grounds that such a prominent display would upset some Afrikaans-speaking people and would provoke the Afrikaans press into attacking the institute. The director of the institute then telephoned leading Afrikaner journalists who assured him that they would not take offence if this photograph were reproduced on the cover. Thereupon the grounds of the objection shifted and it was claimed that the government would be offended by the photograph. Under pressure, and not wanting to offend his major donor agency, the director of the institute ordered the report to be printed with the offending photograph placed inside the report in a less prominent position.

The legislation outlined here restricting access to publications, places, people, information, together with the attacks and constraints on free inquiry, mirror directly the tensions and cleavages of a deeply divided society. In such a society it is scarcely surprising that the guardians of group and ideological purity have become highly suspicious of the social scientist and have acted to constrain his probings into its operations and behind its ideologies.

Conclusion

Constraints on sociological and psychological research, and on the total social research process in South Africa, emanate from a large number of varied sources: from the timidities of social scientists, from their trained incapacities and from direct pressures exerted on free inquiry by the state, government and local communities.

In most societies a 'relevant' social science has an uneasy relationship with the wider society whose operations it is probing. Many of the critical issues that such a social science deals with are controversial, and are ones upon which there is often little agreement, academically or politically, although there is usually a 'dominant' view on them. The social science that probes into and behind these controversial issues and questions the dominant view on them almost inevitably attracts hostility from the groups whose viewpoints and organization are being examined and called into question by such probing.

For these reasons it is not surprising that social research in South Africa has been subjected to attacks and that major restraints have been placed on free inquiry. The society is deeply divided and a growing polarization between its main two groups has produced fears that any clinical examination of social issues could weaken the strength of the dominant viewpoint and expose the dominating group to attack. Power and secrecy thus have become fused together. [47]

Sociology and psychology fit uneasily into the society. Much of their teaching and research is welcomed and needed. But where the sociologist or psychologist probes too deeply into social arrangements then his trade can become a dangerous one, but then he should know this. As the first professor of sociology at the University of the Witwatersrand pointed out in his inaugural lecture in 1937, that 'in every authoritarian country it is the worker in the social sciences who is the first to be tamed'. [48]

Notes

1. The phrase is Maurice Zeitlin's in the introduction to his book *American Society Inc.*, p. x, Chicago, Markham, 1970.
2. See David Welsh and Michael Savage, 'The University in Divided Societies: The Case of South Africa', in H. W. Van der Merwe and D. J. Welsh (eds.), *The Future of the University in Southern Africa*, pp. 130-147, Cape Town, David Philip, 1977, 302 pp.
3. Figures from F. Orkin, L. O. Nicholaysen and M. Price, 'The Future of the Urban University in South Africa', *Social Dynamics* (Cape Town), Vol. 5, No. 1, June 1979.
4. Figures from L. Gordon, et al., *A Survey of Race Relations in South Africa, 1978*, p. 449, Johannesburg, South African Institute of Race Relations, 1979.
5. See Geoff Budlender, *Looking Forward: The University in a Democratic South Africa*, Cape Town, University of Cape Town, 1978, 23 pp.
6. Anonymous, 'Sociology in South Africa', *Network*, 11 May 1978, pp. 7-8.
7. Ibid., p. 7.
8. Richard A. Peterson, 'Sociology and Society: The Case of South Africa', *Sociological Inquiry*, Vol. 36, No. 1, Winter 1966, p. 37.
9. See A. Paul Hare and Michael Savage, 'Sociology and South Africa', *Annual Review of Sociology* (in press).
10. Michael Savage and Gerd Wiendieck, 'Social Awareness of Sociology Students in South Africa'. Unpublished paper presented to the 6th ASSA Conference, Swaziland, 1975.
11. Hansi Pollak, *Sociology Post graduates of South African Universities*, p. 258, Durban, Joint Universities Committee on Sociology and Social Work, 1968.
12. H. C. J. van Rensburg and R. A. Viljoen, *A Bibliography of the South African Sociology*, Potchefstroom, Institute of Contemporary Studies, University of the Orange Free State, 1978, 626 pp.
13. See Hare and Savage, op. cit.
14. Human Sciences Research Council, *First Annual Report*, Pretoria, HSRC, 1970.
15. Human Sciences Research Council, 'Their Future Our Responsibility', *Newsletter*, No. 99, April 1978.
16. David Welsh, 'Social Research in a Divided Society', *Social Dynamics* (Cape Town), Vol. 1, No. 1, June 1975, pp. 19-30.
17. The HSRC has now modified its position and interim reports may be published without reference to it as long as no reference is made to the HSRC as having supported the research.
18. See details in Human Sciences Research Council, *Directory of Research Organizations in the Human Sciences in South Africa*, Pretoria, HSRC, 1972.
19. Barend Van Niekerk, 'Hanged by the Neck', *South African Law Journal* (Johannesburg), Vol. 86, November and February 1969 and 1970, pp. 457-75 and 60-75.
20. Ibid.
21. Barend Van Niekerk, 'The Taboos in Legal Research: A Personal Case History', *Social Dynamics* (Cape Town), Vol. 2, No. 1, June 1976, p. 46.
22. John Dugard, *Human Rights and the South African Legal Order*, p. 301, Princeton, Princeton University Press, 1978.
23. One lawyer comments: 'In practice the law now operates as an effective legal barrier to the publication of any adverse information about prison conditions.'
24. See Pierre L. Van den Berghe, 'Research in South Africa: The Story of my Experiences with Tyranny', in Gideon Sjoberg (ed.), *Ethics, Politics and Social Research*, pp. 183-97, London, Routledge & Kegan Paul, 1967, 358 pp.
25. See Gwendolen Carter, Thomas Karis and Newell M. Stultz, *South Africa's Transkei*, London, Heinemann, 1967.
26. The origins of the Hoek Report are described in Anthony Hocking, *Oppenheimer and Son* (Johannesburg, McGraw Hill, 1973, pp. 429-32). The report was also the subject of an urgent application by Professor P. Hoek to the Supreme Court, when he asked for an order restraining a White mine-workers' leader from publishing any part of it and for all copies of the report in his possession to be surrendered.
27. Anthony Mathews, *The Darker Reaches of Government*, p. 138, Cape Town, Juta, 1978.
28. See, for instance, Barry Dean, 'Censorship and the Law', *Philosophical Papers* (Grahamstown), Vol. V, No. 1, May 1976, pp. 34-52; André Du Toit, 'The Absurdities of Censorship', *Civil Rights Newsletter* (Cape Town), Vol. 25, pp. 1-2; David Welsh, 'Censorship and the Universities', *Philosophical Papers* (Grahamstown), Vol. V, No. 1, May 1976, pp. 19-33.

29. Monica Wilson, . . . *So Truth Be in the Field,* Johannesburg, South African Institute of Race Relations, 1975.
30. Louise Silver, 'The Statistics of Censorship', *South African Law Journal* (Johannesburg), Vol. 76, January 1979, pp. 120-26.
31. Dugard, op. cit., p. 201. A new twist has been added as Afrikaans publications have come to be banned. In August 1978 Justice Snyman, Chairman of the Publications Control Board, said that some Afrikaans writers were dehumanizing mankind and that the *non-reading* Afrikaners had a right to control what was being done to their language *(Sea A Survey of Race Relations in South Africa 1978,* op. cit., p. 132).
32. *Times Literary Supplement,* 24 September 1971. Switzer and Switzer also have commented: 'The copyright libraries only began collecting South African serial publications on an irregular basis from the 1950's and some librarians apparently were so timid about holding 'objectionable' matter that they would not keep copies or would not classify those that were held. Indeed, most public libraries and museums, and even some provincial archives, have never kept black serial publications. In our survey, one university library and one major municipal library actually admitted that black serial publications in this category had been thrown away 'in the past'. . . '.— L. Switzer and D. Switzer, *The Black Press in South Africa and Lesotho,* p. 24, Boston, G. K. Hall, 1979.
33. See Leo Kuper, 'A Matter of Surrogate Censorship', *Race, Class and Power,* London, Duckworth, 1974, 345 pp.
34. Also see Welsh, *Philosophical Papers,* op. cit.
35. *Evening Post* (Port Elizabeth), 19 June 1979.
36. David Hammond-Tooke, 'Anthropology at English-language South African Universities', in M. R. Kettle and R. P. Ross (eds.), *Southern African Studies,* London, African Studies Association of the UK, 1970.
37. John Blacking, 'The Current State of Anthropological Research in the Transvaal', in Kettle and Ross (eds.), op. cit. pp. 77-8.
38. William R. Cotter and T. Karis, 'We Have Nothing to Hide: Contracts Between South Africa and the United States, *Social Dynamics* (Cape Town), Vol. 3, No. 2, December 1977, pp. 3-14.
39. Sean Moroney and Linda Ensor, *The Silenced,* Johannesburg, South African Institute of Race Relations, 1979.
40. See Dugard, op. cit.
41. See Mathews, op. cit.
42. *Cape Times* (Cape Town), 23 September 1978.
43. A. D. Wassenaar, *Assault on Private Enterprise,* Cape Town, Tafelberg, 1977.
44. See Philip Mayer, *Townsmen or Tribesmen,* p. 297, Cape Town, Oxford University Press.
45. H. W. Van der Merwe, N. Charton, M. Ashley and B. Huber, 'Appendices to Study of South African Elites', unpublished report submitted to HSRC, March 1972, pp. 21-2.
46. *Argus* (Cape Town), 20 November 1978.
47. See Mathews, op. cit.
48. J. L. Grey, 'The Comparative Sociology of South Africa', *South African Journal of Economics* (Johannesburg), Vol. 5, No. 3, September 1937, p. 283.

4 Anthropological research in contemporary South Africa

Michael Whisson
Rhodes University, Grahamstown

The only thing we have to fear is fear itself.
F. D. Roosevelt, 1933

Introduction

Research in social anthropology, as in most social sciences, can be divided into five components. These may be summarized as: background theoretical reading in the discipline and general area; the design of a project and choice of a specific problem and area; library and archive research; fieldwork, including participant observations and residence in the field; presentation and publication. Each component presents its own problems both intrinsic to the research itself and consequential upon the social circumstances in which the researcher operates. This chapter will deal primarily with problems of the latter type as the former are the subject of standard textbooks and even series (Spindler and Spindler, 1965) which go far beyond the scope of one chapter.

    The context in South Africa is in certain respects unique, but for the researcher it has situational problems common to many other countries. These common problems are essentially political and ideological. Societies in which the state has appropriated a large proportion of the national wealth, whether through its control of public corporations or in some more obvious way, tend to be governed by men who fear losing power, since, once out, they are unlikely to be able to mobilize the resources necessary to get back in again. Hence they are highly sensitive to the possibility of criticism which may weaken their hold on power. Further, in societies governed by men of a particular ideological persuasion, sustained by reference to an absolute deity or to a corpus of written dogma, any activity which by its nature questions the ideology or attempts to test its usefulness empirically, constitutes a threat to what the leaders perceive as the very basis of society. Finally, in societies where the ruling group believes or knows that it is sustained by force of arms and by the fear that it has implanted in its opponents, activities which might go unnoticed or be tolerated by a popularly based government will tend to be watched and repressed. Each of these elements is present to a greater or lesser degree in most countries and in so far as they exist, the research anthropologist will face difficulties similar to those being discussed in the following pages.

No attempt is made here to compare the problems of doing research in South Africa with the problems an anthropologist might face in other countries. If comparison is implicit, it is with an ideal state, governed by reasonable, popularly chosen men and women, whose interests coincide with those of their electorate. Ironically, in such a state, the need for the anthropologist in the role of interpreter and advocate of the inarticulate would scarcely be needed.

One further qualification should be made. Anthropologists are interpreters of their subjects' perceptions of reality. In much of what follows, the problems articulated are those which many anthropologists *believe* to exist. In some cases there is evidence, much of it circumstantial, much of it possibly unique to specific situations, some of it incontrovertible. But whether the evidence justifies the attribution of 'reality' to the problems or not, the indubitable fact that they are believed to exist by most English-speaking researchers creates its own reality for them. For many researchers from the Afrikaans-medium universities, such problems do not arise. Their assumptions about the nature of man, culture and society are more consistent with those of their rulers, and the research preoccupations of 'Volkekunde' less likely to raise challenging ideological or social issues.

With the foregoing qualifications in mind, the rest of this chapter will discuss the five components to which reference was made in the opening paragraph.

Background theoretical reading in the discipline and general area

Christian National Education, an educational philosophy which has governed the decisions at the political and upper executive levels of the South African education system for the past twenty-five years at least, has as one of its conscious aims the development of a set of values about the nature of cultural differences between groups of men.[1] Orthodoxy or 'right thinking' demands that one should think of a culture as the possession of a people *(volk)* which is precious to them and to which they *should* adhere.[2] Those who reject or water down the uniqueness and integrity of their culture, by confusing it with others, are not merely flying in the face of reality, they are also morally wrong.[3] It is values such as these which justify the legislation which endeavours to segregate people on an 'ethnic' basis and which enables the state to accept as unavoidable costs the unhappiness of those who suffer as a result, and the obloquy of the rest of the world.

Because there is such an orthodoxy, those who teach anthropology, and those who study it, are constantly aware that they are involved in a political activity—supporting, questioning or denying the ideological basis of the state. However cool and objective they endeavour to be, however far they stray from the ethnography of South Africa to make their theoretical points, the awareness remains, especially for those who reject the ideology of apartheid. In certain areas of study, such as the theories and analyses which flow from the Marxist tradition, the confrontation between nationalist orthodoxy and the alternative world view becomes explicit, and a substantial number of theoretical works and Marxist analyses of South African problems are banned. Such bannings may apply to works whose titles catch the eye of inspectors at the ports, to works about which complaints are lodged to the Publications Control Board and to works produced by or citing the words of persons banned in terms of South Africa's internal security legislation. In most cases it is an offence to be in possession of such publications, in all cases an offence to disseminate them[4]. In practice, the law has been applied in few cases involving academics in the pursuit of their normal teaching and research, although in the 'sensitive' areas of political theory and some aspects of economics and law, teachers are obliged to check whether the texts they wish to recommend are legally available or not. The pervasiveness of censorship is made more effective by the belief, enhanced by frequent exposés in the student press, that employees of the police are registered for most courses in which either the topic or the lecturer are known to touch on sensitive issues.

This situation would seem to provoke two forms of response: those who wish to pursue the academic life in reasonable tranquillity seek to avoid the very contentious issues with which scholars should be able to grapple whereas those who become morally involved tend to see the academic life less in terms of a disciplined pursuit of truth and more in terms of an ideological conflict in which the classical canons of non-verification of hypotheses are either subversive or bourgeois (each term being pejorative).

In the area of South African studies, the safest course for teachers of anthropology is for them to concentrate the attention of their students on the reconstruction of pre-colonial social systems or cultures and to derive theory from comparing them. Anthropology then becomes a partner with history and archaeology in its concern with the ways of the past. Anthropological studies of change and urbanization in the region tend to concentrate on family life and the involvement of people in voluntary associations (notably in churches) rather than describing or attempting to analyse the political process at any level, or the dynamics of race relations beyond the domestic level.

At each level of academic advancement the student is encouraged to play safe, partly for his own sake, partly in the interests of the department in which he is registered. Thus the content and style of the academic socialization process leads inexorably to particular outlooks on the part of those beginning research. They may continue along the path of playing safe by selecting topics cognate to their training, avoiding 'policy' issues and identifying themselves with no more than minor reform. By so doing they may engage the state in 'rituals of rebellion', enabling the maintenance of the illusion of freedom of expression, and justifying the state's attention to their activities. Alternatively they may adopt a radical stance, in the knowledge that this will eventually attract the opprobrium of the state and possibly in the hope that they will then be made welcome by their ideological sympathizers in other countries. Such stances, generated through the socialization process should not be seen as necessarily conscious and cynical choices, but as responses appropriate to the values inculcated through the process of academic socialization.

The design of a project and the choice of a specific topic and area

We have indicated how the process of academic socialization tends to polarize the outlook of research students and hence, in the course of time, nearly all researchers. Before commencing research however, it is also necessary for the worker to have some financial security. In the case of anthropological research, which tends to involve much travel and long periods of residence with one's subjects, the exercise is costly in time and in travel expenses, although far cheaper overall than most research in the natural and applied sciences for which specialized equipment is required.

The main sources of finance for postgraduate research in anthropology are the Human Sciences Research Council (a government agency), the Chamber of Mines and its affiliates (notably the Anglo-American Corporation), some smaller charitable foundations and trusts, and the universities' own research funds, postgraduate bursaries and fellowships. A substantial but diminishing amount of research money has come from European and American sources, in some cases through the Churches. Despite their being involved in what is virtually mass education, with staff/student ratios of up to 1 : 80, some full-time members of university staffs are able to maintain a fairly vigorous research programme supported by their normal salaries and modest research funds.

The Human Sciences Research Council is believed to be a very conservative and bureaucratic body with a generally mechanistic concept of the research process. The small reports produced by researchers directly responsible to it, that is not working for a degree through a university or institute, generally involve the administration of a questionnaire (personally or even postally) and the analysis of the results in the light of a limited amount of background reading. Judging from the publications, the necessity for sustained participant observation in the life of a subject population does not appear to be recognized—and may even be felt to be undesirable.

Some academics at English-medium universities believe that their applications for funds from the HSRC would not be considered fairly and that any potentially controversial project either will not be supported or will be subjected to surveillance and control in such a way that the findings cannot be published fully. As scholars in sensitive areas often do not test the bona fides of the council by seeking its support, it is impossible to know how far this belief is soundly based.

From the evidence available, however, it would appear that the council gives modest support to a very wide range of projects at the master's and doctoral levels, including controversial topics. Some promoters of larger projects, whose time span is difficult to predict, have had problems in meeting deadlines initially agreed with the council, and others have had difficulty in getting their work cleared for publication. From the council's side, since its case for state funding is based largely on the volume of finished work that it can show, its long-term interests (and those of its beneficiaries) are best served by the completion of a large number of reports and theses each year. Likewise, the publication of highly controversial findings, based on research supported by the council, could lead to difficulties at the political level between the council and the Department of National Education. Like the individual scholar, and regardless of the predispositions of its individual members, the council must make compromises between the unquantifiable and universalistic ideals of academic research and the pragmatic criteria on which its own performance will be judged and upon which its future funding depends.

A further form of state control has been brought into being with the formation of the Council for Development Research, a body which ostensibly promotes research in the homelands which have not yet become officially 'independent'. Many academics in English-medium institutions suspect that this council will promote research only in the areas and topics of which it positively approves and will make it more difficult for researchers not under its aegis to obtain permits and even funds from other government agencies. The council has been in operation for only a short period and, as in the case of the HSRC, where it is judged before it has any opportunity to demonstrate its bona fides, there is no way that the suspicions of the academics can be allayed or justified.

Financial support from the mining houses and foundations, while not plentiful, appears to be distributed without strings attached and has been used not infrequently to sponsor projects critical of the migrant labour system—which supplies the cheap labour upon which the profitability of those institutions is based. While the controllers of such funds probably tend to favour individuals whose political views are congenial to them—which views are not necessarily those of the shareholders of the executive of the business which provides the funds—there appears to be neither record nor fear of interference or manipulation in the topics, manner of research or publication of results. The cognitive model with which foundation managers work appears to be derived from the business world and involves delegation and confidence in the chosen researcher, rather than any attempt to monitor in detail for public accounting.

To some extent, the range of sources of funds enables researchers to approach the funding body deemed to be most sympathetic to the goals and methods of the research and the researcher. One distinguished scholar observed that if the worker is good enough, then finance is never a problem. This is probably true, but 'good enough' is a qualitative concept and evaluated more by past results than by untried potential.

The choice of topic is inevitably affected by both the academic socialization process of the scholar and by his success in gaining financial support. It is further affected by the freedom with which the work can be carried out. Anthropologists generally work in communities and cultural groups other than their own, although in the case of students who are not White they are often encouraged to study 'their own' community. In an ethnically stratified society, it is more difficult for those ascribed to 'lower' strata to study those 'higher' than it is for the 'higher' to study the 'lower'. The 'higher' tend to view research on them by the 'lower' strata as impertinence, the 'lower' to view research on them by the 'higher' as a part of the human condition. Since most research is aimed at informing the 'higher' strata, it is predictable that the 'lower' should be used primarily to inform the 'higher' about life among 'their own community' rather than be encouraged to make what may be critical observations about their 'betters'. In practice there seems to be no way round this dilemma.

Since White anthropologists work, for the most part, in Black communities, the problem of permits arises for them. They can work in White group areas freely, regardless of their subjects—hence a study of living-in domestic workers or a factory study on Black workers requires no official permit. There are no restrictions on entry into Coloured group areas and reserves, but permission is required if one wishes to stay in premises other than those legally occupied by Whites. Permits to stay in Coloured areas seem to be granted quite readily, provided that suitable accommodation in mission, tent or caravan is available. African areas are subject to more stringent control and a permit is required to enter. For daylight visiting, such permits are granted fairly easily during periods of calm, but the authorities look more carefully at requests for late-evening permits and rarely grant permission for Whites to stay overnight.[5] In the rural areas, it is possible to stay for longer periods provided suitable accommodation is available at a mission station or in a caravan, but applicants often experience discouraging delays in obtaining permits.[6] It is assumed that political scrutiny as well as bureaucratic machinery is responsible for the slow processing of applications. The delays, suspicion that they will be closely watched and the inconvenience, has encouraged several White scholars to choose topics for research which do not involve any contact with permit-granting bodies.

Another set of constraints on the choice of topic and area revolve around the experience and fears of the researcher concerning the reception that he will get from his subjects. Since the 'troubles' of 1976 a greater sense of 'racial' polarization has set in and some White researchers feel that their involvement in Black communities in any role is no longer welcome, constructive or safe. The problem is not new, but the extent of it has grown. Writing of their 'study of social groups in an African township' in the early 1960s, Wilson and Mafeje (1963, p. 11) noted:

> We did not investigate political organizations or trade unions. Questions were not asked about them early in the investigation because that would have aroused suspicion, and during the course of the study the two main political organizations . . . were banned . . . two cases occurred in which journalists were imprisoned for refusing to reveal to the police their sources of information on political matters.

After the report of a workshop on 'Coloured Citizenship in South Africa' was published (Whisson and Van der Merwe, 1972) the editors were described by *The Educational Journal* (the organ of the Teachers' League of South Africa, a small radical organization whose membership is almost wholly 'Coloured') as 'the intellectual wing of BOSS'—BOSS telling the government what the racially oppressed are doing, while the editors of the workshop report, and presumably the participants, told the government what the oppressed were thinking. In 1976, Dr M. Edelstein, who had carried out social research in Soweto high schools and who probably believed he had rapport with the students, was beaten to death by a student mob. During and after those troubles White lecturers believed to be sympathetic to students in Black universitites were told by their pupils: 'Why don't you leave the country? People like you can only complicate the issue now—you can't help.' These examples highlight two issues—constraints upon the researcher in terms of what he believes he can safely study because of the attitude of his subjects, and in terms of what use might be made of what he publishes or even discovers unintentionally in the course of his work. To this latter aspect we shall return in a later section.

Some evidence of the significance of these constraints may be found by comparing the bibliographies of I. Schapera's, *The Bantu-speaking Tribes of South Africa* (1937) with W. D. Hammond-Tooke's *The Bantu-speaking Peoples of South Africa* (1974) in respect of works published in the decade or so before those volumes were compiled. The bibliographies represent the preoccupations of scholars in the field in the period 1920-35 and 1960-70 respectively. In the earlier period, the major preoccupation was with general works and on studies of social structure and kinship work requiring substantial time to be spent in the field. Religious topics came a very poor second with historical references third. In the later period that order is reversed, with many historical and archaeological references, followed by religious topics with kinship and social structure third, and relatively few works on law or politics. To some extent the differences reflect increasing specialization, but the specialization is largely in the 'safe' areas of historical reconstruction and religion.

Library and archive research

South Africa is well endowed with libraries, archives and museums, as well as with that most precious, if unpredictable, human resource—'enthusiasts'. Access to archives is not difficult and staff are generally helpful despite their small number in relation to the materials that they must catalogue and store.

To the researcher, one of the compensations in working in a society which has been in a state of conflict between literate sections for over 180 years is that there are usually at least two sides to every story on record. Each party has bred its own mythology, recreating the past in each generation and hanging on to the evidence which validates it. On many issues, it is not the search for evidence which is challenging, but the interpretation of it.

For the anthropologist, who has tended to concentrate his attention on the non-literate, the urban poor and the generally unheard sections of a diverse population, the problems of interpreting archive material are considerable. The perceptions of the writers of the material which is today in archives were generally middle class. Reports and records were compiled utilizing the categories and values of the *literati* in each generation and overwhelmingly the White *literati* whose world view often differed radically from those of greatest interest to anthropologists.

Under such circumstances the researcher is tempted to turn to oral tradition in order to redress the balance or 'to grasp the native's point of view, his relation to life, to realize *his* vision of *his* world' which Malinowski (1922, p. 25) defined as the goal of anthropological research. Here too, the problems of interpretation are enormous. Memory is highly selective and that which is remembered and passed on from generation to generation develops the authentic qualities of myth—a structure which facilitates its easy transmission and a meaning or function which tends to reflect present - day preoccupations rather than past realities. Oral history generally begins with the tellers' perceptions of the quality of life in times past, his reflections on a golden age, and proceeds from there to the description and interpretation of events. The weekly walk from farm to market, covering many miles over rough tracks, becomes evidence of the heroic character, determination and energy of 'the old people'—implicitly contrasted with the generation which is totally dependent upon the internal combustion engine. The written record for the same period tells of poverty, tuberculosis and the annual spate of deaths from 'apricot sickness' (gastroenteritis) due to malnutrition, ignorance and insanitary conditions.

Such problems are present in all attempts to reconstruct the past, but are sharpened in a situation of social conflict. The analysis of change, which is a major interest among anthropologists, demands a time scale beyond that which the anthropologist can usually spend in the field. He is therefore compelled to use oral history and archives to reconstruct aspects of the past as a preliminary to measuring change. Where statistics are absent, unreliable or incomparable, as in most cases involving anthropological studies over substantial periods of time, the researcher endeavours to capture the quality of life as well as the rules and the elusive facts about living. An account of the past and an analysis of change then becomes a political statement since an improvement in the quality of life implies that colonial and post-colonial rule has been beneficial and a deterioration in the quality of life implies the opposite.

In discussing the process of academic socialization, reference has already been made to the major problem in the availability of published material: that of censorship. It is possible to obtain permission to import and use banned material for '*bona fide* academic purposes' but many scholars prefer neither to become enmeshed in the bureaucracy nor to draw particular attention to what may well be a peripheral aspect of their work.

Thus, despite the richness of the material in the archives and its relative ease of access, the preliminary work in anthropological research is not without its problems and hazards. There is a temptation to sidestep the problems of the analysis of contemporary society—which is the anthropologist's calling—by concentrating on the retrievable past. The hazards are fewer when dealing with the dead, and for those who are active parties to the contemporary political struggle, the use of history to validate ideological stances can be seen as a contribution to the struggle from a fairly safe academic position. The strength of its appeal is indicated by the substantial amount of historical research published in the decade before *The Bantu-speaking Peoples of South Africa.*

Field-work

Anthropological research classically and typically involves spending substantial periods of time in the research area, living, as far as possible, with the people and learning by sharing in their daily lives. Understanding develops through 'osmosis' as much as through formal questioning, although the systematically collected data generally forms the objective base upon which interpretation is built. Moving from the milieu of one's own native culture, and in particular one's academic culture, into the field is analogous to learning to swim—the medium is different and one must learn new techniques in order to feel at home. Most field-workers have stayed within easy reach of 'land' in the form of culturally familiar institutions, like mission stations or the outposts of westernized governmental bureaucracies; few have not been accompanied by cultural life-jackets in the form of equipment, books and some form of communication with their home culture. Having learned to swim, to be at home in the strange culture, re-entry into one's own may present problems. As one experienced research-institute director put it: 'We have to carry them kicking and screaming into the field because they say they aren't ready—and after a year we carry them kicking and screaming out because they say they haven't finished and don't want to leave.'

The field-work experience thus leads the field-worker, almost inevitably, into a set of intimate and affectionate relationships with his subjects. He identifies himself with their aspirations and their values—but then tries to stand back from that experience, recollect it (with the aid of his notes) in tranquillity and communicate it in a manner which will convey the totality of the experience. This process of initiation into being an anthropologist has analogies with initiation into being a diviner, and the roles do indeed have structural parallels as each endeavours to interpret the experience of a reality which he alone can perceive, to enlighten those who have not perceived or who cannot perceive that alien or separate reality.

If the field-worker studies a society far from his own, certain problems can be ignored, or become of minimal significance. But in a poly-ethnic situation, in which a vital element in everyone's life, if not *the* vital element, revolves around the competition for resources and power between the 'group' from which the field-worker comes and the group which he is studying, the process of becoming an anthropologist involves becoming a traitor to one's 'group'. Several field-workers have been asked 'Where are you from?' and, on declaring that they are not South African, have found rapport more easily established. South Africans generally find some 'good link' through a suitably trustworthy institutional or personal intermediary in order to establish rapport, thus denying something of their presumed ethnic identity.

To get into the classical field-work position, permits are required, and the relevant authorities have difficulty in grasping the necessity or the desirability of such intimate contact between anthropologist and subject community. Talking to 'them' is comprehensible—everyone has conversation with people of different groups—but actually living with 'them', sharing the same food, the same houses, that is taking things a bit far. For anyone actually to want to do that sort of thing suggests that he is in some way a corrupted person and hence possibly a danger to society as well as to himself. Many field-workers recognize the problem and so conduct their research from a base which is essentially a part of 'their' community—a mission station or a residence in a White area from which they make daily forays into the community. By so doing they deny themselves or are denied a crucial aspect of the anthropological experience.

Once in the field, the anthropologist is confronted with problems of communication beyond those of language. As the quotation from *Langa* earlier indicated, some topics are felt to be particularly sensitive and the field-worker will avoid them until good rapport is established. The inhibitions in a society where the ear of the state is believed to be ubiquitous are naturally greater than those in a less closely governed society. The dilemma can be resolved by the sort of avoidances practised by Wilson and Mafeje (1963) whereby certain topics are either never discussed or never admitted to be discussed. The field-worker can rationalize this as being in the interests of his subjects, in the interests of his personal security and as pertaining to matters which he could not publish anyway. This resolution of the problem may be highly unsatisfactory, since the topics which are avoided tend to be precisely those which are of the greatest importance to the people in the community, the *foci* of their hopes and fears and the touchstone of true rapport or identity of values and interests. To evade them may be not merely to leave a *lacuna* in one's analysis, but to create a fundamental distortion which pervades the whole.

Further, the field-worker is likely to be challenged, possibly directly, to express his own views on those potentially explosive issues. The political question glosses the more fundamental one—'What do you think should be done about Mandela?' glosses 'Are you on our side or not?' which is the basis of rapport. The testing is continuous in the present decade, not only because the field-worker is an alien, but because in an era of heightened sensitivities all people, both insiders and aliens, are subject to political pressures and hence potentially suspect.

This situation can cripple the over-sensitive field-worker, as his concern not to give offence can itself create inhibitions in his subjects. In practice, it is probably still true to say that the greatest inhibition to the collection of information lies within the field-worker himself. Within very broad limits his confidence, or lack of it, is infectious and when he asks he will be answered.

What applies to the field-worker applies in at least equal measure to his subjects, and generally they are more vulnerable than he is. Blacks believe, with adequate reason, that they are more liable to arbitrary arrest and detention than Whites. If a White person is detained for very long, the case is a *cause célèbre* in the press and the minister is subjected to continual pressure until the person is tried or released. For reasons of numbers, political status and ethnic alienation, Black detainees cannot expect the same sort of support from the enfranchised section of the community. Thus, while it is probably true that the social stigma of detention is less for a Black than for a White within the social contexts in which each normally moves, the risks that a Black faces by being misunderstood, misquoted or betrayed are substantially greater than those faced by a White.

The inhibitions to an easy rapport in the field are heightened by various structural constraints. Reference has already been made to the image of the 'reasonable man' which appears to be in the minds of the officials responsible for issuing permits. Those who do not conform to that image become conspicuous and are liable to be watched. Some students have described how they have visited an informant and returned to their approved residence, only to discover that within a few hours of their leaving the informant he has been visited by a plain-clothes policeman who has inquired about the details of the conversation. Such incidents are very rare, but the existence of a system of surveillance so total that it can pursue individual field-workers from house to house is itself a structural inhibition to the establishment of those easy relationships that lie at the basis of good field-work. In time, the field-worker and his subjects may be able to put such considerations out of their minds, but the problems re-assert themselves during the period of writing up.

A further problem in the field concerns relationships between the field-worker and the various officials with whom he has to deal at the local level. In some areas, but by no means all, the polarization between the ordinary people and those whom they perceive as the imminent arm of an alien government is great. To understand the total social system the field-worker is bound to treat such officials in the same way as he treats the rest of his subjects—since they form an integral part of the community which they, in part, control. Where there is alienation, good rapport in both directions is extraordinarily difficult as it depends upon the field-worker establishing relations of trust with each of the opposing parties, inevitably with the knowledge of both. In situations, such as those which existed in the latter years of the colonial era, the anthropologist was seen as a conduit and potential resource by both sides and his broker role recognized. In South Africa, that role is not always available—if the parties concerned perceive the situation as one of potential, if not actual, civil war, then they seek allies (and possibly spies) rather than mediators or brokers.

The foregoing paragraphs have presented the problems inherent in field-work in a divided society and may have given the impression that it is virtually impossible. Such an impression is not wholly correct, for while there are some topics on which study is extremely difficult, a great deal of work can be done and is done, by field-workers of integrity. Only a fool is unaware of the problems, but a good field-worker will accommodate himself to the social realities of the situation and proceed with his task. Some gaps and distortions may be inevitable, but if he is aware of them, he can usually make allowances and urge those who read his work to do the same. Field-work is possible, it is merely more difficult, more challenging and more dangerous than was the case a generation or so ago.

Presentation and publication

Among the implied pledges that a field-worker makes to his subjects is that of confidentiality. The subject knows that what he is saying is needed by the field-worker for publication, but at the same time he is encouraged to believe that statements will not be attributable to him. Anonymity is protected by the generalizing of information so that it emerges as a corporate opinion, by giving false names to informants and even by giving false names to the area in which the field-work was done. These devices were more than adequate when most field-work was done among non-literate communities, but as more people are able and interested to read what their anthropologists have written about them, so the problems have become greater. These problems are common to social research everywhere, and especially where the topic covers transgressions of the law, or forms of behaviour considered immoral by the community at large.

For the most part the devices to protect anonymity have worked reasonably well because rarely has anyone set out to identify informants and to break through the seals of confidentiality. But in a society in which a police officer and a cabinet minister, referring to totally different events, can affirm the doctrine that when the interests of the country are at stake, there are no binding rules of conduct,[7] the traditional means of protecting confidentiality are inadequate. Whether it be through the field-worker himself, or through a less direct route, the state is able to locate the source of any published statement and the person responsible for it. Further, the powers of the executive are such that a person can be held incommunicado until such time as the police are satisfied that he has told them all that he is able on any subject (Terrorism Act No. 83 of 1967).[8] Very little anthropological writing has attracted the attention of the executive in this way and informants have rarely, if ever, been harrassed following the publication of material, but the possibility creates a constraint upon publication of which all writers are aware.

Further problems arise if it is the intention of the field-worker that his material be published in South Africa. As has been indicated earlier, it is an offence to publish, or cause to be published, any part of any work that is itself banned, or the work or words of any person who is banned. Minor infringements generally escape unnoticed, but publishers are generally very cautious in South Africa itself. Something of a *cause célèbre* was a chapter on African nationalism which appeared in *The Oxford History of South Africa* (Vol. II, 1971). In the edition sold in South Africa the 'chapter' appeared as blank pages, this being the most dramatic, and incidentally most economical, way of producing the book without the banned material.

Subsequently the complete edition was sold without action being taken against the editors, publishers or sellers. The main targets of the censors relevant to anthropology pertain to 'communism' which may be very broadly defined as material which may give moral support to 'the enemies of South Africa' (as opponents of apartheid tend to be called) especially that which promotes in any way the aims of the Black nationalist organizations.

These legal restrictions create some problems in analysing material, though fewer than might appear from the wording of the relevant legislation. Provided that he is familiar with a particular theoretical approach, an author can generally utilize it without reference to specifically banned works or persons.

Far more important for the author is the question of the use to which his work will be put. This is a major moral issue which is generally ignored by scholars who argue that more truth is better than less truth and hence they should publish the truth as they perceive it. This classical position was challenged by *The Educational Journal* in its reference to 'the academic wing of BOSS', as mentioned above, although such an epithet confuses the effect with the intention. In a divided and sensitive society, however, a writer cannot hide behind good intentions to evade responsibility for the effects of his work.

As has been suggested in the discussion about the choice of topics to be studied, one way out of the problems of the uses to which material may be put is to pursue research of no practical use to anyone. It may be, however, culturally enriching, or ideologically comforting to know that, for example, a long-dead hero not only behaved in a manner consistent with the aspirations of his people today but in conformity with a particular set of analytically interesting, ideologically based prescriptions. The closer one gets to the present and to the conflicts which characterize it, the more difficult it is to ignore the possible effects of one's work.

The nub of the problem is the locus of power in the society. If knowledge is power, then pre-existing power can appropriate knowledge to strengthen itself. Thus a detailed study of the violence and strikes among the Black gold-miners in 1973-74, explaining the causes and possible remedies in terms sympathetic to the workers would have been of some value to the miners themselves in pursuing their goals of better wages and conditions, but more as a moral weapon than as a material one. On the other hand, the employers could take such a report and use it as the basis for their own analysis of how to achieve their aim of maximum productivity at minimum cost. The superior bargaining power of the employers, based on law and substantial unemployment, would have been materially enhanced by the knowledge gained from such a report.

The same problem arises in any study which has implications for state policy. Accurate information on the values and aspirations of a community, on the way that it survives in a situation of acute poverty, on the informal institutions which bind its members together and mobilize it for corporate action—matters which are the very stuff of ostensibly uncontentious anthropological research—all are of value to a government which seeks to achieve its goals as economically as possible. Ironically, research carried out by those who do not share their rulers' ideology, and whose conclusions are that the policies flowing from that ideology are impractical or immoral, has probably provided those rulers with more information useful to effective government than the research carried out by ideologues to show that all is well save for the activities of a handful of alien agitators.

This problem is not new. A whole literature has flourished around the theme that anthropologists were the handmaids of colonialism—a judgement not always fair if the intention is implied with the effect. But the words of Radcliffe Brown and Forde are as relevant to South Africa as they were to the colonial empire of which he wrote, and equally relevant to any society where the ruling élite does not reflect the will of the mass of the people:

> The process of change is inevitable. To a very limited extent it can be controlled by the colonial administration, and it is obvious that the effectiveness of any action taken by an administration is dependent on the knowledge they have at their disposal about the native society, its structure and institutions, and what is happening at the present time. (1950, p. 85.)

The moral dilemma is clear. The closer the anthropologist gets in his observations and analysis to the major concerns of the people whom he studies, or, in other words, the closer he gets to achieving the classical ideals of his calling, the greater will be the value of his work to the rulers of those people. If the interests of the people are at variance with those of their rulers, then regardless of his intentions the effect of his work is likely to enhance the power of the rulers.

If the 'rulers' are, in fact, a homogeneous and united group, possessing all power, then the dilemma is insoluble and there can be no place for the anthropologist apart, perhaps, from dabbling in the past and the peripheral. But in most societies, and certainly in South Africa, there are several loci of power and influence in the system—monolithic as it may appear to be to the outsider. Pressure groups exist in the form of local-government bodies which are not necessarily creatures of the state; in the unions, despite their obvious weaknesses; in the business community; in the Churches and other voluntary associations, and in the ethnic councils. Anthropological research can be utilized by such bodies to pursue goals approximating to those traditionally close to the anthropologist's heart in his role of advocate of the oppressed and inarticulate. As the internal and external pressures upon the South African Government have increased, so the power and effectiveness of those bodies has become more circumscribed by law and their potential opposition weakened by the stronger identification of their White members with the united White South African front. But they remain loci of power and influence available to take up relevant information and to act upon it.

A final consideration of relevance to anthropologists whose homes are in South Africa and who have no desire to leave it, is that of the pursuit of further research after the publication of each major piece of work. Each piece of work has to be evaluated by its author, not only in terms of its truth and relevance, but in terms of whether its publication will jeopardize the freedom of the author in his future research. One angry junior official or touchy politician may be able to block permits and, where the anthropologist is aware of the risks, he has to evaluate them accordingly. Since reasons need not be and are, in fact, rarely given for the refusal of permits, funds or access to source material outside the libraries and archives, there is an element of chance involved and hence the researcher is encouraged to play safe if he wishes to continue his work.

Conclusion

The problems outlined in the foregoing pages may have given the impression that serious, long-term anthropological field-work is no longer possible in South Africa and that in so far as it can be done, it must be historical, trivial or supportive of the existing regime. There is much truth in that conclusion, but it is sufficiently far from the whole truth to encourage a substantial number of scholars to stay in or to visit South Africa for the purposes of doing research. To a very considerable extent, the problems have been ignored and the risks taken without obvious damage either to the researcher or to the community studied, and much fine work has emerged as a result of the adoption of that approach.

However, the constraints are real, and one only has to compare the work carried out in the thirty years prior to 1948 with that carried out in the last thirty years to see the differences. What once appeared to be one of the most exciting anthropological laboratories in the world, containing a remarkably wide range of ethnic groups with distinctive lifestyles blending or defending their cultural identities, adopting new strategies to maintain their traditions and to advance their interests, is now largely closed. In part it is closed because of the very qualities which made it an exciting laboratory—the elements are now too explosive to be exposed to each other and the light. From a society in which the dominance of the Whites was so total that research into alternative social arrangements and the dynamics of race relations could be welcomed as interesting and unthreatening, South Africa has changed into a society in which ideological conflict backed by substantial material forces seriously threatens White hegemony.

As has been observed, in a situation of civil war, regardless of whether it is being fought at the ideological, economic or military level, or at some combination of all three, each party demands not interpreters or mediators, but committed allies and partisans. The anthropologist is then cast in the role of spy or intelligence officer. There is a school of thought which argues that in all capitalist societies this sort of conflict is inherent, and that anthropologists should admit it and commit themselves to one side (Aberle, 1968). There is force in that argument in the context not only of capitalist societies, but in all societies where the ruling group controls so much of the wealth and commands so much of the political power that it need not be responsible to the majority of the people.

Academic anthropologists, socialized into a tradition in which they seek to transcend and analyse conflict rather than be involved in it as partisans, are naturally disturbed at these developments in their discipline. Elsewhere, as in South Africa, it would be a tragedy if political circumstances led to a situation in which objectivity in analysis became inevitably associated with irrelevance or triviality in content. However, awareness of the problems, generated in the crucibles of Viet Nam and South Africa, is the necessary first step to their solution.

Notes

1. Classically exemplified by the Minister of Bantu Education, Mr W. A. Maree, addressing Parliament: 'It is the basic principle of Bantu education in general that our aim is to keep the Bantu child a Bantu child. . . . The Bantu must be so educated that they do not want to become imitators (of the Whites, but) that they will want to remain essentially Bantu.' (Horrell, 1964, p. 6).
2. Writing of 'The Basic Race Structure' of South Africa, Dr C. J. Jooste, the director of SABRA (an organization providing academic and ideological support for apartheid policies) stated, as a matter of fact rather than temporal perception: 'Relationships in this sub-continent are built on the principle of recognizing the right of a people to strive towards sovereign independence in its own fatherland.'
3. Basic definitions in Volkekunde/Anthropology texts underline this. 'A people *(volk)* is an aggregation of individuals co-operating to maintain itself and its culture as the means by which it survives as a group; but culture is also the means by which the individual achieves his full potential as a human being.' (UNISA, 1973, p. 12.) 'Culture in fact is the life-form of a people *(volk)* of which the individual members in fact form loose cells.' (Translated from Coertze, 1961, p. 36.)
4. This would appear to be the case since the Publications Amendment Act (79 of 1977) which abolished the exemption on technical, religious, scientific and professional publications which had been provided for in the principal act. (South African Institute of Race Relations, 1977, p. 174.)
5. Example of permit for urban areas:

    BANTU AFFAIRS ADMINISTRATION BOARD Z REGION
    Office of the Regional Manager

    PERMIT TO ENTER .... TOWNSHIP (SECTION 9(9)(b) ACT 25/1945)

    Permission is hereby granted to... Address..
    To enter .... Township for the purpose of...
    This permit is valid for the hours from: ....a.m. to ....p.m.
    For the period from .... to ....
    Date of issue ....
    .... (Signature and Stamp)

6. Proforma permit for rural areas:

    PERMIT
    Under Section 24(1) of Act No. 18 of 1936
    PERMISSION IS HEREBY GIVEN TO .... OF ....
    to enter the Rural Areas for the purpose of: ....
    in the Magisterial Districts of: A: B: C
    subject to the following conditions:
    1. The permit-holder must advise the Bantu Affairs Commissioner of the district concerned when entry to any Bantu area in his district is envisaged.
    2. The permit-holder shall be in possession of an appropriate current licence prescribed by law.
    3. The permit-holder must make his own arrangements for Board and Lodging. Lodging with Bantu is not permitted.
    4. Under no circumstances must the holder of this permit interfere with domestic or other affairs of the Bantu.

5. In his dealings, if any, with the Bantu the holder hereof must behave in a dignified manner and refrain from criticism of the administration of the Government or of any of its officials.
6. This permit is not transferable.
7. This permit may be withdrawn at any time without reason assigned.
8. The holder of this permit shall at all times while he is in a Bantu area have the permit in his possession and shall produce it at the request of any authorized officer.
9. [any other conditions e.g. period for which the permit is valid.]

Chief Bantu Affairs Commissioner
Region Z

Date ....
Reference No ....

7. A senior member of the security police, Col. Goosen, testifying at the inquest of Steve Biko in 1977 and Dr C. Mulder, during the furore over the activities of the former Department of Information in 1978, each expressed himself in very much these terms, according to press reports.

8. The power of the executive extends beyond 'political' issues. In 1978 a student who had produced an academic paper on cannabis-smoking in Grahamstown was detained under Section 13 of the Abuse of Dependence-producing Substances and Rehabilitation Centres Act (No. 41 of 1971) which empowers the police to hold a person 'if there is reason to believe that [he] is withholding any information relating to an offence' under the relevant clauses of the Act, until they are 'satisfied that the detainee has satisfactorily replied to all questions at the said interrogation'. It is believed that the information he gave led directly to the arrest of certain of his informants.

Bibliography

ABERLE, K. G. 1968. Social Responsibilities Symposium. *Current Anthropology.* December, pp. 391-435.

COERTZE, P. J. 1961. *Inleiding tot die algemene Volkekunde.* Voortrekkerpers Bpk., Johannesburg.

HAMMOND-TOOKE, W. D. (ed.). 1974. *The Bantu-speaking Peoples of South Africa.* London, Routlege & Kegan Paul.

HORRELL, M. 1964. *A Decade of Bantu Education.* Johannesburg, South African Institute of Race Relations.

JOOSTE, C. J. 1972. The Basic Race Structure. In: N. Rhoodie (ed.), *South African Dialogue.* Johannesburg, McGraw-Hill.

MALINOWSKI, B. 1922. *Argonauts of the Western Pacific.* London, Routledge & Kegan Paul.

RADCLIFFE BROWN, A. R.; FORDE, C. D. 1950. *African Systems of Kinship and Marriage.* Oxford University Press.

SOUTH AFRICAN INSTITUTE OF RACE RELATIONS. 1977. *A Survey of Race Relations in South Africa, 1977.* Johannesburg, South African Institute of Race Relations.

SCHAPERA, I. (ed.). 1937. *The Bantu-speaking Tribes of South Africa.* Cape Town, Masked Miller.

SPINDLER, G.; SPINDLER, L. (eds.). *Studies in Anthropological Method.* New York, Holt, Rinehart & Winston.

UNISA. 1973. *Anthropology I, Guide 1.* Pretoria.

WHISSON, M. G.; VAN DER MERWE, H. W. 1972. *Coloured Citizenship in South Africa.* Abe Bailey Institute for Inter-group Studies, University of Cape Town.

WILSON, M.; MAFEJE, A. 1963. *Langa.* Cape Town, Oxford University Press.

WILSON, M.; THOMPSON, L. 1971. *The Oxford History of South Africa.* Vol. II, Oxford University Press.

5 Servants of apartheid ?

A survey of social research into industry in South Africa

E. Webster*
Department of Sociology, University of
Witwatersrand

This chapter attempts to analyse the growth and development of social research into industry in South Africa. It was not possible to deal with all social research in industry, however; much research into industry is of a confidential nature. The chapter therefore focuses on selected sociological studies, which highlight some of the main problems of industrial research. It does not deal with research into technology and, in particular, its relationship to the changing nature of capital accumulation.

In Part I, it is argued that management turns increasingly to harness the wider intellectual resources of the social scientific community when faced by challenges arising out of structural changes in the economy and labour organization and unrest. In Part II, the relationship which emerges between industry and social science in the late 1930s and 1940s is located in the context of the crises of that time. However, it is tentatively suggested that the apartheid path, characterized by a lack of an organized labour force, stalls the growth of this relationship.

The 'take-off' in the relationship between industry and social science is dealt with in Part III and six different approaches to research are identified. In Part IV, the argument that apartheid compounds the biases inherent in industrial research, is evaluated.

The chapter concludes by suggesting that, increasingly, capital and the state will call on social scientists to assist them in implementing the new strategy of limited 'reform'.

I

It has become commonplace in the last two decades to argue that much of industrial sociology is 'managerial sociology'. By labelling sociology as 'managerial', it is being suggested that sociology is being used, to put it simply, to facilitate management's task of increasing the profitability of the enterprise. For Merton, 'of the limited body of social research in industry,

* The author wishes to thank Ari Sitas, Alan Simon, Kevin French, Anika Claassens and David Mckibbon for allowing me access to their honours papers delivered in my Industrial Sociology honours course.

the greater part has been oriented towards the needs of management'.[1] Similarly, Tom Burns writes that 'it remains true that for every twenty studies of the lowest ranks of manual operatives, there is perhaps one of managing directors'.[2] Alan Flanders, summing up the literature in industrial and organizational sociology, writes that it does not study how 'to make management formally more accountable to the managed' but rather the 'employees more accountable to management'.[3] Loren Baritz, concluding his comprehensive history of the use of social science in American industry, was to label social scientists as the servants of power.[4]

In trying to account for the 'managerial' nature of industrial sociology, at least four different explanations are usually offered. First, there is the argument of the essentially middle-class social background of the sociologist. C. Wright Mills emphasizes this when he says that

> from after the civil war until only a generation or so ago, the urban middle-class of America was, in part, composed of men with expanding businesses, who were taking over instruments of production and gaining political power as well as social prestige. Many of the academic men of the older generation of sociologists were either recruited from these rising strata or actively mingled with them. Their students—the public of their thought—have been the products of such strata.[5]

Secondly, there is the widespread acceptance of capitalist values by sociologists. Thus Burns writes that 'frequently sociologists may accept more or less uncritically the aim of making industrial and business undertakings more efficient or less troublesome as instruments of private profit-making—with very few exceptions they tend to accept the existence, values and purposes of industry and individual undertakings at their face value'.[6] In the third place, 'this [managerial] bias', Wiendick argues, 'can probably be explained in terms of a sponsorship effect, since most industrial research is paid for by management to solve management's problems'.[7] Or, as Burns states, 'as in the case of educational institutions, central and local government departments, prisons, military units, hospitals and other closed establishments, access to industrial undertakings for research purposes is only granted by the controlling authorities when they are assured that the research will further the interests of the establishment'.[8] 'Therefore', says Brown, 'the problems to be studied are restricted to those preoccupying the clients'.[9] 'Studies into industry', Burns writes, 'reveal that there is ordinarily a large margin between the potential and the actual amount of work done by workers. The task of management was to reduce this margin'.[10] However, the main protagonist of the sponsorship argument is C. Wright Mills. When summarizing the work of 'managerial sociology', in particular that of Elton Mayo, he argues that they have discovered

> one, that within the authority structure of modern industry there are status formations ('informal organization'), two, that often these resist the authorities and operate to protect the workers against the exercise of authority, three, and that, therefore, for the sake of efficiency and to ward off uncollaborative tendencies (union and worker solidarity), managers should not try to break up these formations but should rather try to exploit them for

their own ends. And four, that this might be done by recognizing and studying them, in order to manipulate the workers involved in them rather than merely authoritatively order them.[11]

A final explanation for the direction taken by research into industry is the manner in which it can be used to build up a career in the university. 'It is true that professors certainly welcome the small increases in salary that may come with new research activities and consultantships—the ambitious type of consultant is able to further his career in the university by securing prestige and even small-scale powers outside it.'[12]

Clearly, evidence can be found of managerial bias in industrial sociology to substantiate any one or all of these explanations, yet none of them would explain why industry turned to social science at a particular stage in the development of capitalism. Foucault has suggested that 'the historical emergence of each one of the human sciences was occasioned by a problem, a requirement, an obstacle of a theoretical or practical order'.[13] What was the 'problem' that led to the emergence of industrial sociology? In the first place, argues Baritz, the increase in the size of the firm made the manager 'desperate in his need for assistance—to manage the organization of his firm'.[14] However, the focus of Baritz's explanation for research into industry is not only on developments internal to industry, but also on the growth of organized labour. Describing the massive increase in union membership from 3 million in 1914 to 15 million in 1945 in the United States of America, Baritz suggests that management began to realize that 'the more thoroughly they understood their workers, the less chance would there be to make those drastic errors which had nurtured unionism. If the social scientists were right, an understanding of human behaviour would show how to control men'.[15] Again, in a later chapter, he says that 'during the period [the first fifteen years of the twentieth century] of increasing union militancy, of socialists and 'Wobblies', of violent strikes and violent strike-breaking, a few managers turned to psychology in an effort to solve their labour problems'.[16]

To deal adequately with the challenges facing management, it would be necessary to show how 'capitalism wrenched itself out of the paralysing fetters of the outmoded free market system and on to the open ceiling economics of monopoly capitalism.'[17] Harry Braverman has pointed to the vital interconnection between the crucial developments in the process of production and the consolidation of monopoly capitalism:

> Scientific management and the whole movement for the organization of production in its modern basis had their beginnings in the last two decades of the last century. A scientific technological revolution, based on the systematic use of science for rapid transformation of labour power into capital, also begins... at the same time.... Both chronologically and functionally, they are part of the new stage of capitalist development, and they grow out of monopoly capitalism and make it possible.[18]

However, the concern of this chapter is not to show how scientific management is introduced to facilitate capital accumulation in South

Africa, but rather to show how management, faced by various challenges, turns increasingly to harness the wider intellectual resources of the social scientific community. What is suggested in this chapter is that a dynamic interaction exists between structural change in the economy, particularly the challenge of Black labour, and the emergence and growth of social research into industry.

II

Social research into the mining industry begins in the 1930s, Bozzoli writes, when, faced by a profitability crisis and competition for labour from manufacturing industry, the mining industry, increasingly turned to more 'scientific' methods of management.[19] The application of scientific principles in the management of Black mineworkers proceeded with the help of industrial psychologists, in four main areas. The first task was to develop a series of simple repetitive tests to assist in the placement of new recruits into the categories of semi-skilled, unskilled and 'boss-boys'. According to these tests, workers can be almost instantly classified, thus saving wasted training time. The second was to introduce more systematic methods of acclimatizing a mineworker to get him accustomed to the extremely high temperature underground. For three hours a day for eight days, recruits undergo 'stepping' exercises at a rate of 550 new recruits each month. At the end they are classified, according to their pulse-rate during stepping, into three categories—those able to perform strenuous, less strenuous and light work respectively. The third strategy was training of workers through the standardization of all jobs. Finally, the system of labour control operating through the compounds was increasingly streamlined and bureaucratized.

However, the relationship established in the 1930s was to grow more rapidly with the crisis of the 1940s. The rapid proletarianization of Africans as well as Afrikaners, had led to the growth of industrial unrest as reflected in Table 1.

TABLE 1. Colour breakdown of strikes, 1938-45

Year	Total man-days lost	White man-days lost	White as percentage of total
1938	4 070	479	11.8
1939	4 246	17	0.4
1940	6 475	3 068	47.4
1941	23 199	7 197	31.0
1942	49 547	14 368	29.0
1943	47 719	28 738	60.2
1944	62 709	1 210	1.9
1945	91 180	6 039	6.6

Source: Union Statistics.

This unrest was to culminate in 1946 when 71,000 miners went on strike. The war years saw a marked tendency towards increased and more intensive trade activity. By the end of the war the Council of non-European Trade Unions (CNETU), claimed a membership of 158,000 and 119 unions, covering more than 40 per cent of the 390,000 Africans employed in commerce and industry (see Table 2).

Table 2. CNTU Membership in 1945

Area	No. of unions	Membership
Johannesburg	50	80 000
Pretoria	15	15 000
Bloemfontein	10	5 000
Kimberley	5	3 000
East London	10	15 000
Port Elizabeth	19	30 000
Cape Town	10	10 000
Total	119	158 000

Source: D. Lewis, 'African Trade Unions and the State, 1947-53' (unpublished).

Four developments expressed the growing relationship between social science and industry in the 1940s. First, there was the appointment in 1946 of J. D. Rheinalt-Jones, a leading exponent of the liberalism prominent among some public figures at the time, as adviser to Anglo-American.[20] In a speech to the Institute of Personnel Management in 1948, Rheinalt-Jones stressed the inevitable growth of an organized African labour movement. (He had already been active in encouraging African trade unions through his involvement with the SAIRR, South African Committee on Industrial Relations.) While he quotes the Lansdowns' Commission's conclusion that 'the native mineworkers have not yet reached the stage of development which will enable them safely and usefully to employ unionism as a means of promoting their advancement', he emphasizes the probability that the mineworkers, union will 'gather strength as time goes on'. 'The strike of 1946 was due to the mineworkers having been worked up to a high feeling by the unions' organizers, but the workers anticipated the plans of the union, which was caught unready for a strike at that time. Experience of the workers in secondary industry showed that those Africans at any rate understand the strike weapon and have developed solidarity.'[21] He then goes on to stress the need for personnel management to take five main considerations into account: '(a) the right selection of workers for specific kinds of work; (b) the training of workers in occupations where training will yield greater efficiency; (c) improvements in working conditions and methods; (d) incentives to effort that can be offered to workers; (e) relations between workers and their immediate supervisors'. He then mentions that work is being done by the National Institute of Personnel Research (NIPR) under the direction of Dr Biesheuvel on these areas of research on the mines.

The second development is the growing interest of the universities in academic work on industry and the economy. In 1932, H. P. Pollak published her pioneering sociological study on *Women in Witwatersrand Industries*. This was followed by a number of other studies on the sociology of work: E. Theron on *Fabriekwerksters in Kaapstad* (1942); V. P. Pons on *Social Investigation of Female Workers and a Related Study of Their Absenteeism* (1949); the University of Natal, Department of Economics, on *The African Factory Worker* (1950); and E. Hellman on *Sellgoods: a Sociological Survey of the African Commercial Labour Force* (1953).[22] Similarly, E. Batson was to begin his pioneering work on poverty during this period and the UCT School of Social Science was to publish numerous studies of the PDL. African trade unions became a matter of academic interest at this time. Writing from their perspective of active involvement in trade unions, Eddie Roux published *Time Longer than Rope*, Kadalie and *My Life and the ICU*, in 1949. Similarly Jack Simons was to write a chapter on trade unions for a book edited by E. Hellman entitled *A Handbook of Race Relations in South Africa*. However, the first university-based study of unions was produced by H. G. Ringrose entitled *Trade Union in Natal* (1951), followed by M. Horrell's *South Africa's Non-white Worker* (1956). In 1932 the Report of the Carnegie Commission on the poor-White problem in South Africa was published, recommending *inter alia* that where job reservation is introduced, it should be treated as transitional. Within the Afrikaans universities the 'poor-White question' was to be the main area of focus, particularly after Dr Verwoerd was transferred to the Chair of Sociology and Social Work at the University of Stellenbosch in 1933. Invited to help organize a *Volkskongres* on poverty among Europeans in 1934, F. Meer, addressing the ASSA in Lesotho in 1973, relates that Verwoerd was 'unapologetically ideological and concerned with the urgent need to raise the poor Afrikaner from the Platteland to the industrial heart and finally political helm of the country'. Three classical studies followed in the Afrikaans universities: P. J. de Vos *Die Bywoner* (1937); P. J. Koorts, *Die Armblank vraagstuk* (1935); S. Pauw, *Die Beroepsarbeid van die Afrikaner in die Stad* (1916).[23]

A third development expressing the growth of social research is the establishment in March 1946 of the National Bureau for Personnel Research (later the National Institute of Personnel Research, NIPR), as a division of the state-subsidized Council for Scientific and Industrial Research (CSIR).[24] The initial preoccupations of the bureau were research into problems of job evaluation and selection and training. The South African Air Force, the General Post Office, the Civil Aviation Co., the Transvaal Clothing Manufacturers Association, and the Chamber of Mines were the first organizations to put specific requests to the bureau, to undertake research into the best utilization of labour in industry. Several of the early investigations were 'concerned with the important question of scientifically testing the aptitude of the native for industrial work both as an operative and in more responsible positions'.[25] In 1946, responding to a request from the Transvaal Clothing Manufacturers Association, the bureau undertook 'a study of the factors determining the fatigue and output among operatives in an underwear factory, with special research on behalf of the Chamber of Mines to develop a battery of performance tests which could be administered to African miners and boss-boys, by a relatively untrained White mine employee. The report records that 'included in the battery is a series of physical fitness tests. Different jobs required different degrees of stamina, as well as different requirements in respect of strength of arms, leg or trunk muscles. Aptitude tests which ignored these factors could only be partly effective'.[26] The third annual report of the CSIR in 1947/48 maintained that, due to the number of inquiries received and the increased research undertaken for both industry (under contract) and for government departments, it was evident that interest in personnel research was being sustained. The original staff of the bureau numbered 8 in 1946, 49 in 1948 and 63 in 1949. In this period, industrial personnel research was confined to large undertakings such as ISCOR, the gold mines and the clothing industry. The battery of performance and selection tests used by the mines were systematically reformulated and improved and were extended in 1949 to include methods for the selection of artisans and European officials in the mines.

An industrial research team was set up in ISCOR and by 1949/50 had completed two projects concerned with the development of selection procedures for administrative trainees, and research into the incidence of absenteeism and labour turnover among Africans. Table 3 classifies research undertaken by the NIPR since its foundation in 1946.

TABLE 3. Classification of research undertaken between 1946 and 1978 by the NIPR

Classification	Percentage of total
Selection and training	30
Productivity/efficiency	12
Job evaluation/classification	11
Attitude towards houting/work	10
Motivation	8
Absenteeism	6
Race and utilization of labour	6
Turnover	5
Management strategies	4
Women in employment	4
Industrial accident/safety	2
Industrial relations	1
Organizational sociology	1
Trade unions	0
Industrial conflict	0

Source: CSIR annual reports, 1946-78.

Table 3 clearly indicates the orientation of the NIPR's research —nearly a third of the total social research done since 1946 has been on the selecting and training of personnel. This is followed by studies on productivity and efficiency, job evaluation and classification, attitudes towards work and absenteeism and turnover. The first study undertaken on industrial relations was in 1977, the second in 1978. No study has been undertaken of trade unions or industrial conflict.

A fourth development in the 1940s is the emergence and growth of personnel management. In 1944, the demand in industry for 'welfare supervisors' and personnel managers provided the impulse to institute a postgraduate diploma in personnel welfare and management at Rhodes University. In 1948, the National Development and Management Foundation of South Africa was founded by Sir Ernest Oppenheimer with the object of helping all those involved in management functions, from the supervisor to the managing director. Earlier, in 1945, Mrs I. H. B. White of the Leather Research Institute at Rhodes University was instrumental in establishing the Institute of Personnel Management. Although the institute always maintained articulate and professional leadership, in fact, it only really started to grow in the late 1960s and particularly the early 1970s. Table 4 provides a chronology of the Institute of Personnel Management membership figures.

TABLE 4. Institute of Personnel Management membership, 1946-76.

Year	No	Year	No
1946	147	1960	250
1948	212	1963	362
1949	219	1964	401
1950	243	1965	545
1952	218	1969	870
1953	198	1973	1 277
1955	195	1974	1 546
1956	221	1976	4 000

Source: Bebb, 'The Development an Evolution of an Open Learning Correspondence for the Personnel Profession', Ph.D. 1978 and IPM.

We have suggested that the crisis of the 1940s, in particular the growth of Black labour, was to provide the impetus for a growing relationship between social science and industry as manifested through the involvement of liberal reformers such as Rheinalt-Jones, the involvement of the universities in research in industry, the establishment of the NIPR and the emergence of personnel management. The dilemma facing the state and capital can be succinctly stated:

> On the one hand it was believed that secondary industry required a more skilled, more contented worker, with lower job turnover and less incentive to malinger or sabotage the production process. This meant permanent urbaniza-

tion for the manufacturing work force, at least. On the other hand such a work force could not but acquire the bargaining power to challenge the sociopolitical structures which sustained its comparative cheapness.

Faced by these challenges of the 1940s, two directions were open to the state. The one was to settle the labour force in the urban areas, allow certain rights such as controlled trade unions and improve production in the 'reserves'. This was the path of liberal reform, particularly that of manufacturing, ambiguously and inconsistently represented by the United Party. The other was to try to stem the flow of Africans into the cities, control labour relations through in-plant bargaining instead of trade unions, control its rate and direction of absorption into industry through influx control and labour bureaus, redirect labour to White agriculture and then attempt to deal with the reserve problem. Legassick argues that the latter path is essentially what apartheid constitutes and this direction represented a political victory for a class alliance, in the form once again of Afrikaner nationalism, of White workers, capitalist agriculture, and the petty bourgeoisie.[27] It was this class alliance which was to reject the Botha Commission's cautious proposals for recognition of African unions. In fact African trade unions had, by 1950, declined significantly and approximately, sixty-six had become defunct. Table 5 shows the Botha Commissione estimate's of total paid-up membership of African trade unions as at 31 March 1950.

TABLE 5. Membership of African trade unions in 1950 (estimate).

Area	Membership	Area	Membership
Pretoria	250	Port Elizabeth	604
Witwatersrand	12 078	East London	500
Durban	1 686	Kimberley	0
Cape Town	2 028	Bloemfontein	150
		TOTAL	17 296

Source: Botha Commission Report, para. 1500.

While the late 1930s and 1940s produced boom conditions, these slackened to stagnation and even recession in the 1950s. During the 1950s, the Institute of Personnel Management actually experienced a decline in membership (see Table 4), although it picked up again in the late 1950s. It was at this time that Black workers experienced a new wave of militancy in the form of bus boycotts and stay-aways, on the one hand, and the organization of Black workers into trade unions, on the other. C. Pearce in an address to the Institute of Personnel Management in 1958 made clear the importance of personnel management in monitoring this unrest when he said:

> We have next to no knowledge of how and what our African employees are thinking . . . A discussion group with a number of sound African leaders

> proved most valuable during the period of the Alexandria bus boycott. This was an interesting experiment in joint consultation and a proof of its success was that we were in touch with African leadership, and with African thought and opinion, this at a time when other contact was virtually non-existent and at a period of lamentably bad relations and great hostility.[28]

Similarly, but with more emphasis on control, a personnel manager, Corbett, had this to say to members in 1959:

> Industry and commerce have been calling for consultation between employers and their native employees. This move started during the native bus boycott of 1957 when the Johannesburg Chamber of Commerce negotiated both with government and natives and brought about a settlement of the dispute—before last year's three day strike threat, employers in both commerce and industry were urged to consult their Bantu employees in regard to the move—a strike move broke down after one day's half-hearted demonstration. A careful survey was made of reports specially completed and the lesson is there for all to read—it pays to consult your Bantu employees and generate mutual understanding and respect.[29]

However, in spite of these appeals to use personnel management skills, Langenhoven, in a study of Black personnel management in 1972, was to note how little personnel management's skills were used with Black employees. He records that only 0.9 per cent of the South African employers studied used psychological tests for the selection and placing of African workers, only 21.8 per cent inducted new Black workers and only 33.6 per cent kept records of their job performance.[30]

Similarly Prior records, in a case-study of management in a gold mine, that faced by a protest march because of the long hours workers were kept underground, management

> instead of advocating a stepping up of formal means of communication and admitting of the need for worker representation in the work structure, called for a more vigorous control. This extended to a streamlining of the procedures for getting security personnel, dogs and vehicles to the place of any incident, the procuring of radio equipment and the provision of a riot car for the mine.[31]

Jubber explains the failure of employers to use personnel management's skills in these terms. First, he suggests that 'individual capabilities are of relatively little importance and the kinds of performance which pass for competence are easily achieved by almost anyone'. In other words, most African workers in the manufacturing sector are machine operators doing jobs which require very little skill. Secondly, 'the low average wage paid to Black workers implies that organizations can tolerate fairly low levels of individual competence without the overall competence of the organization being seriously affected'. And thirdly, 'the high rate of labour turnover in certain groups of black workers is cited by some managers as the reason for not inducting training or monitoring the performance of black workers'.[32] However, in an earlier part of the same article, Jubber provides the clue to the stalled relationship which begins in the 1940s between industry and social science and only really takes off in the 1970s—a lack of an organized labour force. 'South Africa', says Jubber 'unlike other developed capitalist societies, does not as yet have an organized working class capable of seriously opposing the organizational structures which the agents of capital and management impose on the workers.' He then goes on to argue that there is the exception of the White 'labour aristocracy' but

> it can be reasonably argued that black workers are caught up in extremely bureaucratic organizations because they are weak and poor. Bureaucracy is an effective instrument of capital and the state for the rationalization and exploitation of black labour. Bureaucratic organization and South Africa's industrial relations system together form a powerful instrument for keeping the black labour force poor and weak.[33]

However, Jubber does not suggest why the Black labour force is poor and weak. Four obstacles to the organization of Black workers can be identified. First, there is the repressive role of the state in containing Black worker organization. Secondly, there are numerous divisions, particularly racial divisions, within the working class. Thirdly, there is the low-wage, low-skill nature of the work-force in a situation where a large reserve army of unemployed workers exist. This weakens the ability to organize and enables management to replace workers who demand their rights. Finally, a central obstacle is the institutionalization of migrant labour through the contract system which makes the contract worker more vulnerable to dismissal if he joins a union.[34]

III

By the 1960s the resurgence of African trade-union activity that characterized the late 1950s and early 1960s had been crushed. South Africa was to experience a decade of relative industrial peace. However, it was a decade in which the economy experienced a structural transformation through the massive influx of foreign capital, accelerated expansion of industry, and a corresponding growth of the African working class, which brought African workers firmly to the centre of the industrial stage. Coupled with these changes is the restructuring of capital and the growing concentration and centralization of firms between the years 1969 and 1973.[35] In particular, we see the growth of a semi-skilled Black labour force—the organizational base for industrial unionism. Or, as Hemson writes:

> With the growth of monopoly capitalism and the concentration of production in large-scale, highly mechanized factories and 'industrial mines', basic production is carried out by a massified black proletariat neither differentiated by traditional skills, nor having experienced the benefits of reform. These are the conditions for a rapid advance in class consciousness as the political resistance to apartheid gains momentum.[36]

From 1972 onwards, this pattern of industrial peace was to change dramatically. Faced by rapid inflation, 60,000-100,000 Black workers in Durban went on strike in February 1973. It was out of this wave of working-class militancy that five distinct Black union groupings of approximately 60,000 workers were to emerge in the 1970s. Although there has been a decline since then in industrial disputes, South Africa's townships were to experience a massive wave of internal unrest culminating in the September stay-aways where nearly half a million participated.[37]

It is in the context of this structural transformation of the economy and growing working-class organization, that social research into industry grew rapidly in the late 1960s and 1970s. In the heady atmosphere of boom conditions, the thesis that the logical imperative of industrialization will break down apartheid assumes widespread acceptance, and becomes the source of a major liberal/radical debate in the 1970s. At the annual conference of the South African Institute of Race Relations in 1968, the theme of industrialization and human relations was chosen and papers on this tropic were presented.[38] In 1968, James Irving, professor of sociology at Rhodes University, published a series of lectures in industrial sociology where he takes up similar issues. In the first lecture, he deals with the effects of industrialization on the social structure of South Africa arguing that 'the South African labour pattern is a deviation from the normal historical development of the capitalist system throughout the rest of the world. Nowhere else had produced a pattern of capitalist development in which a large sector of labour is marked by segregation and virtual prohibition of mobility through a wide occupational range.'[39] The second lecture centres on the problems raised by mechanization for the trade-union movement. This is followed by a lecture on the problems of productivity in the light of the growing alienation from work in affluent societies. The final lecture deals with the effect of mechanization on society, particularly the role of the engineer.

Two other developments indicate the growing involvement of sociologists in industrial questions. First, there is the emergence of separate courses in industrial sociology at various universities. In 1968, the University of the Witwatersrand launched a two-year sub-major in industrial sociology. In the same year the University of Potchefstroom also launched a separate three-year course in industrial sociology. At present, the University of Westville (Durban), University of the Orange Free State, University of Potchefstroom, Rhodes and the University of Cape Town all have separate courses (that is credits) in industrial sociology. Most of the other universities offer industrial sociology as an option at undergraduate and postgraduate level.[40]

The second development is the growing interest of the universities in research into industry. There are two types of institutes which have developed an interest in the study of industrial behaviour. First, there are those institutes, such as the Centre of Applied Social Studies, at the University of Natal (Durban), which were set up in the 1950s, but have increasingly focused on industrial questions in the 1970s. An analysis of the publication lists covering the period 1954 to 1978 reveals little research interest in industry, until 1973 when studies on managerial strategy, employment opportunities and race, organized labour and the African, the African worker, turnover, African occupation advancement, and the effects of economic growth, are published.[41] The second category of research institutes are those set up in the 1970s, many to focus specifically on labour and industrial relations. The first of these was the Institute of Industrial Education (IIE), established by a group of academics at Natal in 1973, to provide a research and teaching service to the emerging African trade-union movement. They initiated the *South African Labour Bulletin* and published its early editions. In 1974, they published *Durban Strikes 1973* and since then have done research on company ownership, comparisons between conditions in Durban and other parts of the world in similar industries, and minimum wage levels. The IIE has also produced six handbooks entitled *Worker Organisation, History of Worker Organisation, Worker in the Factory, Worker in Society, Negotiation Handbook, Legal Handbook*. Since then UNISA has established the Institute of Labour Studies with an impressive list of publications focusing on labour relations and labour law. In 1975, the Anglo-American Corporation initiated the establishment of the Institute of Industrial Relations (IIR) to provide a forum where management and labour could meet to exchange views. The most extensive work to date in this field has been done by UCT's Saldru which, in their current list of working papers, has twenty-three publications. They have held two pioneering conferences in the field of labour—one on farm labour and the other on industrial health. In 1975, the University of Natal in Pietermaritzburg launched a Development Studies Research Group which has published two books on Black employment, as well as numerous working papers on the field of unemployment and labour distribution. In 1978, the University of the Witwatersrand established a Centre for Applied Legal Studies, which has a specific focus in one of the sections on labour law and produces the *Bulletin of Labour Law*. The University of the Western Cape's Institute of Social Development does not focus specifically on labour, but lists in its annual report research on migrant labour, foreign labour and unemployment.

Similarly the establishment of the Merger Institute at the University of the Witwatersrand School of Business Administration in 1978 falls into this category. Established with the purpose of monitoring the mergers in the 1970s and to study the extent to which shareholders in practical terms have economic control over their shares, it is clearly a response to the wider changes in the economy in the 1970s.

We quoted Foucault earlier to the effect that 'each one of the human sciences was occasioned by a problem'. We have suggested that the structural transformation of the South African economy, particularly the challenge of Black labour, is the occasion for the emergence and growth of social research into industry. But, continues Foucault, 'this may explain the set of circumstances that led to this focus, it cannot explain why the human sciences take the form they do'—this, he says, 'is an event in the order of knowledge'.[42] As 'events in the order of knowledge', drawing on different intellectual traditions and focusing on different problems, it seems possible to select six different examples of the type of studies done in the 1970s.

In the first place, there are state-initiated studies, usually in the form of Commissions of Inquiry, which attempt to provide government with a solution to a problem arising in industry. The Wiehahn Commission, set up in part to control the emerging African trade-union movement, is the most recent of this type. Two academics, Wiehahn, a professor of labour law at UNISA, and Van der Merwe, professor of economics at the University of Pretoria, sat on this commission. These commissions tend to rely on academics from the more conservatrice universities as indicated by this commission's use of Van der Merwe's D. Phil. thesis (*Die Bantoe arbeidsmark in Suid Afrika*) for their information on migrant workers and so-called foreign commuters.[43]

Recommending trade-union rights for all workers, the Wiehahn Commission's report was heralded as a 'breakthrough in industrial relations'. Yet closer examination of the report suggests that it was not the intention of the commission that large numbers of Black workers should join registered unions, nor that all unregistered unions achieve registration. On the contrary, the 'dualism' in the system is to be perpetuated but its racial element is to be softened and the working class is to be further fragmented by the incorporation of some categories and the 'freezing' out of others. This disorganization, particularly of the unregistered union movement, is in itself a powerful instrument of control. Furthermore, although many commentators have contrasted the supposedly 'liberal' tenor of the commissions' report with that of the White Paper, the distinction is less clear. In deference to 'international standards', the commission comes out against the legislative exclusion of migrant workers from registered unions, but a close reading of the report suggests that the commission expected 'migrants' to be excluded by the unions themselves and even indicates what measures could be adopted to achieve this. Furthermore, the establishment of a national manpower commission and an industrial court, along with the restrictions imposed on new unions registering, suggests that the *intention* of the report, taken together with the White Paper, is to extend state control over the trade-union movement.

The second type of research is that sponsored by management to investigate a specific problem. Jubber has argued that 'management in South Africa has never strongly supported industrial sociology, as has been the case in the United Kingdom and the United States'.[44] Although he does not provide any specific evidence of this, an analysis of the budget allocation to the HSRC and the Human Resources Laboratory (HRL) of the Chamber of Mines, indicates a very low percentage of total research money spent on social research. In the case of the HSRC it averages 7 per cent between 1975 and 1978 and in the case of HRL about 14 per cent of the total research budget.[45] What is clear is that the bulk of money went into technical research, in particular, in the case of the Chamber of Mines, in attempts to restructure the labour process through mechanization. 'The largest private research effort in South Africa was trebled in 1974 for the prime purpose of revolutionizing gold mining by means of mechanical devices designed to gauge, hammer or bore out the ore. Mechanization should reduce manpower requirements and open higher skilled job opportunities.[16] Nevertheless, two studies indicate the nature of research done in this category. In 1972, Keenan-Smith, a personnel manager, published a study he undertook of productivity. He conducted an experiment to increase the productivity and the profit of a company by improving morale, motivation and general work satisfaction and by reducing absenteeism and labour turnover. Initial tests in the experimental areas showed absenteeism was at times as high as 15 per cent, and productivity was 15 per cent lower than the expected rate of production. Meetings were held at all levels with the factory staff and ideas for improved job content emerged, as well as ideas for changing the job context, such as lighting.

> A dramatic step was taken in issuing charge-hands with white coats which had previously been reserved for foremen—while attending to what appeared to be nothing more than 'maintenance factors', the higher motivators or 'satisfiers', i.e., his wages, were stimulated by giving these employees recognition, opportunities to advance, the feeling of responsibility and a sense of achievement.[47]

Operators were invited to participate in isolating the problems and making suggestions and devising methods aimed at improving productivity. Regular meetings were seen by the foremen as not only appropriate while identifying problems, but also as allowing the formation of natural work groups who were expected to produce possible solutions to problems. If one member of the work group failed to pull his weight, his colleagues would demand his dismissal because he was holding up the team effort for the remainder of the group. 'Internal pressures within the work groups tended to reduce absenteeism for the simple reason that an habitual absentee was found to be a hindrance to productivity and to the group's performance.'[48] Measurable results included the following: labour turnover fell from 100 per cent to an average of 60 per cent during 1971, abstenteeism dropped from 15 per cent to 9 per cent within three months. Productivity rose and production doubled within a relatively short period of time.

A second study under this category is that of van Breda of the Personnel Division of the University of the Orange Free State. The aim of this study, entitled *A Manual on Black Labour,* was to analyse the staffing process and the problems of personnel acquisition and placement with the labour bureau. Data were collected by means of questionnaires sent to firms throughout the country and to labour bureaux. Recommendations are made on how to make the present system of labour allocation more efficient with specific recommendations for employers using tribal labour bureaux. For example, the following: 'Let the remaining applicants run on the spot in order to eliminate the unfit and sick ones—tuberculosis cases are specially reduced drastically in this way.' As well as 'interview each applicant and pay attention to work history, training, education and domestic circumstances, appearance and whether the person has the necessary limbs'.[49]

The third type of research into industry could be loosely labelled interactionist because of the emphasis on the participant's perception of events. Gordon's *Life in a Namibian Compound* describes how Blacks cope with the alien and hostile environment of the compound. African workers, he says, develop two distinct social worlds. One is a private or enclave culture, which is located in the interstices of the formal organizational structure and grounded in the compound. This private culture, of which the White supervisors are largely unaware, is analysed under the blanket term of Brotherhood.[50] Drawing heavily on Goffmann's work on total institutions, Gordon describes the various secondary adjustments Africans make in their work situation. Brotherhood, he says, is the means by which Africans protect their own people.

> It emphasizes the respect, trust, consultation and dignity, and delineates a distinctive universe which specifically excludes all whites, and blacks who, by their action have proved to be non-brothers. Its ideology provides the setting for the private culture in which the blacks can be themselves and masters of their own actions. The most damning label which any black migrant can get from his fellow workers is that of informer or sell-out.[51]

The second social world of the Black workers is the one in which the Black has to interact with the Whites. To describe Black-White relations he draws on the concept of interracial etiquette. He draws an analytical distinction between a basic form of etiquette which is aimed at staying out of trouble and avoiding derogatory remarks and sanctions, and manipulative etiquette whereby Blacks use etiquette to achieve some end such as patronage or material goods. An example he gives of the second type is 'minstralization', where the worker cynically acts out what the White believes are the Blacks' bad qualities in order to ingratiate himself.

Similarly, Moodie is concerned to identify the informal power structure and informal norms in a compound. There are two key aspects to his study. First, Moodie suggests that 'the major cause of tension underground, apart from the danger of the job itself, is the white miner—who for most part of his time underground sits on his box in the haulage, his picanin (personal retainer) on guard, relaxing in the company of fellow white miners—most of the genuine supervision is done by the black team leader'. The second key aspect of his study is the suggestion that the induna is in an ambivalent position in the authority structure—he is expected both to control the compound and represent the inmates to management. Because he is an appointed official he cannot fulfil this role satisfactorily.[52]

The fourth category of research, 'structural-functionalist perspective', is possibly best illustrated by S. P. Cillier's study of absenteeism in a Cape industry. Defining absenteeism as 'a form of deviant industrial behaviour which occurs when individuals or groups in the organization act contrary in terms of the formal structure and goal of the organization', and using a rigorous methodology, he undertook a three-phase study.[53] In the third phase he argues that

> it was found that while absence and labour turnover are generally regarded as forms of deviant industrial behaviour, no direct relationship could be established in its incidence. Further analyses showed that absenteeism among this

category of workers is primarily a function of factors outside the work place. Yet organization practice cannot be disregarded since a definite relationship was established between absentee rates, and the level of worker satisfaction, attractiveness of work and relationship with superiors on the other hand.[54]

The fifth category can be illustrated by the IIE book *The Durban Strikes 1973*. While radical in the sense of locating its critique of capitalism in terms of the inequality of power relationships, it presents, in the last chapter, a 'reformist' solution. 'Trade unions, with the right to organize freely, and the use of the strike weapon as a last resort, organized on democratic lines, and possessing their own sanctions over members, are the pre-conditions for stable industrial peace in South Africa.'[55] In the chapter dealing with the creation of a labour supply and the legitimization of authority, it draws on largely conventional historiographical and sociological literature. No attempt is made to develop a systematic Marxist analysis. The *South African Labour Bulletin* could possibly be similarly classified. Table 6 indicates the range of issues focused on in this journal.

TABLE 6. Classification of articles published in the *South African Labour Bulletin* Vols. 1-4

Classification	Percentage
1. Labour history	20
2. Trade-union structure, organization and strategy	18
3. Industrial relations	15
4. Strikes and boycotts	14
5. Managerial strategy, structure and ideology	7
6. Unemployment	6
7. Migrant labour	4
8. Industrial health	4
9. Labour law	3
10. Labour process	3
11. Labour and underdevelopment	2
12. Women and employment	2
13. Foreign investment	2

The final category is that of studies done clearly within the framework of historical materialism. In large part these do not deal with contemporary South Africa[56] but the recent study of *The Mozambique Miner* by the University of Maputo is one of the exceptions. Concerned essentially with the export of labour from the three southern provinces of Mozambique to South African mines, it focuses on two central issues. First, in the attempt on the part of the mines to establish a more stable labour force, partly through mechanization, WENELA is increasingly pursuing a recruitment strategy that excludes novices and only recruits holders of the re-engagement certificate or bonus cards. This, it is argued, must be understood in the context of the Chamber of Mines 'policy of maximising the number of labour supplier states around South Africa and of distributing the demand for foreign labour across them'.[57] Its second focus is on the degree of penetration of mining capital in these three provinces:

> ... the only men who had never been [to the gold mines] were the sick and the disabled; or teachers or self-employed craftsmen like carpenters. Furthermore, men do not work the occasional contract, say at the beginning of their working lives when they are young men needing to find money to marry. On the contrary, men work large numbers of contracts; they work long contracts; and they spend a large proportion of their working lives as workers in the mines.[58]

The study then goes on to focus on the pattern of rural stratification in these provinces, drawing a distinction between areas with small, medium and large numbers of peasants.

However, the fifth and sixth category of research share two characteristics in common. In the first place, they both involve attempts to apply a class analysis to South African society. In the second place, they both attempt to link their class analysis to organization—in the case of *The Durban Strikes 1973* the last chapter makes a case for trade unions for all industrial workers, while *The Mozambique Miner* laid the basis for a strategy of rural development among peasant-workers in southern Mozambique.

IV

What effect does apartheid have on social research into industry in South Africa? For the President of the HSRC (known until 1968 as the National Council of Social Research and the central state body concerned with funding and directing social research) this question has a simple answer: '.. in the Republic social science research is not a dogma super-imposed from above as an instrument of national policy; the aim of the HSRC is to encourage and stimulate research in the social sciences by free and independent scholars....'.[59] However, while it may be true that the state has not attempted to impose directly an apartheid view of social research on the universities, it has been widely argued that the effect of South Africa's racist structures and governmental policy is to compound the biases inherent in industrial research in a capitalist society in at least two ways: (a) by encouraging social scientists to develop separate theories for Black and White industrial behaviour that take as given the social structure, they legitimize and reproduce intentionally or unintentionally, apartheid; (b) through direct or indirect pressure make it difficult, if not virtually impossible, to undertake research in controversial areas.

The first criticism seems to be the thrust of Gerd Wiendieck's critique of the attempt by industrial psychology to develop a theory of Black motivation.

Servants of apartheid? 103

> The theories of industrial psychology also reflect a capitalist bias, since managerial philosophies are capitalist philosophies in most western countries. South African industrial psychology reveals the same biases, but here the more general biases are compounded by those arising from the racist structures in this society. Given the fact that South Africa is an apartheid society, the South African industrial psychologist is solicited into producing motivation theories for racial groupings, because the society dictates that the various race groups may not be motivated in terms of the same opportunities for development, promotion, self-expression, remuneration, security, achievement, self-determination and so forth. . . . that these biases are inter-related seems quite apparent, but at this stage in South Africa's history it is the bias which tries to peddle the idea that a black worker is somehow different from a white worker and has somehow to be motivated differently which is overtly the most abhorrent.[60]

Thus we see a book by Backer, designed specifically to make research into 'black motivation more accessible to managers', recommended to those 'who might be unaware of some of the important motivational differences between white and black workers'. However, the curious feature of the book is that the sociological evidence reproduced in the book by the NIPR regarding the African worker suggests that no such separate theory of Black workers is possible. Drawing on the rural/urban, tribal/Western dichotomy, Vorster concludes that

> there appear to be no cultural factors which influence the emergence of unique African patterns of work aspirations after he has left the traditional tribal milieu. The aspirations of the African closely resemble those of other western groups as he becomes integrated in the industrial scene. When compared with similar research elsewhere, the findings suggest that there may be greater differences in the work aspirations of different social and occupational groups from the same ethnic group, than between similar social and occupational groups from different ethnic groups. In other words, it may be suggested that ethnic origins are less important than environment and occupation in determining aspirations . . . .. The hierarchy of their aspirations was found to be good wages, good supervision, good and safe working conditions, non-strenuous work, sympathetic management.[61]

Yet in spite of the lack of sociological evidence for such a separate theory based on cultural differences, the author is happy to publish a book with the title *Motivating Black Workers*!

A more direct example of research within the framework of apartheid is that undertaken by the institutes of the HSRC. Of particular relevance to our topic is the Institute of Manpower Research which defines its objective as follows: 'The broad aim of the research undertaken by this institute is to gather data on the manpower potential and its development, as well as to collect and process the supply of, and demand for, and utilization of, manpower, with a view to manpower and educational planning.'[62] In line with this objective a Talent Survey was launched in 1965 to obtain 'a picture of the white manpower potential of the country and to determine the factors which are conducive to the optimum development of this potential'. Similarly, an analysis of their publications since 1969 reveals that 23 per cent of their research publications that deal with industrial behaviour focus on employment opportunities in the homelands and border areas.

David Webster, reviewing the 'popular anthropology' of Raymond Silberbauer and Peter Becker shows how their work rests on the assumption that the most significant fact about the African workers is not that they are workers, but that they belong to a different *culture* which has to be sympathetically understood.[63] These writers, says Webster, are operating from a sympathetic, and at times liberal point of view, but they give the misleading picture that Africans have only recently been exposed to Western culture. 'Becker demonstrates tribal wisdom, and that it should not be underrated, while Silberbauer, speaking from within the work context, tries to show that blacks are different and special steps must be taken to allow for these differences.'[64] Webster then goes on to deal with what he considers 'the most serious charge that can be levelled against them and one which goes to the heart of the matter'. This is that

> neither is prepared to face the dominant facts of South Africa's political and socio-economic life; that the country is subject to the policy of separate development and, in earlier times, was subject to a system which was not so openly coercive, but nevertheless exploitive. To be black in South Africa means one is powerless, subject to influx control, job reservation, inadequate housing and health facilities and the lack of trade union representation. All these factors (and more) affect black workers in a fundamental way and must be considered when judging his productivity and efficiency.[65]

Fisher, reviewing, *The Effective Utilization of Human Resources in S.A.* (1974) by Federale Mynbou's Managing Director, Wim de Villiers, attacks him for his 'crude and absurd psychological reductionism based on inaccurate observations of black and white child-rearing habits'. It is worth quoting de Villiers at some length in order to convey the nature of his argument:

> Unlike the white child who is fed at regular intervals—usually every four hours—the black baby is fed only when he cries for it. From infancy, this develops an expectation in the child that his needs will be satisfied on demand. This tendency is further encouraged by the fact that the baby is fed at the breast up to the age of two whenever the fancy takes him. Later in life the child appears on the scene as the bearer of authority, imbued with a paternalistic responsibility. If he experiences any form of need, he knows he can depend on the tribe to provide on request, within of course the limits of its ability. He will arrive uninvited at every feast, confidently expecting to be allowed to enjoy whatever is available. . . . This ethos of his tribal society he bears with him when he enters the white man's world of economic activity. The new society, with its figures of authority and all that goes with it, assumes the place of the old and at once also inherits the obligations of the old society towards the individual. The employer must not only exercise authority and discipline, but he must also provide for all needs without there being

necessarily any relation to the individual's own contribution. If the worker's material needs are only met in part, he needs simply to ask for complete satisfaction. Against this background he may easily interpret his collective bargaining power merely as a way in which to put demands which must be satisfied, and not as a medium for negotiating the basic agreement.[66]

It is not surprising then that in the government Commission of Inquiry, set up to investigate the causes underlying the conflicts in the mines between 1974 and 1975, the following is reproduced: 'Despite the influence of the white man, civilization, religion and western standards, the tendency to become violent where tribal differences are involved, is practically spontaneous.' Ethnologist and Bantu expert, Dr van Warmelo, stated *inter alia* that 'the Southern Bantu tribes (Xhosa, Basutho, etc.) are particularly inclined to become violent and that they even regard fighting as a form of recreation'.[67] Finally there is the danger of reproducing apartheid in the very research act itself—the White sociologist conceives, the Black research assistant executes.

The second area in which it is argued apartheid affects social research is through the difficulties experienced by social scientists in doing 'controversial' research. Four arguments have been put forward here.

First, it is cautiously questioned by both Unesco and by Welsh whether the HSRC does not prefer to allocate funds for non-controversial research. Unesco, in the 1967 report on the effects of apartheid on education, science, culture, and information said that

> given the policy of the South African government, and the steps it has taken to ensure the implementation of this policy, it may be questioned whether the National Council for Social Research (now the HSRC), which provides funds for research in the social sciences and which is directly administered by the Minister of Education, Arts & Science, would hesitate or not to support research projects that might appear ideologically suspect, and whether projects sponsored by universities, which would be less likely to raise fundamental issues of racial policy, would not be given preference. This suspicion is certainly entertained by some social scientists who are either working in South Africa or who have had recent experience of South Africa. By its nature, however, it is almost impossible to obtain direct evidence of this kind.[68]

Welsh argues that the Advisory Committees, which recommend funding of research projects, are 'numerically dominated by academics from conservative institutions. No blacks serve on any of the committees and nor, indeed, are black universities represented.'[69] Furthermore, 'it is believed by some scholars that the HSRC accords preferential treatment to those research projects that do not impinge upon controversial areas'. Although Welsh makes it clear that it is not possible to confirm or deny the validity of these feelings, 'those who make this assertion do so emphatically and cite examples of refusals in support'.[70] Hammond-Tooke feels that 'it has not been too difficult to obtain research funds and some important work has been done under the auspices of the Council, for example Mayers' well-known work on migrancy and urbanization'. However he does add the rider that difficulties sometimes arise in publishing material if the findings do not meet with the Council's approval.[71] Lever, on the other hand, suggests that the HSRC, which is in a position to discourage research in the controversial field of race relations, does not do so.[72]

An analysis of the Advisory Committees for 1977, bears out Welsh's argument that they tend to be numerically dominated by academics from the conservative universities, although at least one of the committees does now have—for what it is worth—a representative from a Black university. Furthermore, an analysis of research money granted in the field of industrial research, reported in the HSRC bulletin, does not indicate any obvious direction and quite likely represents the sort of interests held by postgraduate researchers at the universities. Research into 'race and the utilization of labour' received the most support, while industrial conflict was ranked third. However, ultimately, such an analysis would not be able to prove that bias did not exist, as those who fear discrimination may simply not apply for funds in the first place.

Secondly, research into controversial areas is made difficult by the hierarchic structure of society which leads the subordinate groups to structure their communication with the superordinate groups in such a way as not to antagonize them.[73] Alverson, in his study of informal organization, writes that 'one of the African's secrets of survival in South Africa is to keep the white man as ignorant of him as possible'.[74] On the other hand, racial tension is such that one may well experience sharp hostility from respondents to being interviewed. Webster and Kuzwayo record a high refusal rate in their survey among African workers in Durban, because fear and suspicion in the townships aggravated the feeling that the interviewer was involved in the feud between Buthelezi and a cabinet colleague.[75] But even when respondents are not hostile they may not want to talk. 'Refusal to be interviewed', they write, 'seems to be related to the mundane point that African workers have very little leisure at home and prefer to spend it on household chores or with their friends and family, rather than on an hour-long interview with a stranger on abstract questions which seem of little immediate relevance'.[76]

Thirdly, it is argued that research on controversial areas is controlled by the government through the requirement that scholars who wish to conduct research in the African reserves must first obtain a permit from the relevant government department. Hammond-Tooke writes that

> permits are necessary for entrance to non-white areas and can be summarily withdrawn with no reasons given. One suspects that reasons for withdrawing permits are in some cases trivial and in some cases based on the information or opinion of some petty local official. The general effect of the uncertainty is to force the research worker to 'play it safe', either by selecting as politically neutral topics as possible, or by failing to push his interaction with the people or questioning as far as he should. This uncertainty also affects publication of results—there is a danger that if a report is published which criticises government policy either implicitly or explicitly, further field-work facilities will be withdrawn.[77]

This reproduction of a permit from the Secretary for Plural Relations and Development indicates the areas of control that a permit involves:

1. The permit holder(s) must advise the Commissioner of the district concerned when entry to any Black Area in his district is envisaged.
2. (a) The permit holder(s) must make his/her/their own arrangements for board and lodging. Lodging with Blacks is not permitted.
   (b) The permit holder(s) must advise the officer in charge beforehand if he intends to enter any Forest reserve.
3. Under no circumstances must the holder(s) of this permit interfere with the domestic or other affairs of the Blacks.
4. In his/her/their dealings, if any, with the Blacks the holder(s) hereof must behave in a dignified manner.
5. This permit is valid for a period from .....to ..... but may be withdrawn at any time without reasons being assigned.
6. The holder(s) must be in possession of this permit when in a Black Area, and must produce it to any authorized official upon request.
7. The permit holder(s) shall not enter any proclaimed Black Rural Township without the prior consent of the Commissioner of the area concerned AND the Superintendent of such township.
8. The concept of the book to be published must be forwarded to this Department for approval before it is submitted to the publishers for publication.

A final but crucial area is the discouragement of research through prosecutions, detentions, deportations, banning, withdrawal of passports, censorship and suppression of vital information and statistics. In 1971, Dr Barend Van Niekerk was charged with contempt of court for two articles he had published in the *South African Law Journal* suggesting a racial bias in the number of cases of capital punishment.[78] In 1977, David Russell was sentenced to three months' imprisonment for refusing to divulge the names of three people who made statements to him for his publication *The Role of the Riot Police and the Suppression of Truth*.[79] Toine Eggenhuizen was deported shortly after the publication of *Another Blanket,* a sharply critical study of compounds in Anglo-American mines in late 1975. A number of research assistants attached to the Centre of Applied Social Studies in Durban have been detained at length (one for as long as nine months) and interrogated about information obtained in the course of their investigations. While it may be true that they were not detained because of their research activity, but rather because of alleged political offences, the effect of detention is to discourage or delay research work in controversial areas.[80] Clearly research into political attitudes can be a hazardous task. Welsh describes several cases where security police have tailed research workers and subsequently questioned informants. 'This is naturally intimidating both to investigator and investigated, the former fearing that the information he has obtained could land his informant into trouble, and the latter fearing that the information could be prised out of the investigator.'[81] In their study of Langa, Monica Wilson and Archie Mafeje elected not to investigate political organizations or trade unions. They said that questions were not asked about them early in the investigation because they would have aroused suspicion, and during the course of the study the two main political organizations, the African National Congress and the Pan African Congress, were banned. Furthermore, two cases occurred where journalists were imprisoned for refusing to reveal to the police their sources of information on political matters.[82]

However, it is in the banning of books and journals dealing with controversial subjects that the state's disapproval or discouragement of research activities of a potentially controversial kind is made clear. In giving reasons for the banning of an edition of the *South African Labour Bulletin,* the Directorate of Publications submitted that 'any article advancing the application of Marxist theory to South African black labour problems, however academically it may be done, could be furthering the aims of communism. To do so is a statutory crime in South Africa'.[83] The Publications Appeal Board, in giving reasons as to why it believed the journal 'was prejudicial to the safety of the state, the general welfare of the peace and good order' said 'dozens of examples of illegal strikes appear in the publication, yet these strikes are nowhere condemned. If a paper serves an educational purpose, it should consistently oppose, deprecate and condemn these illegal and often criminal operations'.

A major research problem is the difficulty in obtaining adequate statistical information, best illustrated by the fact that until last year, no government department produced any statistics on Black unemployment. 'South Africa produces no regular statistics measuring unemployment for the population as a whole. Regular figures for registration of non-African unemployed are published and these can be taken to be an indicator of the state of the business cycle. They are no guide to overall unemployment, however, unemployment being disproportionately concentrated among Africans.'[84]

Research into, and publication of, information of a critical nature relating to the Defence Force, the Department of Prisons, the Police, as well as foreign investment, is made extremely difficult by legislation. Publication without ministerial authority of any statement, comment or rumour relating to any member or activity of the Defence Force which is 'calculated to prejudice or embarrass the government in its foreign relations or to alarm or depress members of the public', constitutes a criminal offence.[85] The Prisons Act makes it a criminal offence to publish false information about prisons without taking reasonable steps to verify the information.[86] Since neither the legislators nor the courts have spelled out what the words 'reasonable steps' mean, a great deal of uncertainty exists to the extent of discouraging a recent postgraduate student from embarking on a research project on prison labour.

The recent amendment to the Police Act similarly makes it an offence to publish 'any matter' about the police 'without having reasonable grounds for believing that the statement is true'. Section 2(2)(f) of the Terrorism Act states:

> A person is conclusively guilty of terrorism if he does not prove beyond a reasonable doubt that he did not, *inter alia,* intend to further or encourage the achievement of any political aim, including the bringing about of any social or economic change, by violence or forcible means or by intervention of or in accordance with the direction or under the guidance of or in cooperation with or with the assistance of any foreign government or any foreign or international body or institution.[87]

The wording of this section of the Act, which carried a mandatory five-year gaol sentence, could be read to mean that, for example, a study of the role of foreign investment in South Africa that recommended disengagement was an offence. This is certainly the fear among scholars and has led some to avoid this area of research. A final, but disturbing, incident was the tarring and feathering of Afrikaner historian, F. A. van Jaarsveld, by the Afrikaner Weerstand Beweeging, for questioning the religious nature of the Day of the Covenant.[88]

The effect of apartheid on social research will remain a matter of controversy. On the one hand, we see the bland optimism of Henry Lever when he concludes that 'the impediments to social research in South Africa are not very great. South African sociologists are far freer to pose controversial questions than their colleagues in . . . most African countries and have fewer restrictions placed on their choice of topics or on the manner in which they are discussed'.[89] On the other hand, there is the cautious optimism of David Welsh: 'There are ways around most, if not all problems; but the investigator's ingenuity and resourcefulness may often be taxed to the limit. Social research, it seems to me, is the art of the impossible; it can be done even in the most hostile of environments.'[90] In part, the differences between these two conclusions indicate a difference in their understanding of sociology and of South African society. What is clear is that, for any sociologist who wants to go beyond a sociological analysis, from a liberal, and certainly from a radical or Marxist perspective, to link up with practical activity, South Africa can become a very dangerous society. The banning of sociologists such as Richard Turner, Fatima Meer, Loet Douws-Decker, Charles Simkins, Mary Simons and Jack Simons is evidence for this assertion. The editor of *The Durban Strikes 1973* writes in his 'acknowledgements' that

> This study was originally designed and initiated by Richard Turner . . . but restrictions placed upon him by the government at the end of February 1973, made it illegal for him to take any further part in the study. . . Two other participants, Halton Cheadle and David Hemsen, have also since been banned and can, likewise, no longer be associated with this publication.[91]

Similarly, the director of *The Mozambique Miner*, Ruth First, is in exile, and, as a listed 'communist', her work may not be published inside South Africa.

The pressures on South African sociologists to serve apartheid are likely to increase in the unfolding of 'total strategy' as expressed by P. W. Botha. In the 1977 White Paper, he wrote that the process of ensuring and maintaining the sovereignty of a state's authority in a conflict situation has, through the evolution of warfare, shifted from a purely military to an integrated national action: the resolution of a conflict in the times in which we now live demands interdependent and coordinated action in all fields—military, psychological, economic, political, sociological, technical, diplomatic, ideological, cultural, etc. Germany had already realized this before World War II, and Russia has maintained a multi-dimensional campaign against the West since this war. Consequently we are today involved in a war, whether we wish to accept it or not.[92]

The establishment, recently, of the National Manpower Commission with the task of monitoring and undertaking research into the field of labour, is presumably part of the unfolding total strategy mentioned by P. W. Botha. Faced by the crisis of the 1970's, the apartheid state is finding it increasingly necessary to mobilize social scientists to serve apartheid.[93]

Similarly the strategy of capital is now becoming clearer. Harry Oppenheimer expressed this best when, at the 1979 annual conference of the South African Institute of Race Relations, he called on liberal institutions to move away from 'the politics of protest to the politics of power'. He goes on to suggest that 'all liberal institutions must examine how they can become more directly and positively engaged in promoting and encouraging the process of change which is now underway in South Africa'.[94] The initiative by H. F. Oppenheimer and Anton Rupert, in November 1976, in establishing the Urban Foundation, with the clear objective of creating a 'black middle class' illustrates this strategy. Its director, Justice Steyn, describes the foundation's objectives in these terms: 'Urban distortions and their exploitation played a significant role in the tragic events of 1976. The elimination of these distortions or at least their amelioration must lie close to the heart of every thinking South African. I cannot see any thinking businessman declining to participate in South Africa's future through the U.F. His dividend will be the emergence of a black middle class and greater stability in our urban societies.'[95]

The response of university social scientists to P. W. Botha's 'total strategy' and Oppenheimer's call to encourage 'evolutionary change' is not yet clear.[96] However, constrained in direct and indirect ways to avoid controversial areas of research, most sociologists will be tempted to take advantage of the money and access offered to do research to assist capital and the state in their new strategy of limited 'reform'. Increasingly, the social scientific community will find it difficult to avoid 'taking sides' in the wider ideological debate surrounding the form and nature of change in South Africa. Influenced by the growing presence of the liberation movements in Southern Africa, university social science departments will increasingly become areas of ideological debate.

Notes

1. R. Merton, *Social Theory and Social Structure*, p. 625, Chicago Free Press, 1957.
2. T. Burns, 'The Sociology of Industry', in A. Welford, *Society*, p. 196.
3. A. Flanders, *Management and Unions*, p. 131, Faber & Faber, 1970.
4. L. Baritz, *Servants of Power*, Wiley & Sons, 1965.
5. C. Wright Mills, *The Sociological Imagination*, p. 89, Penguin, 1959.
6. Burns, op. cit., p. 185.
7. G. Wiendieck, 'The Motivation of Black Workers', in K. Jubber (ed.), *Industrial Relations and Industrial Sociology*, pp. 231-2, Juta & Co., 1979.
8. Burns, op. cit., p. 195.
9. R. Brown, 'Research and Consultancy in Industrial Enterprises', *Sociology*, 1967, p. 41.
10. Burns, op. cit., p. 197.
11. Mills, op. cit., p. 94.
12. Ibid., p. 98.
13. M. Foucault, *The Order of Things: An Archeology of the Human Sciences*, p. 345.
14. Baritz, op. cit., p. 7.
15. Ibid., p. 11.
16. Ibid., p. 17.
17. Sohn-Rethel, *Intellectual and Manual Labour*, p. 147, Macmillan, 1978.
18. Harry Braverman, *Labour and Monopoly Capital*, Monthly Review Press, 1974.
19. B. Bozzoli, 'Managerialism and the Mode of Production in South Africa', *South African Labour Bulletin*, Vol. 3, No. 8. Scientific management and personnel management are not, at least in South Africa, chronologically distinct; they were introduced at similar times.
20. See Erwin and Webster, 'Ideology and Capitalism in South Africa', in L. Schlemmer and E. Webster (eds.), *Change, Reform and Economic Growth in South Africa*, pp. 92-3, Ravan, 1977, for a discussion of the emergence and nature of liberalism.
21. J. A. Reinhalt-Jones, 'Adaptation of Personnel Management to Native Labour on the Gold Mines', (address delivered to the Institute of Personnel Management, 28 September 1948, and housed in the Department of Historical and Literary Papers, University of the Witwatersrand, (memorandum AN/A 22/48).
22. For detailed references to these publications see H. C. J. van Rensburg and R. A. Viljoen, *A Bibliography of the South African Sociology*, Institute of Contemporary Studies (UOFS).
23. See note 22.
24. Council for Scientific and Industrial Research, *First Annual Report, 1945-6*, p. 11.
25. Council for Scientific and Industrial Research, *Second Annual Report, 1946-7*, p. 26.
26. Ibid., p. 27.
27. M. Legassick, 'Legislation, Ideology and Economy in Post-1948 South Africa', *Journal of Southern African Studies*, Vol. 1, 1974.
28. *Personnel Management*, No. 1, 1958, p. 21.
29. *Personnel Management*, No. 1, 1959, p. 28.
30. H. P. Langenhoven, *Die Huidige Stand van Swart Personeelbestuur in Suid Afrika*, Universiteit van die Oranje Vrystaat, 1975.
31. A. Prior, 'Managerial Ideology: A Case Study', *South African Labour Bulletin*, Vol. 3, No. 8, p. 69.
32. K. Jubber, 'A Sociology of Industrial Organizations' in Jubber (ed.), op. cit., p. 194.
33. Ibid., p. 187.
34. E. Webster, 'A Profile of Unregistered Union Members in Durban', *South African Labour Bulletin*, Vol. 4, No. 8, pp. 65-6.
35. P. G. du Plessis, 'Concentration of Economic Power in the South African Manufacturing Industry', *South African Journal of Economics*, Vol. 41, No. 3, 1978.
36. D. Hemson, 'Trade Unionism and the Struggle for Liberation in South Africa', *Capital and Class*, No. 6, 1978.
37. E. Webster, 'Stay-aways and the Black Working Class' (unpublished), 1979.
38. South African Institute of Race Relations, *Industrialization and Human Relations* (papers given at the 38th Annual Conference, 1968).

39. J. Irving, *Man, Machines and Society,* p. 27, Institute of Social and Economic Research, Rhodes University, 1968.
40. For further information on the teaching of industrial sociology see the *Journal of Labour Relations,* Vol. 2, No. 4, and *Die Suid Afrikaanse Tydskrif van Sociologie,* No. 17, April 1978.
41. Center of Applied Social Studies, *Publications List,* University of Natal, Durban, 1978.
42. Foucault, op. cit., p. 345.
43. *Report of the Commission of Inquiry into Labour Legislation,* Part 1, p. 23 (RP47/1979).
44. Jubber (ed.), op. cit., p. VII.
45. These calculations are based on the annual reports of these organizations between 1975 and 1978.
46. S. Hannig, 'The Changing Face of South African Mine Labour', *African Institute Bulletin,* Vol. 13, No. 5, 1975.
47. Keenan-Smith, *Personnel Management,* Vol. 23, No. 6, 1972, p. 8.
48. Ibid., pp. 10-11.
49. For a review of this book see R. de Villiers, *South African Labour Bulletin,* Vol. 4, No. 6.
50. R. Gordon, *Mines, Masters and Migrants,* p. 82, Ravan Press, 1977.
51. Ibid., p. 102.
52. D. Moodie, 'The Rules are there to Protect those in Power Only: Structures of Domination on a South African Gold Mine', History Workshop, University of the Witwatersrand, 1978.
53. S. P. Cilliers, 'Absenteeism in Cape Industries' in Jubber (ed.), op. cit., p. 220.
54. Ibid., p. 229.
55. Institute of Industrial Education, *The Durban Strikes 1973,* IIE, 1974.
56. The work of the South African Trade Union Research Project at the University of Warwick (England) is another example. Of course the extensive work on the history of capitalist development done over the last decade within a framework of historical materialism is crucial to any understanding of research in southern Africa, but falls outside the terms of reference of this survey. However, it is worth mentioning the conferences and material published at the University of the Witwatersrand, in particular those activities, such as the 1978 History Workshop on 'Labour, Townships and Patterns of Protest', held under the umbrella of the Institute of African Studies.
57. *The Mozambique Miner,* p. 52, University of Maputo, 1977.
58. Ibid., p. 143.
59. Human Sciences Research Council, *First Annual Report, 1969-1970.*
60. Wiendieck, op. cit., p. 232. It is not clear whether he sees *all* attempts to develop a separate theory for racial groups as racist. For a discussion of the changing forms of 'racism' and their relationship to the reproduction of South African capitalism, see D. Innes and M. Legassick, 'Capital Restructuring and Apartheid; A Critique of "Constructive Engagement," *African Affairs,* 1977.
61. Backer, *Motivating Black Workers,* pp. 34-5, McGraw-Hill, 1973.
62. Human Sciences Research Council, op. cit.
63. D. Webster, *South African Labour Bulletin,* Vol. 3, No. 1.
64. Ibid, p. 63.
65. Ibid, pp. 53-4.
66. Fisher, *South African Labour Bulletin,* Vol. 2, No. 3, pp. 59-60.
67. 'Extracts from the Report of the Interdepartmental Committee of Inquiry into Riots on the Mines', *South African Labour Bulletin,* Vol. 4, No. 5.
68. *Apartheid: Its Effects on Education, Science, Culture and Information,* Paris, Unesco, 1967.
69. D. Welsh, 'Social Research in a Divided Society', in Hare, Wiendieck and van Broembsen (eds.), *South Africa: Sociological Analysis,* p. 391, Oxford University Press, 1979.
70. Ibid., p. 392.
71. D. Hammond-Tooke, *Bulletin of the African Studies Association of the United Kingdom,* special issue on African studies, 1970.
72. H. Lever, 'Some Problems in Race Relations Research in South Africa', op. cit., p. 402.
73. J. Rex, *Race Relations in Sociological Theory,* pp. 83-4, Weidenfeld & Nicolson, 1970.
74. H. Alverson, 'The Human Dimension in Industry', in Orpen and Morse, *Contemporary South Africa,* Juta, 1975.
75. E. Webster and J. Kuzwayo, 'A Research Note on Consciousness and the Problem of Organisation', in Schlemmer and Webster (eds.), op. cit.
76. Webster and Kuzwayo, op. cit., p. 221.

77. Hammond-Tooke, op. cit.
78. *A Survey of Race Relations in South Africa, 1971,* p. 74.
79. *A Survey of Race Relations in South Africa, 1977,* p. 112.
80. Webster, op. cit., p. 33.
81. Welsh, op. cit., p. 395.
82. M. Wilson and A. Mafeje, *Langa,* pp. 11-12, Oxford University Press, 1963.
83. Directorate of Publications, *Reasons for Banning of South African Labour Bulletin, Vol. 2, No. 5.*
84. C. Simkins, *Measuring and Predicting Unemployment in South Africa 1960-1978,* Development Studies Group, University of Natal, Pietermaritzburg, 1978.
85. J. Dugard, *Human Rights and the South African Legal Order,* pp. 1-2, Princeton University Press, 1978.
86. Ibid., p. 183.
87. A. S. Mathews, *Law, Order and Liberty in South Africa,* p. 170, Juta, 1971.
88. *Rand Daily Mail,* 26 June 1979.
89. Lever, op. cit., p. 403.
90. Welsh, op. cit., p. 398.
91. Institute of Industrial Education, op. cit.
92. *Work in Progress,* No. 8, May 1978, p. 5.
93. Jubber (ed.), op. cit.
94. H. F. Oppenheimer, in an address on the fiftieth anniversary of the SAIRR, July 1979, University of Witwatersrand, Johannesburg.
95. *Financial Mail,* 11 March 1977.
96. An indication of the directions of government thinking was a newspaper report on a Cabinet decision to co-ordinate all state-subsidized research. Apparently the newspaper had in their possession a draft 'national' plan drawn up by the HSRC stipulating that all social science research concentrate on 'areas of national concern' so that it can be used as a tool by policy-makers. The main objectives of the plan are: (a) the identification, with the aid of researchers, academics and policy-makers, of problems of national concern; (b) the design of research projects in such a way that they will be as useful as possible to 'decision-makers', be completed in a reasonable space of time and enable problems of the highest priority to be dealt with first; (c) the 'screening' of research applications to eliminate undesirable overlapping of projects, and to accomplish the necessary co-ordinating between researchers and policy-makers so that research findings are useful to the policy-makers; (d) the mobilization of research manpower to investigate 'urgent problems in South African society.'
The plan had been sent to universities for comment. Official comments from most universities appeared to be favourable. However, David Welsh, commenting in his personal capacity, said: 'It is obviously part of the Prime Minister's total strategy and we now find that when Mr P. W. Botha says "total" he means "total" even down to dictating what research should be done.' (*Sunday Times,* 25 November 1979.)

6 The vocation of a sociologist in South Africa

Heribert Adam[*]
Simon Fraser University, British Columbia

I

Any critical inquiry about the various kinds of sociology and its practitioners in South Africa presupposes the prior question: is sociology at all possible in a repressive society, which legally determines life-chances exclusively according to birth into racially defined castes? Sociology here refers to the free analysis of the South African social structure, its historical origin, its beneficiaries and victims, its unique and common features, compared with similar oppressive systems, and likely developments in the future. Such a notion of meaningful sociology precludes the label for well-trained professionals, who intentionally and uncritically serve the powers that be. Such service may consist of supplying ideologies that justify the system, or social research aimed at its smoother functioning. In other words, whether sociology is possible in South Africa does not depend on the existence of academics by this name, but whether a plurality of approaches is tolerated, whether dissident sociologists can find equal employment, can teach their unhindered research without censorship and other sanctions. A specific analysis of the obvious limitations of such an ideal type of freedom results in an answer which is relative. Whether sociology in South Africa is trivial or relevant, constitutes ideology or enlightenment, depends on the society with which it is compared.

Pierre Van den Berghe (1979, p. 10) has recently suggested that, contrary to conventional assumptions, the 'free' societies of Western liberal democracies do not provide the optimum milieu for an active and creative intelligentsia 'but a grossly unjust and indefensible social order backed up by a moderately and inefficiently repressive regime'. Indeed, British and American social science departments are full of distinguished scholars who spent their most formative years exposed to the unique intricacies of a divided society in South Africa. In their grasp of crucial issues they frequently stand head and shoulders above their colleagues, who were

---

[*] The author is grateful to Hamish Dickie-Clark and Kogila A. Moodley for discussions on the topic.

trained in the self-serving tradition of fleeting disputes. Similar observations apply to some sociologists at present living in South Africa. Even after the immense brain drain of most liberal academics in the 1960s, there are still a few individuals left in South Africa whose writings measure up well to the best products of a much more pampered milieu outside. If a renowned tradition of social anthropology is included in a broader definition of an interdisciplinary social science, adding sociologically oriented historians, psychologists and, above all, political economists, the ostracized South African universities compare well with their counterparts anywhere.[1] To be sure, there are great differences in the foci between individual sociologists and between the English, Afrikaans and Black institutions which will be discussed later. It suffices to conclude here that a relevant South African sociology is alive and well, especially if the continuous work on South Africa by exiles is included.

Van den Berghe's speculation that the very obstacles for dissent stimulate intellectual inquiry needs to be pursued further for South Africa. As is well known, there are special risks involved in publicly insisting on political stances that are considered 'enemy' alternatives. Apart from police surveillance, the tampering with the mail and telephone of 'dangerous' opponents, the academic analyses of several sociologists were banned. A few were themselves put under house arrest, gaoled for times or forced into exile for political activities. One banned political scientist (Richard Turner) was mysteriously shot in 1978, several prominent academics received repeated threats and even a relatively loyal Afrikaner historian was tarred and feathered for his unorthodox views in 1979. Although this unofficial violence by fanatic fringe groups or zealous policemen has not reached the proportions it has in some countries, the potential victims have to take it seriously, particularly if they are Black. Intragroup terror increases with the escalating intergroup conflict. These real sanctions encourage solidarity among the serious government opponents, much like the mutual support and friendship among dissidents in other regimes. Unlike the risk-free protests of Western intellectuals, signing an anti-government resolution or even publishing an unorthodox article can cost an Afrikaner sociologist his promotion chances and a Black lecturer at a tribal university his/her contract renewal.

Yet the scope of freedom for dissenting intellectuals in South Africa, so far, remains greater than in other past and present dictatorial systems. Despite intimidation and widespread self-censorship, journalists and academics still can and regularly do expose the South African system inside, as few sociologists could do better from the outside. This 'repressive tolerance' needs to be understood in order to assess the vocation of sociologists in its midst.

Among the reasons for the South African relative academic freedom, the ineffectual aspect of sociological analysis stands out. White solidarity is strong. It remains unshaken by obscurely formulated liberal utopias or Marxist histories. Their appeal is limited among a politically illiterate White electorate and a tiny Black bourgeoisie alike. The censorship board considers it far more important to prohibit certain magazines or licentious novels, particularly in Afrikaans. They do undermine the traditional morale of the *Volk,* and open suppressed desires far more dangerous to a conformist group existence than political criticism.

Moreover, a semi-free opposition stabilizes Afrikaner rule. It contributes to Afrikaner cohesion, if the leadership has internal traitors to rally against. Despite their nuisance in holding the regime accountable, their value in demonstrating 'civilized' democratic standards towards foreign friends proves much greater. After all, an active opposition and particularly critical social scientists point out frictions and forestall them before they become explosive.

In censoring some academic products, usually when they come out in cheaper paperback, Pretoria has been credited with taking its ideology seriously. Many liberal observers see 'the stridency and the relevance of ideology . . . inevitably heightened' (Van den Berghe, 1979, p. 7). On the other hand, it may be argued that apartheid no longer constitutes an ideology, and South Africa's ruling group is characterized by the very absence of a common political blueprint, save the determination to secure Afrikaner survival. If we define ideology as a shared belief to justify power and to mobilize followers, then apartheid has long lost its support among many of its former advocates. Even its high priests, such as the chairman of the Broederbond, now announce 'separate development' as an 'open-ended method', not a dogma or end in itself, but with 'the options quite open for changes towards what is mutually acceptable' (Gerrit Viljoen, cited in Starcke, 1978, p. 177). Such propaganda indicates insecurity and splits over strategies within the ruling group. Unlike some other rigid party doctrines, apartheid represents more of a holding operation. The millennium lies in an inevitably lost past. Unlike other enshrined paths to salvation, religious or secularized, apartheid resembles a blueprint of experience. It is, therefore, open to all kinds of deals and *ad hoc* arrangements, despite the cultivated rhetoric of intransigent Calvinism. The socalled puritans of Africa have long become corrupted by the spoils of political power.[2] The pragmatism which was needed to entrench themselves has undermined the former zeal. South Africa's rulers are faced with a genuine 'legitimation crisis'. Among the subordinates their legitimacy was never deeply rooted. The increasing doubts about the traditional way among their own group is a new phenomenon.

It is this ideological vacuum, rather than rigidly imposed silence or strident disputes, which offers social scientists some special scope. Despite the sabre-rattling on all sides, there is still curiosity among thinking persons in all camps about the reasons for the lurking agony. More people venture out of their intellectual garrisons before the doors are finally shut. Sociologists can contribute to opening up the horizons. To be effective, though, they have to discard their own inherited group lenses first. John Rex (1974, p. 232) has suggested that 'no one should pretend to be a sociologist who has not studied and lived spiritually within less than three or four separate cultures widely separated from each other in time and space'. Black and Whites hardly study each other in South Africa. The widely separated group lives of master and servant prohibit such endeavours, despite close physical contact. Among the subordinates too, the psychological barriers are high and cleavages deep, despite Black alliances and the much asserted 'unity of the oppressed'. This mutual isolation is not surprising in light of the Group Areas Act for residential and educational segregation, including tribal universities. In the one area which is of necessity physically integrated, the workplace, the biggest employer in the country proves to be ahead of many sociologists who peddle 'identity-maintenance' above anything else. In the view of the Chairman of Anglo-American, Harry Oppenheimer (cited in Starcke, 1978, p. 156):

> We have made interesting findings in our group that indicate that ethnicity is on the way out in the urban areas. For instance, recently we've been putting in a housing scheme in Sasolburg and we consulted very carefully with the people who were going to live there—they insisted there should be no housing based on separating the different tribes. In the mine hostels too we have found that by mixing people we get fewer disturbances than where tribal groups are separated.

Ethnically perceived rivalry then does not inevitably emerge in the melting pot where people of different backgrounds share common interests. Only because manipulators exploit the competition for scarce goods and mobilize along spurious ethnic lines for entitlements against outsiders, does ethnicity become an issue. South African sociologists have not even started to educate an indoctrinated public with such banal truths. And yet the liberal optimism that ethnicity will finally fade out and human brotherhood begin when the legal apartheid barriers have broken down, may well be doomed. It is when the real scramble for scarce amenities begins and cherished life styles are threatened, that the crucial problems will come to the fore.[3] What role can intellectuals in each group play in this conflict? The models, to be discussed later, comprise at least four alternatives: (a) partisan commitment to one's group (nationalism); (b) bridgebuilding, reasoning, aimed at strengthening the diminishing middle-ground between the extremes (liberalism); (c) withdrawal into the ivory tower of uncontroversial research (privatism); (d) exile.

It will be argued here that none of these roles fits the vocation of a sociologist. He/she is specifically challenged by the very magnitude of the problem in South Africa, and by the fact that these are basically sociopolitical problems. At the same time, South African society poses great moral questions and arouses resulting passions which are long dead in Western societies. This offers the South African sociologists unique tasks and rewards, compared with those of their colleagues abroad.

South Africa, embodies *in nuce* the major problems of the globe, ready to be interpreted and tackled. The North-South conflict is duplicated in the widening gap between highly industrialized urban areas and an overpopulated, impoverished, rural hinterland. The migration into the metropolitan areas, enforced ghetto-dwelling, tense intergroup relations to the possible extent of mutual destruction, resemble long-diffused classical problems. The major ideologies in various versions—nationalism, Christianity, liberalism and Marxism—compete as nowhere else in offering salvation for the benefit of their sponsors. In South Africa, the social scientist is indeed challenged to deliver insights, perhaps even 'solutions' as a political innovator.

What is the record of South African sociologists in this respect? Which theoretical lenses have been employed to make sense of this society? Which sociological perspectives have been advanced and which major issues focused upon? Four schools of sociologists with different mentors and different emphases may be distinguished according to the four main political traditions: (a) Afrikaner nationalism; (b) African nationalism/Black Consciousness; (c) liberalism; (d) Marxism.

II

Afrikaner nationalism defines individual self-fulfilment exclusively within the limits of in-group boundaries. Allegiance and loyalty to the ethnic unit and its legitimate leadership is expected from the intellectual. Sociologists in this tradition are expected to serve their group. Dissent may be aired only from within. Most Afrikaner academics still adhere with great dedication to this role. Sociologists are in particular demand. After all, Verwoerd demonstrated the usefulness of social science expertise. In this view, the Blacks need to be 'administered' and 'properly serviced', so that they function without friction in their prescribed role. The paternalistic sociological administrator in all his wisdom knows what the subordinates want and what is good for them. Until very recently, there have not even been opinion surveys to detect Black grievances. Many Black sociologists at the five tribal universities could write satires about the racism, callousness or at best paternalism of their Afrikaner colleagues, frequently promoted from civil service positions to these academic outposts (Moodley, 1979).

In the Afrikaner universities, mainstream sociology is similarly traditional: criminology ('Black deviance'), demography ('Black overpopulation, migration and development'), concern with modern management techniques, ('poverty datum lines') and productivity dominate an essentially social engineering approach. Fatima Meer (1979, p. 74) has characterized this scene simply as 'academic colonialism'. Even a more pragmatic and politically sophisticated Afrikaner sociologist such as Nic Rhoodie, who appeals to the enlightened self-interest of his group by advocating constitutional alternatives, still stresses the role of Whites as 'senior partners' in newly proposed political arrangements.

The second major concern of Nationalist Afrikaner academics may be described as the ideological battle against the English liberal attack and liberal deviations within Afrikanerdom. The South African Bureau of Racial Affairs (SABRA) had been initially founded as an Afrikaner counter to the Institute of Race Relations. However, when it did not toe the government line in the 1950s, distinguished sociologists such as S. P. Cillier were purged and henceforth pursued independent work. Subsequent splits between some academics, particularly from Stellenbosch, with official policy related in the main to the role of the Cape Coloured group. In 1978, the government rejected the more fundamental recommendations of a commission, headed by sociologist Erika Theron, which aimed at a reintegration of the Coloureds into White Afrikanerdom. Whether a Stellenbosch Bureau for Future Research with more ambitious technocratic designs for diffusing the conflict will have a different reception remains to be seen.

In the meantime, confusion and doubts about the political assumptions of ethnic cohesion increase within the Afrikaner intellectual élite. There are younger Afrikaner academics and sociologists who are fully versed in the radical analysis of South African society and have themselves adopted decisive conceptualizations of this approach. The Afrikaner press no longer supports the party uncritically, and most Afrikaner playwrights and novelists are ostracized to varying degrees. Radical Calvinists at Potchefstroom challenge the official complacency. This ferment among parts of the Afrikaner intelligentsia may eventually percolate down to the 93 per cent of the *'volk'*, who have not had a university education.

Black nationalism, particularly at the five tribal universities, operates of course under much tighter restrictions, and, therefore, has to be much more cautious in its articulation, than radical White scholarship. It is, therefore, difficult to form a coherent picture of specific sociological approaches, inspired by Black consciousness.

As is well known, the Black Consciousness movement which started to grip the younger Black intelligentsia during the early 1970s was first tolerated as presumed 'separate development desires' but after the Soweto upheavals in 1976 the Black Consciousness movement was rigidly suppressed by the authorities. Its main difference from the earlier nationalist resistance, driven underground and into exile in the early 1960s, lies in the rejection of liberal allies. Unlike the Congress organizations, particularly the 'Africanists' in the PAC (Pan-African Congress), the Black Consciousness students aimed at political integration of all three subordinate groups into one movement of the oppressed. The most crucial assumption proceeded from a sociological factor frequently forgotten or underestimated in the conventional analysis of South Africa: the psychological self-colonization of many subordinates. Recent opinion surveys (Hanf et al., 1978, p. 338) have again confirmed reliable evidence of comparatively widespread internalized feelings of helplessness, low self-esteem, and deep de-politicization among urban African workers, let alone farm labourers and migrants.

Starting at the tribal universities with a breakaway drive from the liberal National Union of South African Students (NUSAS), the psychological liberation of the Black students developed at an astonishing pace. Similar to the student rebellion elsewhere, the politicizing wave swept through high schools and churches, and culminated in the mass euphoria of 1976, only to be severely repressed. However, all Black intellectuals have been more or less affected by the crusade. Some writing under other disciplinary labels—Black theology, for example—have furnished incisive analyses of South African society. Indeed, what constitutes the psychic glue of such a system, how objective stigmatization is transformed into subjective reality, constitutes one of the most crucial and neglected areas of social research. The dominant focus on the pronouncements of the few militant activists may mask quite a different reality of inferiorization.

An emphasis on the subjective, ideological articulations of the conflict—race, prejudice, nationalism—characterizes liberal scholarship on South Africa. Starting with attitude studies by McCrone in the 1930s, followed by studies of group perceptions by Allport, Pettigrew, Kuper, Danziger, Van den Berghe, Dickie-Clark, Lever and several other distinguished social scientists, South Africa's so-called 'laboratory' of intergroup relations has been the ideal setting for the comparative application of social distance scales, marginality perspectives and other empirical studies of ethnocentrism and authoritarianism. Most of these perspectives, however, assumed prejudice as the cause of apartheid and neglected its economic functions. The same can be said of the pluralism school, which sometimes tended to overstate and reify ethnic resilience rather than explore its manipulation.

At the same time the preoccupation of liberal political economists focused on the contradictions between assumed colour-blind market forces and an irrational political order. The central thesis, named after Oppenheimer or one of his economists' O'Dowd, asserts that the intrinsic rationality of a capitalist economy will inevitably sweep away the archaic relics of apartheid. However, liberal scholarship in South Africa has never systematically examined the extent to which nineteenth century European conditions—a progressive powerful bourgeoisie striving for *laissez faire* and civil liberties against a restrictive feudal order—apply to a colonial settler society. Not only political prescriptions, derived from the European class constellation, but many liberal assumptions about human nature in general, have seldom been critically examined by South African adherents, as Dickie-Clark (1979) has recently shown. Instead, the achieved role has been seen to have a historical inevitability over the ascribed role in the colonial periphery as well. For this reason the practical rationality of opposing forces has been overlooked (Adam, 1971).

Marxist-oriented studies thrive on the liberal neglect of the changing beneficiaries of apartheid and its class base. These studies argue that apartheid represents only a specific form of class struggle in response to two main changing contradictions: the internal struggle between labour and capital and the external conflict between centre and periphery or a weak national bourgeoisie. A continuing pre-capitalist mode of production in the reserves and, therefore, a greater diversity of classes than in the European case, is considered causal for the greater state power in the realm of civil rights and economic interference. The so-called revisionist school made up mostly of South African exiles (H. Wolpe, M. Legassick, S. Trapido, F. Johnstone) has analysed in detail how the comparatively cheap labour, due to the retarded full proletarianization under segregation and apartheid policies, has benefited capital and White workers alike. For example, Edna Bonacich, who also considers the race issue 'essentially a product of class struggle between capital and white labour', contends that 'the Nationalist government is, in large measure, a 'white labour' regime'. She sees the Nationalist Party as speaking 'especially for workers at the lower end of the economic spectrum who are most directly threatened with displacement'. However, this is surely no longer the case, if it ever was true in this simplistic expression. The assertion represents a good example of how such a reductionist focus misses even a changing interest constellation (Adam and Giliomee, 1979, Chapter 7), let alone the non-materialist aspects of Afrikaner mobilization. It also loses sight of the present trends in South Africa where English liberal interests and Afrikaner capital together with political allies establish common ground in policies of gradual de-racialization and co-optation. The reductionist focus on the 'articulation of fractions of capital, both in the centre and in the South African formation' (Erwin and Webster, 1977, p. 96), still does not come to grips with the full power of ethnic ideologies in the social and political realm. Neither economic nor ideological forces can be ascribed primacy; both have their independent dynamic at times and must be analysed in their historical interaction.

III

Fatima Meer (1979, pp. 71-2), herself banned but allowed to teach at Natal University, has charged that 'South African sociologists are stuck with the Apartheid model as the ultimate reality', that they keep 'away from considerations of what ought to be', that they 'will not predict' the inevitable change, 'let alone act as midwives'. She considers the entire history of the discipline 'a history of intellectual support for the status quo', since sociology emerged as 'an invention of Western capitalism', innocently operating as its left hand, just as Christianity is said to have operated as its right hand. Such sweeping claims are, emotionally appealing though they may be factually incorrect. As was shown in the foregoing discussion, consensus-oriented Parsonian conceptualizations or a Comtean search for predictable order are but one and not the most influential lens of sociologists dealing with South Africa. If there is one topic with which South African sociologists are obsessed for different reasons, it is the ongoing socio-political change, particularly the impact of economic growth on the racial system. Few would be so naïve as to think that they can arrest this change or bring it about overnight, even if they would like to. Even fewer would claim 'objectivity' or 'ethical neutrality' in a polarizing conflict which affects them directly. All slightly sophisticated practitioners of the trade do not assume that the facts speak for themselves, but that they have to be interpreted. Fortunately, ethno-methodology has not yet come to South Africa. Even most social psychologists now recognize that everyday attitudes are not the whole truth, but that they can be manufactured and are always anchored in a social reality with which perceptions interact. Therefore, sociologists are inevitably biased already in the selection of their research by the cognitive limitations of their own socialization. The intense debate on objectivity in the social sciences since Weber and Mannheim should have made this clear. Nor can sociologists legitimately claim special skills which would afford them privileged insights. Socially sensitive journalists or novelists can compete well with most professional sociologists. Their label 'science' for a historically informed, interpretative art represents a misnomer, except for the hardened positivists. In their search for data to verify non-political middle-range theories they hardly play a role in the real South African debate.

Yet there are legitimate decisive differences among politically committed sociologists about their vocation. They concern the expression of this commitment and political considerations of means in relation to goals. This writer has been criticised for advocating as much as possible realistic, dispassionate analysis, free of wishful thinking and emotional abhorrence, which may cloud the selection of evidence and lead to illusionary conclusions. To this effect Hilda Kuper (1979, p. 42) questions my proposition: 'Is objectivity advanced in any way by not expressing that indignation? And, indeed, would it not be more consistent with the integrity of scholarship, and with personal integrity, to declare, with anger and commitment, one's revulsion of apartheid'?

The problem with this dominant perspective of writers about South Africa seems to be that it is more concerned with personal confessions at the expense of effect. Frequently, the declaration becomes an end in itself. The need to allay Black suspicions and demonstrate solidarity has blinded many White academics to the obstacles of liberation. Thus in the 1950s and 1960s a whole generation of highly sophisticated observers predicted as a certain fact what they wanted to see: the imminent downfall of White supremacy, complete with timetable attached. Their focus on the irrationality of racism led them to underestimate the pragmatic rationality of their opponents. This often occurred at tragic costs to those who believed in the prediction. Such incorrect prophecies of sociologists are not as politically inconsequential as a error of an historian might be. Disappointed hopes may lead to a climate of demoralization or widespread cynicism, defeating the very purpose of broader commitment. More tragic, unnecessary victims can be created by an atmosphere of moral instead of political approaches to injustice. As Margo Russell (1979) has aptly observed for the early 1960s:

> The pressure to do and to be seen doing probably also accounted for the speed with which the police were able to infiltrate the sabotage movement and eliminate it. The severe sanctions in themselves provided the cathartic opportunity for public affirmation of allegiance. The emotional appeal of sabotage outweighed its strategic irrationality.[4]

More frequently, however, the required expression of moral outrage, sincere as it may be, merely serves as an alibi to leave things at that. United Nations condemnations of South Africa must number in the hundreds since 1948. In a similar fashion, South African scholars are frequently satisfied with the 'testimony' they have given. They pride themselves on being 'fearless', on having had the 'courage to be decent in an indecent society' (Van den Berghe, 1979, p. 11). In celebrating such notions, they merely cultivate individual heroism, apart from denigrating lesser mortals who supposedly do not live up to these verbal standards of decency. Such self-styled élitism seems particularly dominant among the economically and professionally secure South Africans who can afford to be 'fearless'. 'Fearlessness', however, is the virtue of a good soldier. It is realistic fear, pragmatic assessment of obstacles and the chances of success without being paralysed and losing sight of the goals that characterizes the successful activist. And yet the achievements of fearlessness do not seem of great concern to those engaged in the ritual. As Alan Paton (1957, p. 212) writes: 'Creative suffering changed no laws, it softened no customs, but it made the country a better place to live in.' Such glorification of martyrdom may be self-gratifying to those who seek personal purity first. Those politically committed scholars interested in outcomes rather than gestures must think twice before they join this fashionable chorus.

IV

What else then could sociologists do, if not raising their voices first and foremost? Perhaps sociologists should examine the taboos which accompany the rhetorical condemnation of White supremacy. To mention only one glaring example: it could well be that retarding economic growth in South Africa through disinvestment, if it were possible at all, may well have the opposite effect to that which its proponents predict. From a moral point of view, of course, the issue is unambiguous: from a political perspective the consequences of a severe recession may turn out to be counter-productive to Black power. It is true that the conservatives fear what radical analysts revel in: political instability because of labour unrest by displaced migrants who cannot find employment in a recession. However, both may be mistaken. If comparative socio-historical research about the causes of revolution has proved anything, it is that the down-trodden become more de-politicized in their desperate struggle for survival. Crowds of illiterate migrants collaborated with the police in crushing radical students in Soweto. One does not have to cite the worn-out notion of frustrated rising expectations in explaining political upheavals. Barrington Moore (1978) has recently shown convincingly that an emerging sense of injustice by the slightly better off motivates these subjects to rise. It is triggered when the rulers break an established contract of domination. South Africa's ruling caste so far has shown little weakness in applying repression, and thereby kept the threshold of hope low. This has had the effect that relatively minor concessions are frequently seen out of all proportion by some recipients. An expanding economy would further aggravate the existing skill shortage and draw Africans into strategic economic positions. More Blacks would have to be trained. It is more likely that *their* industrial action would cripple the South African economy far more than strikes by interchangeable migrants. Such considerations have not even taken into account the many other political implications of an educated urban work force.

Another topic in the taboo areas may include the unintended consequences of separate development institutions, which could provide political platforms and shelters for undermining the central power. It would seem that such undogmatic investigations could constitute important research for committed sociologists.

However, there can be no prescriptions as to what sociologists in South Africa should research. Nor can there be general rules about appropriate political behaviour. As soon as the sociologist follows orders, be it from the government or the liberation movement, he loses the capacity to include his sponsor in his critical probe.

For the politically committed scholar in particular, appropriate action depends entirely on his/her specific situation and the individual assessment of priorities. Sociologists should be cautious about their rash dismissal of colleagues who seriously work from within a repressive system to bring about its change. It is their prerogative to decide how. To demand confessions from them would obviously render them ineffective. Those in safe exile have no moral right to urge others on to prove their purity by denouncing them as otherwise guilty of complicity.

John Rex (1974, p. 231) has defined the proper posture of a sociologist as 'moral nihilism'. By this attitude he means disassociation from one's ideological socialization: 'deliberately displacing, dislodging and detaching themselves, intellectually, and perhaps practically and politically, from the sacred values of their society'. While this attitude surely remains a necessary condition for any wisdom, it is questionable whether it is sufficient for political effectiveness of intellectuals in the South African context. Given this reality of firmly entrenched group conflict, could it not be conceivable that, on the contrary, sociologists ought to place themselves firmly within their respective group, in order to maximize their political impact? Black Consciousness has drawn this conclusion in rejecting White liberal sympathizers. In an extremely unequal structure, such as South Africa, the respective life experiences remain so far apart that members of the advantaged group cannot in fact speak with any authenticity for the disadvantaged groups, regardless of their noble intentions.

This does not mean that sociologists should embrace their group sentiments and group interests uncritically. In reality, though, the collective emotions are likely to overwhelm the critical analyst as well. What Margo Russell (1979, p. 149) observes for one side, applies equally to the other: 'The ground swell of popular Black resentment carries the educated with them rather than relying on the educated to mobilise support by articulating dissent.'

What can be expected from those few who still adhere to their professional commitment amounts to a cost-benefit assessment. Sociologists can calculate realistically the likely advantages and costs of collective action or inaction. Sociologists may deter or inspire some active participants with such cost-benefit calculations. The course of history, however, will hardly be altered by these sane voices. But at least those who are actively involved in shaping events do not maintain their blindness and cannot claim innocence, and the sociologist has remained true to his professional and political challenge.

Notes

1. For evidence the volume edited by Leonard Thompson and Jeffrey Butler (1975) stands out. The Cape Town journal *Social Dynamics,* edited by Michael Savage, is the best South African social science forum. Since 1971, H. W. Van der Merwe at his Institute of Intergroup Relations publishes the proceedings of annual conferences on crucial themes. So does an Association of Southern African Sociologists, but, above all, the Johannesburg Institute of Race Relations. F. Van Zyl Slabbert and Lawrence Schlemmer, to my mind, have distinguished themselves as the two sociological commentators with the most insight in South Africa. This overview has only included sociological activity at the English-language universities.
2. For a further elaboration of this theme, together with an analysis of recent trends within the Afrikaner ruling group, see Adam and Giliomee (1979).
3. A point well made by Lawrence Schlemmer (1977, p. 118) who concludes 'that there is a sphere of institutionalized racism in public life which is to a large degree immune to the immediate influence of the rational colour-blind norms of modern industry'. However, one should also add that this social racism where Whites paradoxically show a far greater resistance than towards economic and political demands (Hanf et al., 1978), is the least important sphere. Presumably, if Blacks could buy their own *equal* life-style as a result of their own economic and political equality, White racist exclusivism would hardly matter to them. Indeed, in surveys about priorities among Blacks, demands for social integration rank far below economic concerns.
4. Earlier predictions of an imminent collapse of White power have sometimes been replaced with equally unreal scenarios. Thus Van den Berghe (1979, pp. 16, 62) now maintains that once the level of internal unrest and insurgency has risen, most of the Whites 'can be expected to emigrate'. He considers this 'the most desirable and humane solution to the Southern African problem'. I would consider this not only highly unlikely (beyond a relatively small percentage of selected individuals with options abroad), but also undesirable and inhumane. It hardly matters whether such exodus arises from explicit government orders or is relatively 'voluntary' in that people are deprived of their security and livelihood beyond reasonable measures of redistribution. That does not mean that Whites should not be expected to change their life-style radically after their monopoly of political power and unequal wealth has been broken. It is this very prospect which makes some Afrikaners contemplate policies of co-optation while the majority favours dividing power rather than sharing it, so that in a shrunken territory they could still exercise sovereignty. It is an unresolved and rather academic question what would constitute a just partition of the country or, more likely, a division of political control in a federal or confederal system. The ahistoric and undialectical conceptualization of the problem in terms of final solutions—oppression versus liberation—ignores the fact that such a conflict is ongoing, with different expressions according to the varying responses of the main contending forces.

Bibliography

ADAM, Heribert. 1971. *Modernizing Racial Domination.* Berkeley, University of California Press.
ADAM, Heribert; GILIOMEE, Hermann. 1979. *Ethnic Power Mobilized: Can South Africa Change?* New Haven and London, Yale University Press.
DICKIE-CLARK, Hamish. 1979. On the Liberal Definition of the South African Situation. In: Van den Berghe (ed.), 1979, pp. 56-67.
ERWIN, Alec; WEBSTER, Eddie. 1977. Ideology and Capitalism in South Africa. In: Schlemmer and Webster (eds.), 1977, pp. 91-110.
HANF, Theodor et al. 1978. *Südafrika: Friedlicher Wandel?* Munich, Kaiser.
KUPER, Hilda. 1979. Commitment: The Liberal as Scholar in South Africa. In: Van den Berghe (ed.), 1979, pp. 30-47.
MEER, Fatima. 1979. Sociology and Universal Reality: South African Implications. In: Van den Berghe (ed.), 1979, pp. 68-76.

MOODLEY, Kogila A. 1979. The Politicisation of Ethnic Universities: Experiences with South Africa's 'College Brews'. In: Van den Berghe (ed.), 1979, pp. 117-132.

MOORE, Barrington. 1978. *Injustice. The Social Bases of Obedience and Revolt.* White Plains, New York, M. E. Sharpe.

REX, John. 1974. *Sociology and the Demystification of the Modern World.* London, Routledge & Kegan Paul.

RUSSELL, Margo. 1979. Intellectuals and Academic Apartheid, 1950-1965'. In: Van den Berghe (ed.), 1979, pp. 133-152.

STARCKE, Anna. 1978. *Survival. Taped Interviews with South Africa's Power Elite.* Cape Town, Tafelberg.

SCHLEMMER, Lawrence; WEBSTER, Eddie (eds.). 1977. *Change, Reform and Economic Growth in South Africa.* Johannesburg, Ravan Press.

THOMPSON, Leonard; BUTLER, Jeffrey (eds.). 1975. *Change in Contemporary South Africa.* Berkeley, University of California Press.

VAN DEN BERGHE, Pierre L. (ed.). 1979. *The Liberal Dilemma in South Africa.* London, Croom Helm.

7 Social research and the Black academic in South Africa

Anonymous*

Municipal administration

There is nothing available on the state of research by Black academics in South Africa. It has therefore become necessary for the purpose of this chapter to look at sources of social research in the country and develop from these a set of indices to evaluate the status and problems of the Black social researcher. Accordingly, Black participation in social research has been examined from the points of view of representation on the councils and committees of research bodies, opportunities for writing and publishing, availability of funds, job opportunities, training facilities, and relationships with fellow White colleagues.

The most glaring aspect of social research in South Africa is the non-presence of the Black. In the last three centuries, starting with the first European commander at the Cape, Jan van Riebeck, who was instructed to keep a journal of daily events, there has accumulated in the country's libraries and resource centres a great volume of empirical records contributed by missionaries, travellers, administrators and their wives. To these have been added the many works of modern social scientists. Missing from this vast tapestry of recorded knowledge are the impressions and interpretations of Black South Africans.

From the Afrikaner point of view, the omission is a result of intent —there is no room for the Black researcher and writer; it is the prerogative of the White to structure the South African reality and place the component 'race' groups into their appointed positions. He even signs charters with the independent homeland governments for the right to research in their areas. The English White laments the absence of trained Blacks and continues to run his White enterprise. The result is that both Afrikaner and English research institutes exclude Blacks from the research enterprise

---

* For political reasons the author of this paper remains anonymous. This is itself a comment on the effect of apartheid on social research.

though the nature of the exclusion differs: the exclusion of the Afrikaner is explicit, that of the 'English' is blurred by tokenism. The Afrikaner recognizes that the Black can do it and therefore stipulates that he does it in his own area where he will not suffer the pain of competing with him; the 'English' doubts that he can do it at all and so contains him in the status of ward.

South African research institutes

The non-presence of the Black becomes apparent in an analysis of the institutions of social research in the country. These fall into two categories—those that are directly or indirectly financed by the Government, and are Nationalist in orientation and Afrikaner in concern; and those that are administered by the English-speaking White establishment, liberal in concern and financed to some considerable extent by overseas foundations. An attempt in 1976 to found a national Black research body was destroyed at its inception by a frontal government attack, which resulted in the detention and banning of the key organizers. The research programme of the Black Community Project, closely allied with the South African Students Organization (SASO) and the Black Peoples' Convention (BPC), was banned in 1977, together with these two organizations, and all their resources confiscated. The only existing Black research body, the Institute of Black Research, continues a precarious existence. In 1976, its vice-president, secretary and research officer were detained and subsequently banned. Two members of the new executive elected in 1977 were also detained. The resultant effect has been a shrinking in membership and activity and the abandoning of several projects for which considerable research had already been done. Apart from funds raised from the sale of donations, the institute has received two small grants from the Anglo-American Corporation. It functions on a shoestring budget.

The Black research institutes were initiated directly in response to a feeling that neither of the two White research groupings were genuinely interested in creating research opportunities for Blacks, or in orienting research from other than the point of view of White interest. The government, however, is extremely worried about Black academic groupings, and rather than risk the effect they might have, the tendency is to destroy them through intimidation. Two student organizations which emerged in the last two years in Soweto, both of which might well have developed research interests, were attacked within weeks of their formation, their executive members detained and subsequently banned.

Afrikaner research bodies

The Afrikaner research organizations are by far the more important from the point of view of government funding, and influence on the White electorate. But precisely because they are so close to the government, there is doubt about their academic credibility. The recent 'information scandal' revealed that a number were recipients of secret funds. The government's subsequent decision to finance some of these publicly—the Institute of Plural Societies and the Institute of Strategic Studies at the University of Pretoria, the Institute of Human Rights at the University of South Africa, and the Centre of International Politics at the University of Potchefstroom—has deepened the doubt. It is hardly remarkable that when a minority government has held sway for over twenty-five years, the lines between research and propaganda should become blurred.

The overarching social research body in the country is the Human Sciences Research Council, quite explicitly Afrikaner in control, orientation and content. It grew out of the National Bureau of Education Research founded in 1929 to advance White education, and while its interests are wider, White education still remains a prime concern. The council functions in the main to create research and publication opportunities for Afrikaner academics, develop a tradition of the Afrikaner intellectual attainment and project Afrikaner models of the structure and content of South African society. Its Afrikaner commitment is obvious in its research interests, beneficiaries of grants, and in the composition of its staff and councils. Its 1977 report reveals only one Black name, in its vast staff of councillors, committee members and researchers, and no Black names appear in its list of 188 research projects. There are only 2 English names on its executive and only 14 on its 123-member finance advisory committee. The Afrikaner theme predominates in practically all of its constituent institutes. Thus the Institute of Historical Research concentrates on Afrikaner genealogies and diaries; the Institute for Languages, Literature and Art on the Afrikaans language and literature; the Institutes of Educational, Manpower and Psychometric Research on expanding the innate Afrikaner potential. While there is some recognition of the English genius, the Black is totally ignored. There is no research into the Black literature and Black languages. Whereas White children are tested to promote their scholarship, Blacks are tested to identify factors which promote their mechanical aptitude and gifts.

The HSRC's Institute for Communication Research is a euphemism for keeping a close tag on the government's propaganda machinery. So it computes reports on the content of the mass media—television, radio and newspaper. The newspaper, the only element not under government control, since by far the greater and more important sector is in the English language and in private hands, is cause for some considerable concern, even though it is generally supportive of the racial boundaries, and gives only the barest, unavoidable coverage to Black politics operating outside government-structured institutions.

An examination of the Africa Institute of South Africa founded in 1960, and financed primarily by the Department of National Education, presents an even more overt view of Nationalist ties. It claims that: 'Indeed, it would be an error to think that because the authors are part of the establishment, they are mere adulators of their Government.' (*Chairman's Report*, p. 12.) The institute concentrates on putting out short term-reports on assignments received from ministries, universities and private firms, and these are used on the popular media—radio, television, newspapers, magazines, and in public lectures. It has a staff of twenty-nine of which three are apparently English-speaking, and five, categorized as messengers and assistants, Blacks. All four senior researchers, and the director, are Afrikaners. The institute has, however, some carefully selected token Blacks on its committee.

The liberal English research institutes

The South African Institute of Race Relations (SAIRR) is the oldest and most important of the 'English' social research institutes. Other institutes in the group are to be found on the English-speaking university campuses. The fifty-year-old SAIRR had a closer association with the Establishment in its pre-Nationalist existence. It now stands to the far left of the Nationalist Government which by statutory definition attempts to class it as communistic.

The SAIRR has amassed over the years an impressive volume of empirical material, and has brought to the fore some very cogent views on the politics, economics and society of South Africa. Yet it has done little to stimulate research and writing among Blacks and until recently had few positions for Blacks even at an administrative and clerical level. Today thirty of its seventy-three posts are held by Blacks; but these do not include a single research post. In fact only four of the appointments are of a senior nature, and the rest being fairly junior posts. For all that, the institute is making a concerted though belated attempt to improve the balance between Black and White participation, and with the co-operation of the Ford Foundation has set up a programme to assist Blacks with post-graduate scholarships to be taken up in the United States.

Its updated classification of publications, lists over 1,500 thousand items, ranging from books and pamphlets to memoranda, contributed by some 321 writers of which 42 are Black—40 of the 60 Black contributions, however, fall in the category of informative memoranda; the list includes only fourteen journal articles and six pamphlets from Blacks, some written in collaboration with Whites.

The SAIRR has also compiled a list of 269 works in Zulu and English, relating to the Zulu people and associated matter. These cover ethnographic, sociological, anthropological, political and economic studies, fiction, drama and poetry. Of the 131 authors listed, the majority, 74, are White. The 57 African writers are responsible for 125 contributions, 101 of which are in Zulu, in the main fictional or biographical works (70) and including 13 dramas, and 16 Zulu dictionaries. There is only 1 African contributor in the 16 translations into English from the Zulu oral tradition, whereas 5 of the 22 compilations in Zulu are by Whites.

The relative fertility of African-language writings in the country is due primarily to their demand as set works in African schools, where the medium of instruction remains the 'Bantu' languages up to the lower secondary stage. There is thus a lucrative market for Zulu writings and South African publishers, who usually ignore Black writers, actually seek them out in this instance, often paying them retainers to urge them on into literary pursuits.

The Centre for Intergroup Studies in Cape Town was founded in 1968 to establish intergroup studies for 'better understanding of and among race groups'. Its latest catalogue lists nine books and ten reprints. Not one bears a Black name, though some Black names are included between the covers of one or two. This situation is all the more surprising since the Cape has a fairly long history of Black scholarship, especially among the Cape Coloured. A large-scale study of the Coloured community was even undertaken by Whites. The administration of the centre also appears to be entirely White. Coming into existence on the threshold of the Black Consciousness Protest, the centre could have shown greater foresight and integrated Black academics into its organization.

The Centre for Applied Social Sciences of the University of Natal, formerly the Institute for Social Research, lists seventy-three publications based on research conducted at that centre: twenty-eight concern the Black populations directly. Except in two cases where credits are shared with Blacks, the authors remain Whites. The total list includes 111 publications; only nine have Black authors, in four cases the Blacks being co-authors with Whites. The other 'publications' are theses or extracts from theses submitted for academic degrees.

A substantial proportion of the research subjects reflect White entrepreneurial or White Establishment interests. Thus even when the subject-matter is Black, it is from the point of view of White interests in Blacks, albeit enlightened industrial interest. Accordingly, three of the four reports relating to Indians are guidelines for local authorities in assessing housing needs and rent structures. The African studies revolve around his role as worker and consumer in the urban complex—his labour stability and turnover, his minimum economic requirements, his attitudes to blood donation, his preferences in advertising.

The subjects pursued by the White bodies show concern for problems which Blacks do not find problematic, and an evasion of issues which constitute the problems from the Black point of view and which in the final analysis are entrenched in the monopoly of White power.

Though the 'English' institutes may show appreciable concern for Black problems and a capacity to probe and expose sensitive areas of race relations, in the final analysis they constitute yet another White view of the South African reality, albeit a more proximate and sympathetic one. They do not provide opportunities for Black scholarship. Blacks are brought in as agents because of their key positions in an ethnic sense, as community leaders, or activists, or academics, to provide in-depth reports on issues that become problematic in their ethnic areas from the White point of view—a Moodley on 'Indian Housing', an Ngakane on 'African Juvenile Delinquents', a Golding on 'The Legal Rights of Coloureds'. They are thus programmed in and rarely, if ever, come in on the programming. There have been several cases when Blacks have had their own programmes for research and publication rejected out of hand by the liberal institutes. In two known instances the studies were subsequently published and received good reviews.

The Black researcher

The White director of a South African research institute well-known for liberal leanings gave two reasons for the absence of Black contributions to social research: a lack of academically trained personnel, and a lack of motivation to take up training. In his estimation, opportunities were available, but Blacks were not making the effort to utilize them. The reality is that an infinitesimal proportion of the Blacks, and in particular the Africans, reach university, and of this in turn another infinitesimal proportion aspire to postgraduate studies. Those aspiring to positions in the realm of social research will have to await research projects designed for their ethnic areas. While every research field is seen to be at the command of a White researcher, it is unthinkable that a Black researcher could conduct research into any ethnic area other than his own. Thus an Indian researcher would only be engaged for research in the Indian group area and an African researcher would be restricted to his township or homeland.

The operational value of a Black researcher is thus, in the first instance, limited by the liability of his race. There are too few jobs available for him. As a teacher, he is confined to his own ethnic school or university.

The Black interviewer

The Black interviewer is indispensable for research in Black areas, and it is primarily in this capacity that Blacks have made their contributions to social research. Though termed research technicians at times and remaining as anonymous as the computer, they bring specialized insight to the White undertaking, providing it with a meaning and content which would otherwise remain inaccessible. They can be a great asset in the designing of the questionnaire and they alone can administer it, there being nearly always language and relational problems across the colour line, and where open questions are concerned, he will code and provide the meaning of the spoken idiom. The White researcher feels himself at liberty to use the data he provides without any obligation to share credits.

This 'taking' of knowledge from Blacks to advance White scholarship and develop White research institutes is so commonplace that it goes without comment. Black informants are often highly skilled, and with some patience and some solid material support could become fully fledged researchers and writers in their own right. Unfortunately it rarely occurs to the liberal institutes that an ethical obligation devolves upon them to develop that expertise into scholarship and not to plagiarise it.

The liberal academic, establishment finds it very difficult indeed to accept that Blacks can analyze and interpret data. There appears to be an implicit belief that this is a White prerogative. Thus fairly senior responsibility would be given to a young White graduate with an honours degree, but great resistance and emotional conflict will be experienced in making the same decision in relation to a similarly trained Black student. There is suspicion of his training, his culture, a suspicion of the unknown and unfamiliar. There is no doubt at all that Black and White see the social reality differently but rather than explore and understand the significance of those differences, the liberal institutes find it easier and simpler to take on the familiar White applicant who adjusts with greater facility because of his own familiarity with the new situation.

The Black applicant also brings with him the burden of inferiority nurtured by the system: there is little doubt that it affects his competence. Black academics sit in insecure silence in the company of their White colleagues. As children their mothers have warned them not to leave the valley and climb the hill. 'The white folk there will push you down.' The child grown man, grown academic, learns that so long as he remains in the symbolic valley, and accepts his designated status, there are few problems, and few tensions. Those who challenge this position earn themselves the reputation of being opinionated, ambitious, aggressive, not nice, and above all, ungrateful for all that their White colleagues have done for them. On rare occasions, the inhibited tensions have exploded into open conflict: such conflicts were more apparent during the reign of Black consciousness—they are quiescent for the time being.

Training

The Black student is at a grave disadvantage in terms of his opportunities for training. The Black universities are of a lower standard, largely because of the type of staff they are able to attract, but also because the students are in a state of perpetual hostility against the institution and so do not identify with it and through such identification, develop a tradition of scholarship. A student with a post-graduate degree from a Black university will stand practically no chance of a job against a White postgraduate student on an open market. He may also find himself unacceptable as a student at a White university, even after the government concedes his enrolment there, because of his presumed low standard.

The more sensitive Black student is more likely to come into conflict with the regimented authoritarianism of the Black campus and as a result suffers expulsion. He usually completes his first degree on a part-time correspondence basis, often gaining no more than a third-class pass. He may thereafter seek enrolment for a post-graduate degree at a residential White university, but may find, as it has happened, that he is excluded on the grounds that he does not have a second-class pass. Thus though the liberal establishment mourns the absence of trained Blacks, its over-concern with standards precludes it from stretching out a helping hand to correct the situation. The University of Cape Town is a notable exception in this respect. The liberal establishment accepts that Blacks are as helpless against their lowered standard as they are against their race, but it applies no compensatory measures, and those who have applied them on their own initiative have been castigated for practising racism in reverse, or aggravating discrimination against Blacks, through double standards.

The non-help situation appears to have been worse in the social sciences, judging by the fact that few of the Black postgraduate degrees have been gained in the country. Of eleven postgraduate degrees in sociology conferred on Blacks up to 1968, only two had been obtained in the country. Some of these sociologists had applied for registration at local White universities before going abroad and had been rejected as unsuitable.

Few postgraduate degrees have been conferred in the social sciences at the Black universities. Of a list of eighty-three dissertations submitted at the master's and doctoral levels up to 1977, sixty-two were in education, nine in psychology, three in anthropology, four in philosophy and two in sociology. The choice of discipline is related to the potential job situation. Education takes preference because of both the availability of jobs and promotion on additional qualification at the schools. Post-graduate qualification in the other areas is invariably a dead-end exercise. The dissertations are so tied up with the race of the student and influenced by the invariable Afrikaner supervisor, as to make them into yet another White view of the South African scene. The students appear to be the agents of their supervisors, closely pursuing the interests of the HSRC. The titles include: *Rorschach Tests of Bantu, Standard Scores on Physical Fitness of Indian Girls, Problems of Malnutrition of Black Workers, Ethnic Personality Ideals, Significance of Differential Education, Attitudes of Zulus to Indians, Tribal Crafts and Customs, Initiation Ceremonies, Social Pathologies of Ethnic Deviants*. The treatment of the subject is usually historical and descriptive; there is a pointed evasion of sensitive areas and a structured attempt to emphasize and cultivate ethnic differences and to project racially irreconcilable personalities and folkways, each happiest when left to its separated component.

The problem of standards

Blacks have no part in the construction of academic standards and separate as they are, throughout their educational career, they have little knowledge of them. They thus struggle in the dark to reach out to something which remains inscrutable. Success in a public examination is regarded as much, if not more, a matter of luck as of hard work. The system cultivates a sense of intellectual inferiority and uncertainty. Education is dangled as the means to success, but unless acquired in a field where it leads to independent vocational pursuit, it rarely leads to success. Thus African teachers with a university degree earn little more than unskilled labourers—the compensation lies more in the prestige than in the material reward, but even that is contained within the ethnic grouping and is not 'universal'.

Academic standards are constructed and preserved for Whites, by Whites. Blacks must rise up to them, and the intellectual myth is perpetrated that they can and must if they wish to be measured against and counted among Whites, and if they do not, it is because they are different inherently, or made different by their inherent culture.

In the final analysis, the liberal White interpretation of the situation in which they find themselves is probably more frustrating than the Afrikaner one. The Afrikaner pursuing his policy of *eier soort* (own kind) and separate development, explains the different standard as an appropriate adjustment to a different life-style—the English liberal, who is the prime architect of White academic standards, sees his first duty as being to those standards. While he has been forced to accept redefinition of those standards by the emergent Afrikaner academic who today controls the intellectual entreprise, he guards rigorously against violations from the Black side. The Black is rejected on grounds of unacceptable standard; a ground against which he finds himself defenceless. He can cope with rejection based on race and knows that he has universal support against such rejection, it does not touch him personally—it concerns his whole group: but how does he cope with a rejection based on the mystique of standard? He is forced to accept the evaluation and judgement against him, or bide his time until like the Afrikaner, he can structure his own standard and make his own evaluations.

Appointments

There appears to be an unspoken, hidden resistance to Black academic promotions, a subtle practice of job reservation, which has never needed a formal enactment due to the protective mystique of academic rationalization. In 1968, of eleven Black sociologists, only one of the five who had remained in the country had found a job as a university teacher, one with a doctorate was teaching at a high school; the others were pursuing further studies. The remaining six had gone abroad and all were holding academic jobs, two in senior positions, professor and research fellow respectively.

Recently a distinguished Black scholar with an international ranking in African literature returned from abroad where he had been heading an academic department at a well-known university. He has had to assuage his homesickness at the expense of taking on a job as a circuit inspector of schools.

A few years ago, a Black academic applied for the post of head of department which fell vacant in a Black medical college incorporated in a White university. The college had up to then not made a single senior Black appointment though it had been in existence for almost twenty-five years and a number of its Black graduates were holding senior positions in universities and medical departments overseas. The government (the post being a joint hospital and university post) accepted the Black applicant but the liberal academy rejected him in favour of a White applicant from outside the country. The university held that the government, through the Province, was making a political appointment, based on colour (a Black head, in a Black college) not on academic merit. When the university's case appeared to be failing, there was a veiled attack on the Black applicant's character, and he was advised not to make any public statements as an inquiry was in the offing. The inquiry did not materialize, but the post was filled by the White applicant.

Finance

Black research is finally undermined by the economic factor. Few postgraduate Black students can afford to continue as full-time students, and while some may find their fees paid, practically all find that they have to seek employment to cope with family demands. The chances of obtaining research grants by themselves, without the mediation of a university or recognized research institute are practically nil. Apart from government funding, several overseas foundations are know to be making liberal grants to South African universities and research institutions. Very little of this trickles down to Blacks. The funds are directed by the Whites in authority and with hardly an exception are used to finance White scholarships, sharpen White expertise and create White jobs. Little, if any, attempt is made to familiarize potential Black applicants with their existence, so that they may be encouraged to apply, and be motivated to pursue a career in social research.

The White liberal deplores the absence of Black motivation and Black training, but the problem is very complex. The Black is caught in a vicious circle where he will not get the job because he is not trained for it, and where he will not be trained for it because there are no jobs for him in that training.

The Black academic in South Africa trains neither for himself nor his people. He is fitted into a university system which takes over his thoughts and monitors his intellect in the interest of White domination, either to feed it with the information it needs, or to perpetuate it in growing Black minds. His standards are deliberately kept low, his self-confidence warped and his opportunities for self-development and self-fulfilment, smothered. His awareness of this position is implicit and symptomised by periodic strikes and the chronic state of conflict between undergraduates and administration. It is rarely, if ever, made explicit, even by Blacks to themselves, for the Black academic who is qualified to do this is either an employee of the system or a post-graduate student, who is made cautious by the realization that his only opportunity for academic appointment is with and within the system. The tensions are thus repressed and the Black academic is sucked up by the intellectual machinery of apartheid. One or two may even be invited to sit on the committees of some of the lesser, 'outward going', and for that reason alone, relatively more propaganda oriented organizations. The rare exceptions break away and move into protest politics, where they face bannings and detentions, or leave the country to fulfil themselves in exile.

Appendix: Educational status of South Africans by race and sex

According to the 1970 census, 8,058 Whites had postgraduate degrees, master's and doctorates, as against 77 Indians, 87 Coloureds and 97 Africans. This is detailed in the following tables:

TABLE 1. University training attained by South Africans, 1970

		White	Indian	Coloured	African
Bachelor's degrees	M	51 822	1 509	644	1 111
	F	10 641	267	144	203
	T	62 463	1 776	788	1 304
Master's	M	6 136	37	42	72[1]
	F	1 253	12	20	25[1]
	T	7 389	49	62	97
Doctorates	M	3 335	26	12	
	F	334	2	3	
	TOTAL	669	28	15	

1. Master's degrees and doctorates.

Source: Population Census 1970, Nature of Education. Pretoria, Government Printer (Report No. 02-05-02).

TABLE 2. University training by age and sex in major academic areas

	White	Post-grad.	Indian	Post-grad.	Coloured	Post-grad.	African	Post-grad.
Arts	19 644	(1 884)	488	(9)	221	(8)	573	(74)
Science	12 688	(3 925)	184	(8)	116	(15)	153	(11)
Education	6 923	(1 125)	311	(9)	231	(14)	293	(29)
Medicine	7 470	(1 120)	486	(33)	118	(12)	119	(10)
Dentistry	1 082	(79)	8	(—)	2	(—)	3	(1)
Law	4 079	(303)	79	(4)	14	(1)	43	(4)
Pharmacy	928	(68)	35	(1)	4	(—)	2	(—)
Architecture	1 226	(50)	14	(—)	3	(—)	4	(—)
Social welfare	1 885	(95)	22	(1)	26	(—)	48	(—)
Theology	1 853	(376)	6	(—)	24	(3)	31	(6)
Commerce	10 151	(1 021)	141	(1)	33	(1)	36	(—)

Source: Population Census 1970, Nature of Education. Pretoria, Government Printer (Report No. 02-05-02).

The total number of students enrolled in south African universities in 1978 (207,561) can be broker down by race as follows: 178,580 Whites, 6,309 Coloureds, 9,2111 Indians and 13,461 Africans. A large proportion of the Black students (over half in the case of Africans and a third in the cases of Coloureds and Indians), were part-time correspondence students enrolled with the University of South Africa. By contrast, over 70 per cent of the White students were full-time students at residential universities.

TABLE 3. University staff by race on the Black campuses, 1978

University for:	White	Indian	Coloured	African	Total
Whites [1]	6 080	38	9	27	6 154
Indians	193	96	–	–	289
Coloureds	253	6	53	1	373
Africans (1977)	301	–	–	133	437

1. The Black staff at White universities are in the main employed at the Black Medical School of the University of Natal as lecturers/instructors in African languages.
Source: Figures extracted from: South African Institute of Race Relations, *A Survey of Race Relations in South Africa, 1978,* Johannesburg, SAIRR.

In 1974, only eleven of the Black members of staff were professors: six Africans and five Indians. This situation remains little changed today.

Bibliography

AFRICA INSTITUTE OF SOUTH AFRICA. *Chairman's Report.* Pretoria, 1978.
CENTER FOR INTERGROUP STUDIES. *Annual Report.* University of Cape Town, 1978.
COPE, I. *The Zulu People: A Select Bibliography.* Durban, University of Natal, 1974.
HUMAN SCIENCES RESEARCH COUNCIL. *Annual Report,* Pretoria, 1977.
POLLAK, H. P. *Sociology Post-Graduates of South African Universities.* Durban, Institute for Social Research, 1968.
Population Census 1970. Nature of Education. Pretoria, Government Printed. (Report No. 02-05-02.)
Publications List. Durban, Centre for Applied Social Sciences, University of Natal, 1978.
SOUTH AFRICAN INSTITUTE OF RACE RELATIONS. *Survey of Race Relations in South Africa,* 1978. Johannesburg, SAIRR, 1978.
——. *Classification of Publications.* Johannesburg, SAIRR, 1971.

8 The Black universities in South Africa

Marcus Malusi Balintulo
University of Nigeria, Nsukka

Introduction

The negative effects of the policy of apartheid on human development and on relations between members of different racial groups both within the Republic of South Africa and outside its borders have, over the last two decades, been subject to increased scientific study and discussion. This development has, in our view, been inspired by two interrelated factors, namely the growing worldwide opposition to the system of apartheid, as well as a recognition by its opponents of the fact that its architects and perpetrators are dedicated to its consolidation, perpetuation and defence to a degree that makes its dismantling a formidable task fraught with potentially grave repercussions for the world community.

This chapter examines the effects of the apartheid policy on social research and teaching with special reference to the Black universities in South Africa. With the exception of the University of Fort Hare, these universities are themselves a historical product of the pursuance of apartheid by the present regime, in the field of higher education.

While the establishment of Fort Hare predates 1948,[1] the general restructuring that has taken place within that institution since 1960 has made it qualitatively similar to the other Black universities in terms of being essentially (intended as) an instrument for promoting the policy of apartheid.

The central theme of this chapter is that by its very nature the doctrine of apartheid as a rationalization for the perpetuation of minority racist rule, based on the economic exploitation and political subjugation of the Black groups by the White minority, is inherently incompatible with those forms of social research and teaching that are committed to an objective scientific understanding by man of his social environment in its varied dimensions. Rather, it promotes those kinds of research and teaching that serve the interests of the ruling class in general and more specifically the narrower philosophy of minority racist rule.

In the light of the above observations, it is, therefore, not surprising that in these institutions, designed and run as instruments not of human liberation in terms of promoting the creative potential of the trainees, but of oppression in terms of propagating chauvinistic doctrines of an ethnicist and racist type, no infrastructure exists for any form of meaningful social research.

Indeed, it is our view that the existence of such an infrastructure and its utilization for the purposes of meaningful social research would, by definition, represent a negation of the fundamental principles of the theory and practice of apartheid as a system of minority race rule.

Origins of Black-university education

The origins of Black university education in South Africa date back to the establishment of the South African Native College, near the small town of Alice, in the eastern part of the Cape Province in 1916. This institution later became the University College of Fort Hare in 1951 affiliated to Rhodes University, a White English-medium university in Grahamstown in the eastern Cape.

The establishment of the South African Native College in 1916 was a result of an increasing demand for higher education by Africans. There had been widespread opposition to the proposal among the White population. According to C. T. Loram:[2]

> The fear of ultimate black supremacy, which looms large in the eyes of many European inhabitants in South Africa, has made them inclined to scrutinize closely any attempts at the higher education of the Natives. . . . The appearance, again, within recent years of Native political associations founded and officered by educated Natives has not tended to allay the suspicions of the Europeans that higher education and political aspirations are indissolubly connected. When, therefore, the proposal for an Inter-State Native College was so enthusiastically taken up by the South African Natives, there was a distinct feeling among a large section of the Europeans that this movement was due, in considerable part, to the teachings of 'Ethiopianism'.[3]

The government's yielding to this proposal in the face of wide-scale White opposition to the scheme was itself a result of a combination of circumstances. These were summed up by the Principal of the college:

> He [the Principal] explained that there had been plans and propaganda by friends of the natives before 1916 and that the surrender made by the Government, that is by Botha, was partly political. In the War, the fear of native trouble was intensified, and the establishment of the College was a sop, an amicable gesture. Also, because otherwise they would get higher education in the United States and were, indeed, already beginning to go there.[4]

Initially, the college was essentially a Christian institution catering for African students and offering matriculation as well as university courses examined by the University of South Africa. Thirteen years after its establishment, for instance, up to about 75 per cent of the students at the college were enrolled in the pre-university matriculation programme. Of the remaining 25 per cent some were involved in non-degree courses in agriculture, arts and theology. Thus only a tiny minority were registered for degree work.

The slow pace of development can be gleaned from the fact that after thirteen years of existence (in 1929) the college had produced no more than nine graduates (degree). This of course was a reflection of the scanty educational opportunity structure at lower levels which had to depend, as in most African countries, almost entirely on Christian missionary initiatives.

The initial funding was by the Union Government, endowments from private foundations—Carnegie, Rockefeller and Rhodes Trust, plus students' fees. A substantial number of the students were on bursaries raised by their respective local communities, notably in the Transkei and in Basutoland. The Christian Missionary Societies—Anglican, Presbyterian and Methodist—provided the hostels in which the students lived.

The college became affiliated to Rhodes University in 1951 with the students pursuing Rhodes University syllabuses and receiving Rhodes University degrees. This remained so until the passing of the Extension of University Education Act in 1959.

Though, as stated above, the college was initially intended to cater for African students, as it evolved it came to cater for other Black groups. For instance on the verge of its takeover by the government in 1958 the breakdown of the student population by racial group was as:

TABLE 1. Student population by racial group at Fort Hare (1958)[5]

Racial group	Number	Percentage of total
African	292	67.0
Coloured	59	13.5
Indian	59	13.5
Other [1]	28	6.0
TOTAL	438	100.0

1. South-West Africa, High Commission Territories, Southern and Northern Rhodesia, and East Africa.

Besides Fort Hare, facilities also existed for Black students in the so-called open English-medium universities. Needless to say, Black students were subjected to all forms of racial discrimination in these institutions.

Black-university education and White supremacy

At this stage it might be useful to place the development of Fort Hare in the wider setting within the context of the dynamics of a society ruled by a White settler minority committed to a total monopoly of political power.

Among commentators on the subject of higher education in South Africa there is a firm view that the Fort Hare 'tradition' represented something special in terms of its deviation from the wider racist societal norm. In this vein, one author has asserted that before 1960 Fort Hare represented 'to an extent a microcosm of a relatively successful non-racial society'. [6] Another one laments the government take-over of the institution in the following terms: 'The great tradition of a college that in some forty years had produced many of Africa's most notable leaders was destroyed.' [7]

This problem, in our view, cannot be fully grasped without reference to some of the 'dilemmas' that arise in an acute fashion regarding the education of indigenous people in a colonial setting. These 'dilemmas' arise from the fact that colonialism as a process of capitalist expansion, through political and military conquest, in its essence was an instrument of exploitation for the benefit of the colonizing power. This fundamental premise is reflected in all the institutions that arose in colonial societies—whether they be types of forced labour or in the field of political structures.

It is therefore not surprising that in virtually all the African countries the initial infrastructure for Western-type education was provided by the Christian missionaries (as an instrument for their mission) and not by the colonial state.

The general attitude of the colonial administration to the question of African education was neatly summed up by a British educationist who observed that the overall purpose of colonial enterprise was 'one of exploitation and development for the people of Britain—it was to this purpose that whatever education as was given was directed'. [8]

The consequences of this historical fact are manifold. However, two most salient ones can be easily identified:

At the time of independence, there was, in all these countries, no viable educational infrastructure and hence no adequate pool of qualified manpower to fill the available jobs. As a result, education has been one of the major priorities for the governments of these countries in their bid to reduce the degree of dependence on expatriate manpower.

While the general educational underdevelopment of the indigenous peoples is a common phenomenon of colonialism, the peculiarity of the South African situation lies in at least two factors, namely the relative size of the White settler population and the fact that this settler population is itself not ethnically homogeneous.

The size of the settler population is relevant in terms of the ability of the capitalist economy to attain a relatively high level of industrialization, albeit rather fortuitously (with gold-mining and foreign capital as a basis), without depending on Black skilled manpower but on cheap Black labour in a racially stratified labour market. Further, for the purposes of manning the vast repressive bureaucratic machinery on which the day-to-day operation of the apartheid system depends, the availability of a sizeable pool of Whites has been crucial. More pertinent, however, to the field of higher education has been the existence of a minor ethnic contradiction within the White minority.

Within this group there have been at least two identifiable strands on the issue of university education, based on their respective perceptions of the best method of perpetuating White domination in that society. Cecil Rhodes, for instance, envisaged the university as an integrative institution 'within whose walls the students from all parts of the country, both English and Dutch, would be bound together to form a single, united nation, possessing common ideals and a common culture'.[9]

The same viewpoint was reiterated by F. S. Malan, the first Minister of Education in the Union Government, in 1912 when he said:

> I believe, that it is of supreme importance to the future of our Union, that [the youth of both sections of the white population] should be brought together during the most impressionable time of their lives, and thus learn to understand and respect each other. Any scheme, which would have as a result the separation of these two sections, whatever advantages—academical or otherwise—may be claimed for it should ... be rejected, at least until it has been definitely shown by experience that the solution here suggested is impractical and unworkable. But I refuse to believe, that the prejudices on either side are or will be strong enough to prevent permanently the fusion of the two races into one nation.[10]

A contrary view was expressed by the University Vigilance Committee in 1913. They saw the Victoria College as being 'intimately connected with the spiritual, and national life of the Dutch-speaking section of the people'.

> It is the place where the Dutch South African people can most effectively realize its ideals, and whence it can exercise the greatest influence on South Africa. It is the most satisfactory realization yet found by the people of its deepest need. It embodies an idea. And therefore it has become for our people not a mere educational institution among others, but the emblem of and a security for its own vigorous, growing national life, seeking self-expression.[11]

These two opposing ideas as to what the function of university education should be in the South African context have been interpreted by some scholars[12] as manifestations of two irreconcilable world views represented in Parsonian[13] pattern—variable terminology as the particularistic conception of the university as a *volks* institution, as opposed to the universalistic conception that sees it as an instrument for promoting liberal political and racial attitudes.

There is a certain amount of validity in the above view, even though it is on a superficial level. After all, the struggle to keep Fort Hare under Rhodes University and away from the clutches of the Ministry of Bantu Education was partly a reflection of this perception.

However, viewed in a broader perspective of overall intergroup and interclass relations and interests, these two strands, in our opinion, represent variations on an essentially 'ideological' (in Karl Mannheim's usage)[14] theme, namely the preservation of White supremacy. The only difference, in our view, is that on the one hand the particularistic *volks* conception vigorously asserts the superiority of the White race, and combines this with a narrow ethnic jingoism as a weapon in inter-group conflict in a historically determined conjuncture. On the other, the universalistic 'liberal' conception asserts the same superiority of the White race with the stress on the superiority of British culture as a weapon in the same historically determined struggle.

We have termed these perspectives ideological to the extent that they are undoubtedly committed to the perpetuation of White rule. Even more importantly, however, they can be regarded as being ideological in a yet more fundamental sense, namely in terms of obfuscating or mystifying the contradiction between capital and labour which provides the structural anchor to which these themes are dialectically related.

There is no doubt that the existence of these two strands affected and continue to determine the particular direction of Black university education in several respects. There is also little doubt that what was dominant before the transfer of Fort Hare to the Department of Bantu Education was the 'universalistic-liberal' tradition. Several factors were responsible for this, namely: (a) that the establishment of Fort Hare predated the crystallization of White rule into a systematic policy of racial segregation under the apartheid framework as from 1948; (b) the types of Christian missionary influence that were behind the establishment of the institution; (c) the numerical preponderance of academic and senior administrative staff (Black and White) who more or less shared this perspective; and (d) the structural links that developed between Fort Hare and institutional representatives of this persuasion especially its affiliation to Rhodes University in 1951 as well as its links, on the student level, with the National Union of South African Students.

The above observations should not be interpreted to mean that Fort Hare as an institution of higher learning represented anything like a generator of critical consciousness. In so far as the normal functions of a university were concerned, this was essentially a teaching institution with very little research going on.

Further, the overall pedagogy was essentially a domesticating one in line with the wider liberal illusions of peaceful persuasion and passive resistance in the political arena.

In this respect it is quite interesting, in view of the eulogies of the old Fort Hare by liberals, to note that the expulsion of student activists for essentially political reasons did not start until 1960.

The college was closed down temporarily in 1955 because of student unrest. Before the college was reopened a circular was sent to all the students requiring them to sign undertakings to abide by all the rules and regulations and also to disclose to the authorities the names of the students who had been politically active during the events leading up to the closure.

An accurate summary of the general atmosphere prevailing at Fort Hare on the eve of its take-over by the government is given by T. V. R. Beard:

> It is necessary to point out that by 1960 Fort Hare had not outgrown its mission-school background. The rules and regulations, the Christian nature of

the institution with its denominational halls of residence run by the churches, were at once apparent to the newcomer. Fort Hare had a paternalist heritage and some of the churchmen and many of the staff were paternalists. This paternalism was mostly well intentioned, but it was paternalism none the less, which at its worst involved a failure to recognize the capabilities and initiatives of Black students. The rules and regulations reflected this paternalism, which was also manifest to an extent in the general attitudes of the college authorities towards the students. Perhaps the main consequence of this paternalist attitude was political, expressed in the reluctance on the part of many staff to believe that students had the ability or initiative to organize anything without the supervision of staff members, and this led in turn to a tendency to look for white 'agitators' behind any student political activities. The other component of this was the inability of most staff to comprehend the very meaning of the 'political struggle'.[15]

The Extension of University Education Act, 1959— a strategy for ethnic fragmentation

The establishment of ethnic colleges (often referred to as 'tribal' or 'bush' colleges by South African Blacks) through the above Act represented a further step in the implementation of the policy of apartheid in the field of education. Four new ethnic colleges were established in this process: the University College of Zululand at Ngoye for the Zulu- and Swazi-speaking groups; the University College of the North at Turfloop for the Sotho-, Venda-, Tswana- and Tsonga-speaking groups; the University College at Durban, Westville, for Indians; and the University of the Western Cape for the Coloured group. The University College of Fort Hare, which as we have seen had catered for all the Black groups was designated a Xhosa institution and there was a lot of talk about removing it from Alice to Umtata in the Transkei. In addition to these institutions, there is now also the University of Transkei started as a branch of Fort Hare in anticipation of the granting of 'independence' to that territory in September 1976.

While these institutions initially took University of South Africa examinations and degrees, in 1969 they were granted 'autonomous' status and now offer their own degrees and diplomas.

This development represented the extension of the apartheid doctrine to the field of higher education. Some writers have observed that this was an extension of the particularistic *volks* conception of the university to the other racial groups, hence the strict ethnic separation.

What needs to be stressed in this regard is that while the Afrikaners assert their imaginary, ethnic purity and their *volks-Weltanschauung* as a basis for the perpetuation of minority rule, when it comes to Black education, it is the White minority regime that determines not only the structural framework but also the entire purpose, and hence the content of what is taught in these government-imposed 'tribal' institutions.

The essence of the scheme is not only to fragment the oppressed groups and thus weaken their collective resistance but also systematically but subtly to indoctrinate them in their own inferiority. We are aware of the ideological shift from assertions of racial superiority by the regime to the ideology of ethnic separation and cultural difference which has been commented upon by some writers.[16] It is, however, essential to observe that this shift does not represent any departure from the essence of racist ideology since their conception of culture is essentially racially deterministic.

It can therefore be asserted that the purpose of creating these ethnic institutions of higher learning—if they can be so described—is to supplement the racist pedagogy that instils a sense of a God-given mission of domination to the Afrikaner youth with a more domesticating tribal-oriented pedagogy for the oppressed groups.

The architects of the scheme have expressed this purpose with outstanding clarity. For instance when D. F. Malan became Prime Minister in 1948 he asserted that

> An intolerable state of affairs has arisen here in the past few years in our university institutions, a state of affairs which gives rise to friction, to an unpleasant relationship between European and non-European . . . we will take every possible step to give both the natives and the coloured peoples university training as soon as we can, but in their own sphere in other words in separate institutions.[17]

In the same vein Dr H. F. Verwoerd then in charge of Native Affairs in moving the Bantu Education Act in Parliament in 1953 asserted:

> I just want to remind honourable members that if the Native in South Africa today in any kind of school in existence is being taught to expect that he will live his adult life under a policy of equal rights, he is making a big mistake.[18]

This is because

> There is no place for him in the European Community above the level of certain forms of labour . . . until now, he had been subjected to a school system which drew him away from his own community and misled him by showing him the green pastures of European society, in which he is not allowed to graze.[19]

It follows logically that

> My department's policy is that education should stand with both feet in the reserves and have its roots in the spirit and being of Bantu Society . . .
> The basis of the provision and organization of education in the Bantu Community should, where possible, be tribal organization.[20]

The fact that after centuries of the disruption and distortion of indigenous modes of production and social organization by the logic of settler expansionism through violent conquest the above statements could be the cornerstone of educational policy should not be dismissed as either naïvety or arrogant racist cynicism. Rather, it is a manifestation of a well-designed strategy of intergroup combat devised to perpetuate exploitative and colonial-type relations between the different racial groups.

In the same vein in 1957 the Minister of Bantu Education explained that

> Control of [Black universities] by the government was needed as it was necessary to prevent undesirable ideological developments—such as had disturbed the non-White institutions not directly under the charge of the Government, and as the 'Bantu authorities' had not developed to take over this control.[21]

And, speaking in support of the transfer of the University College of Fort Hare Bill in 1959 the same minister observed that

> Where one has to deal with under-developed peoples, where the State has planned a process of development for those peoples, and where a university can play a decisive role in the process and directions of that development, it must surely be clear to everyone that the State alone is competent to exercise the powers of guardianship in this field.[22]

It is therefore not surprising that the senior administrative and academic positions in these institutions were filled by these hard-core racists who were committed to promoting this 'tribalization' mission.

The first Rector of the University College of Zululand, for instance, was proud of the fact that the college was situated in 'purely Zulu territory' and that its student body was homogeneous. He outlined its aims as being:

> the development of the Zulu community; the development of new patterns of thought and behaviour in the life of students and staff which will later spread to the wider community, the development of the Zulu language not merely as a medium of instruction but as a transmitter of culture and the instrument of cultural growth and acculturation; the training of staff (both European and Zulu) to be expert in the Zulu culture and the problems of education affecting the Zulu; and the encouragement of research in problems of importance to the Zulu.[23]

In other words, he saw his duty as being to spearhead the discovery and development of this fragmented and mythical Zulu reality.

The recruitment of academic staff into these instruments of apartheid is carefully designed to burden the Black students, especially in the humanities and social sciences, with the most reactionary products of the established Afrikaans-medium universities.

Nowhere were these processes more dramatically manifested than at Fort Hare. A brief look at what happened there immediately after the government take-over of the institution may help throw light on some of these issues.

There had been widespread opposition to the proposed take-over of the institution by the Department of Bantu Education. At Fort Hare itself the students and the vast majority of the staff (Black and White) were united in their campaign to stop the proposed move. The students referred to the

Extension of University Education Bill as the 'extermination of university education bill' and their protest reached its climax when a team of new administrators came on a familiarization tour of the institution.

The Minister of Bantu Education dismissed eight White members of staff and stated that he would not hesitate to sack any member of staff who 'sabotaged' apartheid. Further, the Department of Bantu Education declared all participation in political activities by African members of staff, even in then legal organizations, as contrary to the university regulations.

Many of the senior administrative and academic staff resigned their positions, thus making way for a team of government-approved personnel who saw their mandate as essentially being to transform what they considered to be a hotbed of liberalism, communism and revolution into an acquiescent tribal institution producing manpower for the Bantustans.

In the few departments in which the senior 'liberal' academics remained, the new regime's strategy was to appoint their own men, some of them recent graduates invariably from the Afrikaans-medium universities and promote them rapidly while doing everything to isolate and ignore the senior staff members.

The conflict was also partly reflected in the syllabuses that were introduced. For instance, whereas under Rhodes University, students in the field of administration had been able to register for Public Administration, in the new structure they could only do Native Administration in line with the apartheid policy.

Moreover, whereas an African, teaching this course and opposed to government policy would proceed by examining the historical dispossession of the African people through military conquest, and the various repressive laws that have over time become more and more draconian in nature, the external examiners at the University of South Africa interpreted the situation from exactly the opposite angle, namely the White man's mission of spreading Western civilization and the necessity for discriminatory laws. There certainly was no meeting-ground. The situation was far from that of Karl Mannheim' free-floating intelligentsia, who are supposed to be capable of effecting a dynamic synthesis of opposing standpoints.[24]

The students, therefore, often found themselves in difficulties when it came to examinations: either to write what they knew was the truth and face the prospect of certain failure or to write what was expected of them and get their degrees.

These problems were not as acute in the natural sciences and languages (the latter included Latin and Afrikaans). In the case of the Department of History where they might have been expected to arise, the staff ensured that the teaching was designed to leave the student without any meaningful understanding of the historical processes surrounding the subjugation of the Black people.

On the level of student politics, a very curious situation arose. The opposition to the take-over continued to manifest itself in a somewhat strange fashion. For instance, the first group of students to register under the new structure (in 1960) met with a lot of hostility from their senior colleagues. It was implied that their presence in some way condoned the establishment of these 'tribal' institutions. This, however, had no basis in fact since this was a *fait accompli* and the new students themselves hardly had any choice in the matter.

Some student leaders were expelled and calls for their reinstatement were ignored by the new authorities. Student protest was overtaken by the Sharpeville crisis in 1960 and the national stay-at-home that was called by the Black nationalist movements to protest the declaration of a republic by the minority White regime in 1961.

What followed was a systematic arrest of members of the banned African National Congress and Pan Africanist Congress, with reports of torture by the police. These developments affected Black students and staff both at high-school and university level.

It was in an atmosphere of wide-scale intimidation and political repression that these instruments of apartheid took shape amidst declarations of separate development palliatives by the ruling class. The arrests and expulsions led to the adoption of more negative methods of opposition by the students; notably the refusal to elect any Students Representative Council for alleged fear of victimization by the authorities.

During these years, growing disaffection with White liberals led to a move by a considerable section of the student body (mainly members of the Pan Africanist Congress and the Non-European Unity Movement) to disaffiliate from the National Union of South African Students. These moves received extremely adverse publicity from the 'liberal' press in the eastern Cape. The outcome was that students could belong to this union as individuals while the institution disaffiliated. Attempts to form students' unions and associations on the basis of political party affiliation did not materialize since the two main nationalist movements had been banned in 1960. All political activity had to be strictly underground.

It follows from the above sketch that the introduction of the new structure amidst a wave of repression in the wider society transformed the nature and thrust of teaching in this institution. Intellectual life was being deliberately tailored to the philosophy and policy of apartheid with all its consequences.

As far as social research was concerned, there was nothing worth that name. The few projects that were conducted in the Department of Anthropology, for instance, centred around such trivialities as Xhosa cosmetics, while the social work projects were based on a blaming-the-victim theoretical posture.

On the other hand, ethnographic studies conducted by some of the new members of staff were aimed at discovering pure tribes; an important undertaking from the point of view of government policy. There certainly was no question of education for critical consciousness, rather education was being shaped to fit in with government policy.

In the area of staff recruitment, though the government paid lip-service to the policy of 'tribalization', in reality this was not achieved even on its own terms. Apart from one or two departments that were headed by Africans, specifically Bantu Languages and Education (where incidentally there were no White staff since it would presumably not have been in line with separate-but-equal apartheid for a White to work under a Black), all the departments were preponderantly staffed by Whites especially graduates of the Afrikaans-medium universities.

In 1971, a decade after the establishment of these universities, the racial composition of the staff reflected the above observations in that, in the African universities, there were 235 White staff-members compared with 57 Black; in the Coloured universities, 72 Whites and 2 Blacks; and in the Indian universities, 122 Whites and 28 Blacks.[25]

It is therefore true to say that the early 1960s, the years during which the government spent considerable amounts of money to create physical infrastructures for Black higher education, were, in reality, the grimmest years for Black higher education.

The political paralysis that followed the unleashing of nationwide repression could not but adversely affect the campuses. Besides factors like wide-ranging government censorship of publications, which militate against the spirit and practice of free scientific inquiry, the structural matrix established by the government was in line with its declared policy of creating Bantustans—in essence a strategy for ethnic fragmentation as a means of perpetuating White rule.

The Black universities and Black Consciousness

It was only with the rise and growth of the Black Consciousness movement in the late 1960s and early 1970s that this political paralysis was transcended. It is significant that the young people in the Black universities were in the vanguard of this movement. The centrality of the race theme in this ideology was itself a dialectical response to the consolidation of apartheid following the wide-scale intimidation of the opponents of the government.

Certainly the formation and growth of the South African Students' Organization (SASO) in the late 1960s and early 1970s had nothing to do with the intentions of the architects of the apartheid scheme. Indeed, their initial response to this development was one of favourable ambiguity. The implication was that breaking away from the White National Union of South African Students by Black students was in line with the government's policy of ethnic separation. In other words, the regime initially failed to grasp the radical implications of the race theme in the ideology of the new movement.

It is also clear, however, that the rise of SASO is partly traceable to the specific conditions that prevailed in these 'tribal' universities.

In this connection two questions suggest themselves. First, how was it possible for what we have termed a domesticating 'tribal-oriented' pedagogy to generate a radical student response? Secondly, why was it that the race theme came to dominate this response. The latter question is legitimate in view of the fact that the militant nationalism of the Pan Africanist Congress had been subjected to severe criticism for being racist. This was why for instance in the early 1960s at Fort Hare a great deal of time was spent by members of the newly formed Pan Africanist Congress in trying to exonerate their movement from this charge by insisting that they were committed to non-racialism, as against the multiracialist policy of the African National Congress.

The answers to these questions are to be found in the nature and dynamics of the South African social situation in recent times. The contradictions within it are so sharp that in the field of education, for instance, it is true to say that even the apparently peaceful White-teacher/Black-students classroom situation is in essence a conflict situation.

Prior to the systematic implementation of the apartheid policy, some of these contradictions could be obscured by a paternalistic ideology, but apartheid ideology and practice unmasked the true intentions of the White minority, namely perpetual supremacy through political repression.

Such a system presents the students with a clear choice between acquiescence and collaboration on the one hand, and struggle on the other. It must be added that these are, to a large extent, conscious choices in view of the fact that collaboration is frequently rationalized in terms of a strategy of opposition from within or the use of apartheid structures to undermine the apartheid system. Thus, to the extent that the system is openly exploitative and ruthlessly oppressive the impact of what we have described as a domesticating pedagogy is, by definition, severely limited. Hence the system has to depend increasingly on open coercion at all levels.

Thus, there develops a syndrome of institutionalized repression. Within the university setting this takes the form of all sorts of regimentation through stringent regulations. Some of these include the prohibition of visits by outsiders without the permission of the authorities; requirements for students to sign undertakings not to take part in protests as a condition for admission; strict surveillance by the authorities and the security police including a network of informers; dictatorial powers in the hands of the authorities resulting in arbitrary expulsions and rustications; arrogant attitudes and practices by the predominantly White staff and the use of police force at the slightest sign of non-compliance by the students.

In these circumstances, the struggle to democratize the universities becomes organically linked with the struggle for liberation in the wider concept of the society.

Some of these factors were brilliantly summarized by the late O. R. Tiro, a student leader, in his graduation address at the University of the North in 1972. Commenting on the nature of education in South Africa he observed:

> Speaking on the occasion of the formal opening of this university, Mr Phatudi, a Lebowa [Bantustan] Territorial officer said that in as much as there is American education there had to be Bantu education. I am conscientiously bound to differ with him. In America there is nothing like negro education, Red Indian education and white American education. We do not have a system of education common to all South Africans. What is there in European education which is not good for Africans? We want a system of education common to all South Africans. . . .

After noting the myriad of discriminatory practices on the campus he observed that

> these are injustices which no normal student can tolerate—no matter who he is or where he comes from. In the light of what has been said, the challenge to every Black graduate in this country lies in the fact that the guilt of all wrongful actions in South Africa, restrictions without trial, repugnant legislation, expulsions from schools rest on all those who do not actively disassociate themselves from, and work for the system breeding such evils ...

In the light of these observations, his final message to his fellow-graduands was that 'if your education is not linked with the struggle on the whole continent of Africa it is meaningless'.

Mr Tiro was expelled from the university the following day and the nationwide student protest that followed (which involved students in some of the English-medium White universities) was met with repressive government action.

Black student radicalism is therefore a response to the government-imposed indignities and humiliations that Black students suffer as Blacks in apartheid society.

While over the years some cosmetic changes have been made in some of these universities as part of 'management of crisis' tactics—for instance appointment of Black rectors and salary improvements—nothing has fundamentally changed to make them anything other than instruments of apartheid.

In the area of staff recruitment, for example, in the words of the registrar of the University of Fort Hare,

> the University policy is positively one of Africanization, particularly academic staff. Where there is a suitable African applicant for a teaching post, he will be appointed in preference to a better qualified White applicant.[26]

Such protestations notwithstanding, there has been no significant change in the racial imbalance in staff numbers. Further, both the postgraduate programme provisions plus staff recruitment are conditional on 'good personal qualities'. This is a euphemism for censorship on political grounds. While the regime can rationalize the numerical preponderance of Whites

TABLE 2. Racial composition of university senates and councils

University	Senates		Councils	
	Whites	Blacks	Whites	Blacks
Fort Hare	51	7	15	4
North	46	5	13	5
Zululand	49	6	11	4
Western Cape	45	1	11	5
Durban	44	4	11	4
TOTAL	235	23	61	22

on the academic and senior administrative staff positions in terms of the unavailability of qualified Blacks, the position is equally skewed in the senates and councils of these institutions as Table 2 shows.

Further, those Black staff-members who are known to be opponents of the regime are targets for victimization and imprisonment whenever there is student unrest. Nor is the political censorship confined to staff. For instance, in the words of one commentator:

> There are many South African Black students who are currently stranded in the country with respect to furthering their education. Most of these are victims of the after-effects of the recent years, mass walkouts from black campuses. Most of these students cannot be registered with the correspondence University of South Africa, which demands a certificate of 'good conduct' to be supplied by the previous University, prior to the registration of the applicant.[27]

It is therefore true to say that underneath the government's assertions about ethnic self-determination and 'separate-but-equal' facilities is a well-designed strategy for perpetuating minority rule. In line with this grand design it is therefore imperative that the Black universities—themselves a product of apartheid policy—should remain under tight government control in order to ensure that they serve their originally intended function of stabilizing the situation rather than promoting liberation.

It is because of this fundamental contradiction that these institutions have been in a state of more or less permanent crisis since the early 1970s.

The causes of this state of crisis are the same as those which generate the crisis in the larger society, namely the policy of apartheid itself and its attendant dehumanization of the oppressed groups. It therefore follows that, without the dismantling of apartheid structures and democratization of the society, whatever resources the regime can boast of having ploughed into the field of Black education (which incidentally are a pittance compared to expenditure on White education) in its pursuit of the separate-development 'palliative' must be seen in terms of a wider goal of providing education for subservience, which indeed is a contradiction in terms.

Nor is this crisis subject only to the internal dynamics of the apartheid republic. South Africa, being as it is the centre of an essentially subregional system of colonialist domination through settler minority regimes, is bound to be affected by the momentum which the liberation struggle, in that region, has gathered since the early 1970s.

It is therefore not surprising that some of the manifestations of the crisis of apartheid are directly traceable to 'external' developments. A case in point was the explosive situation that developed in the Black university campuses towards the end of 1974.

The collapse of Portuguese colonialism in Africa was greeted with tremendous enthusiasm by the Black people of South Africa. One of the manifestations of this enthusiasm was the decision by the major Black Consciousness organizations, namely the Black People's Convention and SASO, to hold Pro-Frelimo rallies in Durban, Cape Town, Johannesburg and Port Elizabeth to coincide with the installation of the transitional government in Mozambique on 25 September 1974. The aim of the rallies in the words of the organizers was 'to show our solidarity with the people of Mozambique who have been freed by Frelimo'.

The student body of the University of the North also decided to hold a rally. Thus when the Black People's Convention and SASO decided to go ahead with the rallies despite a hasty government ban under the provisions of the Riotous Assemblies Act of 1956 the students also decided to continue with their plans.

What happened on the day of the rally was described by one commentator in the following terms:

> According to information from students spoken to on the campus, a thousand-odd students gathered in the University hall and listened to speeches. While one speech was in process police arrived in riot vans and parked inside the campus. They were armed with rifles, pistols, sten guns, scatter guns, and batons. They also had dogs.[28]

Lamenting these developments the rector, Professor J. L. Boshoff, remarked:

> When the Government closed the open universities to black students in 1959, and created all-black universities, it was warned that these all-black universities would become hotbeds of black nationalism. What we experienced this week was naked, satanic, anti-white racism. If this does not pull us up short I don't know what will bring us to our senses.[29]

The *Rand Daily Mail* (a 'liberal' English-medium newspaper) was quick to point out that

> What Professor Boshoff is saying, whether he realizes it or not, is that the fault lies in segregation; that anti-whiteism comes from the heart of the black community. [Further] the creation of segregated black universities was one of the most dangerous, irresponsible acts ever taken by the Nationalist Government.[30]

Immediately after this unrest five White members of staff resigned their positions.

A few months later (in February 1975) the rector banned SASO on the campus. Further, it was reported that he also refused to readmit active SASO members or any of their relatives.

In the meantime, the government had set up a one-man commission of inquiry (the Snyman Commission) to look into the disturbances. This was hardly a year after the one-man Commission (the Van Wyk Commission) inquiring into the 1973 disturbances at the University of the Western Cape had recommended that the following activities at all South African universities be made punishable by law:

1. Disruption of classes or interference with the activities of the members of staff.

2. Incitement by anyone towards disrupting classes or preventing staff members from carrying out their duties.
3. Any other conduct aimed at disrupting the normal functioning of the university, for example by encouraging students or lecturers to boycott classes.

There is no doubt that the university authorities saw SASO as the main cause of their problems and did everything to cripple its activities on the campuses even before the official government ban on the Black Consciousness movement and allied organizations in October 1977.

For instance, following the 1972 disturbances at Fort Hare and further confrontation and mass walk-outs from the university in 1973 the rector, Dr. de Wet, asserted that 'there is ample proof that it is the outspoken policy of SASO to endeavour to effect the closure of black universities'.[31] To which the Eastern Cape Regional Secretary of SASO, Mr S. Sokupa, replied in the following terms:

> We are not out to destroy any university. All we stand for is the upholding of the black man's human dignity in every sphere of life. We also seek to make students aware of the needs of their community, which they are supposed to serve with their education. It is a pity that our message has been misinterpreted by so many.[32]

Later, in 1975, the SASO General Secretary, Mr Thami Zani, observed that

> On the University Campuses the position remains somewhat confused as the forces of Bantu Education, coupled with the State's administrative machinery continue to thwart the development of the Black personality. Black students who are only after the truth have been heavily victimized in these universities.[33]

It is, therefore, not surprising that the university campuses exploded during the June 1976 Soweto uprising. This was followed by the usual repressive measures by the state. With the subsequent killing of Black schoolchildren, the mass arrests, torture and deaths in detention the apartheid-generated ferment continues to deepen.

Conclusion

In examining the effects of apartheid on teaching and research in the Black universities, this chapter has tried to highlight the contradictions that continue to manifest themselves in these instruments of apartheid. It has also shown that the 'tribally oriented' domesticating pedagogy which characterizes the nature of teaching in these institutions has failed abysmally in its intended purpose of producing politically acquiescent bureaucrats for the Bantustans.

This failure, we have argued, is a result of the fact that apartheid is a fundamentally unacceptable policy from the point of view of the oppressed groups. Hence the development of what we have characterized as a syndrome of institutionalized repression. This generates its twin response, namely resistance and struggle by the oppressed. In this respect, it is interesting to note that while, for instance, in the 1974/75 financial year the government allocated up to 16.3 per cent of the country's budget to 'defence' and only 1.4 per cent to Black education, in the 1975/76 budget the ratio had increased, as 'defense' expenditure rose to 18.7 per cent of the total budget while expenditure on Black education fell to 1.3 per cent of the total.[34]

This is during a time, as it has recently been revealed, when the government was spending millions of Rands secretly to promote South Africa's image abroad.

In these circumstances, it is not surprising that the total number of degrees awarded to Blacks in 1977 was 534, of which only 77 were in the sciences—that is for a Black population of over 17 million.[35]

As far as research in these universities is concerned there is really nothing worthy of that term. This is partly due to the wider government strategy of establishing research infrastructures with no direct connection with universities: the South African Council for Scientific and Industrial Research and the National Council for Social Research. While White academics are heavily represented on the organs of these councils, in line with apartheid principles Blacks are excluded. The logic of the system is that, while universities in the rest of the continent are establishing Development and African Studies Institutes, in South Africa we are likely to see Zulu or Xhosa Studies Institutes.

One commentator, after noting that the majority of students qualifying from these universities are mainly in the field of education and humanities, aptly summed up the situation in the following terms:

> By and large, higher education for Blacks still remains education for subservience. This has resulted in most educated Blacks having to depend on civil service employment for their main livelihood, which makes them and their educational wisdom and experience completely useless for the real development of the community from which they come. This cannot be surprising because any meaningful involvement in real community development almost invariably incurs the disfavour of the powers that be.[36]

Notes

1. The year in which the National Party came into power.
2. C. T. Loram, *The Education of the South African Native,* pp. 301-2, London, 1917, as quoted in David Welsh and H. W. Van der Merwe (eds.), *Student Perspectives on South Africa,* Cape Town, David Philip, 1972.
3. 'Ethiopianism' refers to African independent Church movements whose message was interpreted as being purely political by most of the Whites.
4. M. Perham, *African Apprenticeship: An Autobiographical Journey in Southern Africa 1929,* p. 44, London, Faber & Faber, 1974.

5. T. V. R. Beard, 'Background to Student Activities at the University College of Fort Hare', in Welsh and Van der Merwe (eds.), op. cit., p. 156.
6. Ibid.
7. Mary Benson, *The African Patriots: The Story of the African National Congress of South Africa*, p. 260, London, Faber & Faber, 1963.
8. H. S. Scott, 'The Development of the Education of the African in Relation to Western Contact', *Yearbook of Education*, p. 737, London, Evans Bros, 1938.
9. E. G. Malherbe, 'The Universities of the Union of South Africa', *Yearbook of Education*, p. 744, London, Evans Bros, 1934.
10. F. S. Malan, *The University South Africa Needs*, pp. 7-8, Cape Town, 1912, as quoted in Welsh and Van der Merwe (eds.), op. cit., p. 17.
11. 'Memorandum Issued by the University Vigilance Committee in Connection with the Bill', Appendix A of *Select Committee 13*, 1913, p. iii, as quoted in Welsh and Van der Merwe (eds.), op. cit., p. 16.
12. David Welsh, op. cit., p. 16.
13. Talcott Parsons, *The Social System*, pp. 102-12, Tavistock Publications Ltd, 1952.
14. Karl Mannheim, *Ideology and Utopia, An Introduction to the Sociology of Knowledge*, pp. 49-67, London, Routledge & Kegan Paul Ltd, 1954.
15. Beard, op. cit., p. 165.
16. Heribert Adam, *Modernizing Racial Domination: South Africa's, Political Dynamics*, Berkeley, University of California Press, 1971.
17. *House of Assembly Debates (Hansard)*, Vol. 64, 1948, Col. 219, as quoted in Kogila Adam, 'Dialectic of Higher Education in South Africa', *South Africa: Sociological Perspectives*, p. 199, London, Oxford University Press, 1971.
18. H. F. Verwoerd as quoted in B. Pityana, 'Power and Social Change in South Africa' in Welsh and Van der Merwe (eds.), op. cit., p. 177.
19. H. F. Verwoerd as quoted in Adam, op. cit., p. 201.
20. Ibid.
21. Minister of Education, *House of Assembly Debates (Hansard)*, 27-29 May 1957, as quoted in *Apartheid: Its Effects on Education, Science, Culture and Information*, p. 87, Paris, Unesco, 1967.
22. W. A. Maree, speech delivered in the Senate on 26 June 1959, as quoted in *Apartheid . . .*, op. cit. (1972 ed.), p. 110.
23. P. A. W. Cook, 'Some Aims and Objectives of a Bantu University College', in R. G. Mac Millan, P. D. Hey and J. W. MacQarrie (eds.), *Education and our Expanding Horizons*, pp. 314-15, Pietermaritzburg, 1962.
24. Mannheim, op. cit., p. 142.
25. *Sechaba* (official organ of the African National Congress of South Africa), Vol. 6, No. 8, August 1972, p. 3.
26. Registrar, University College of Fort Hare, as quoted in *Black Review, 1974/75*, p. 165, Lovedale Press, 1975.
27. Ibid., p. 187.
28. Ibid., pp. 78-9.
29. Ibid., pp. 170-1.
30. *Rand Daily Mail*, 6 November 1974, as quoted in *Black Review, 1974/75*, op. cit., pp. 170-1.
31. *Black Review, 1974/75*, op. cit., p. 173.
32. Ibid., p. 174.
33. Ibid., p. 113-14.
34. Republic of South Africa, *Estimate of Expenditure to be Defrayed from Revenue Account During the Year Ended 31st March, 1976* (Government Printers, 1975), as cited in Ann and Neva Seidman, *U. S. Multinationals in Southern Africa*, p. 145, Dar es Salaam, Tanzania Publishing House, 1977.
35. *House of Assembly Debates (Hansard)*, 14 April 1978, as cited in P. F. Wilmot, 'The Economics of Apartheid and the Future of Africa: An Essay in Demystification', unpublished mimeo, 1979.
36. *Black Review, 1974/75*, op. cit., pp. 185-6.

9 The Black Consciousness movement and social research

Nyameko Pityana

The Black Consciousness movement is a term of convenience that refers not only to the organizations that sprang up in South Africa after 1968 but also to the widespread mood of Black pride that encompasses the Black man's commitment to a search for human dignity and liberation from all those forces that seek to oppress him psychologically and physically. In time, this mood was to become a political movement that moved from protest to open revolt in 1976.

Black Consciousness was defined by the South African Students' Organisation (SASO)[1] as '. . . an attitude of the mind, a way of life'.[2] Therefore SASO saw itself as verbalizing, giving shape and direction to feelings of anger and resentment that lay embedded in the psyche of the ordinary Black people. Black Consciousness according to the SASO Policy Manifesto implied 'the awareness by Black people of the power they wield as a group, both economically and politically'.[3] The Manifesto also defined Black people as

> those who are by law or tradition politically, economically and socially discriminated against as a group in the South African society and identifying themselves as a unit in the struggle towards the realization of their aspirations.[4]

This definition may be assumed to imply that all those who suffer victimization at the hands of a common oppressor share the same aspirations. Yet SASO made it very clear that such Black people had to be 'identifying themselves as a unit'.[5] Therefore whereas SASO clearly saw the question of colour—and not race—as a factor in seeking unification of all oppressed people towards a national consciousness, it certainly does not exclude the clear possibility that there may be factors which may cause some, who would otherwise fit into this category, not to identify themselves with the aspirations of the Black people and their struggle for liberation. The message of the oppressed classes accordingly was to be spread to reach all sections of the Black community.

This brief discussion of the Black Consciousness philosophy is essential if we are to understand the subsequent developments in the commitment by Black people to the total liberation of the Black community. SASO, incidentally, was the first organization to enunciate this theory in this form in South Africa, but soon the philosophy was to spread to embrace all aspects of Black life so as to grip the very souls of a people who were continuing their centuries-old search for a means towards self-determination and resumption of total political and economic control over their fatherland.

Social research is understood to mean a careful, scientific search of inquiry or a course of critical investigation into the mutual relations of classes of human beings (*Concise Oxford Dictionary*). Though the Black Consciousness movement was not interested in erudite, academic understanding of society and its social and political concerns, it set out a critique of the position of the Black man, an understanding of the true nature of the oppressive society in South Africa and sought to motivate the oppressed masses and to galvanize them into a formidable force that could bring about a social revolution.

SASO expressed this commitment as representing the interests of students 'on all issues that affect them in their academic and community situation'.[6] This objective necessitated a critique of South African society and in particular the education system that was then available for Black people in terms of Bantu, Coloured and Indian education departments of the Nationalist Government.

It is now useful to analyse the aims and ideological foundations of Bantu education. It shall be accepted in this chapter that the education programme for Coloureds and Indians also falls into this category of government policy.

In this chapter I shall seek to point out that not all those who oppose Bantu education do so for the same reasons. I shall also argue that for Black people the alternative to Bantu education is not necessarily the same education that the Whites in South Africa receive. I suggest that the national objectives of the two peoples are so divergent as to be in conflict with each other. I shall seek to establish the thesis that what Blacks seek in the current South African situation are mental tools that will enable them to reach their national goal. It seems to me fair to say that most of the creative thinking within the Black Consciousness movement was possible because for once, being on their own, Blacks could determine their own goals unobstructed by competing claims upon them by liberal White people who seek to soothe their own consciences. There was a move from Black visibility within the National Union of South African Students (NUSAS) to Black participation and creativity in the Black Consciousness movement.

A word of explanation about the terms used in this text is necessary. Whenever convenient the words used officially by the government will be retained. This does not imply in any way this author's acceptance of what the Black Students' Manifesto calls 'definitions that have been imposed upon (the Black man) by an arrogant White world'. Black will be used to refer to Africans, Coloured and Indian South Africans. Whenever it becomes necessary to differentiate between them the above terms will be used. Terms like 'Native', and 'Bantu' belong to government terminology at various stages.

This chapter dwells extensively on the activities of the South African Students' Organization. That is unavoidable in a discussion of this nature because SASO had concerned itself with these matters even before other Black Consciousness organizations did so. But it will be fair to say, I think, that the views expressed here are an accurate representation of the thinking within the Black Consciousness movement.

In his short account of *The Education for the Bantu of South Africa*,[7] G. W. Sneesby hopes that what he calls a 'factual account' will be of value to people in the United Kingdom and elsewhere. While Sneesby states that 'far from the present system of Bantu education being completely revolutionary, one imposed in recent years, it has very largely grown out of the old order of things'.[8] He also seeks to demonstrate that 'very substantial progress in the education of the Bantu has been made'.[9] It is not the intention of this writer to refute the extravagant claims of the apologists for Bantu education; suffice it to say that the former statement is only a half-truth and the latter can be proved to be altogether false.

Bantu education must be and was seen by the Nationalists as a revolutionary step away from the system, in their eyes, that had the effect of creating Blacks who aspired to be Whites and thus threatened their monopoly of intellectual and political superiority. M. D. C. de Wet Nel[10] stated in Parliament on 2 April 1945:

> I say there should be a reform of the whole educational system and it must be based on the culture and background and the whole life of the native himself in his tribe.[11]

De Wet Nel later became Minister in charge of Bantu education. According to J. N. le Roux[12] the threat posed by the system of education then available was that there would be no one to do manual labour if everybody is offered academic education: '... we should so conduct our schools that the native who attends those schools will know that to a great extent he must be a labourer in the country'.[13]

De Wet Nel's use of the word 'reform' was a classic understatement because what indeed happened after 1955 was of a revolutionary nature. Its ripples were to be felt in the events that led to the Soweto uprisings of 1976.

What Bantu education did was to remove the partnership between the education authorities and the Churches who were jointly responsible for the provision of Black education. In terms of this policy the syllabuses were set by the education authorities and the same examinations were taken by all the students in the same level of education. It is true that, in terms of this system, Black people had no say in the education of their children. However, even when Black education was placed on an unashamedly political footing, Blacks still had no voice in policy-making. A whole array of advisory channels were created which led to administrative ineptitude and tied Black education much more tightly to the apron-strings of doctrinaire Afrikaner political ideology. By this process, therefore, Black education was to become a political football thrown hither and thither at the whim of an oppressive machinery.

From colonial days, education for Black people had always been destined to conquer the minds of the Black people of South Africa through the advent of dominion status and up to the Nationalists today. For a long time Blacks were given only enough education to enable them to become useful members of the conquered race. Honour and respect, if not awe for the master-race, were inculcated very studiously. Therefore very few Blacks passed through the ranks of the educated. Many who were educated were absorbed by the system as teachers (often very lowly qualified) and clergymen. Leadership had to remain firmly in White hands. The result was that attitudes of élitism were prevalent among the educated class.

In his so-called historical approach G. W. Sneesby conveniently omits mentioning the ideological foundations of what the Nationalists came to call Bantu education. In her book *Forbidden Pastures*[14] Freda Troup traces the development of ideas on education since the Nationalists took over as the governing party in South Africa. The Eiselen[15] Commission's terms of reference were clearly based on the principles of the Christian National Education which had been the bedrock of Nationalist ideological thinking since the beginning of the Second World War. The brief stated that the commission of enquiry must

> formulate the principles and aims of education for Natives as an independent race, in which their past and present, their inherent racial qualities, their distinctive characteristics and aptitude and their needs under ever-changing social conditions are taken into consideration . . .[16]

It must be observed from these terms of reference that the so-called 'Natives' had 'distinctive characteristics and aptitude'. Their educational needs were so fundamentally different from those of the Whites as to demand a commission of inquiry to look into them and make recommendations. This was to lead Freda Troup to comment:

> This idea has become part of the stock-in-trade of the rationale of discriminatory and inferior education for Africans in South Africa.[17]

Indeed, what at first seemed to be an acknowledgement of 'difference' was to be emblazoned as inferior in subsequent practice and administration of what was later to be known as Bantu education. In many ways Blacks are being treated as inferior. The funds allocated by the government are a mere handout while attempts by Blacks themselves trying to establish an alternative system of education are being frustrated.

According to Christian National Education: 'Education should enable the young to take over from their cultural heritage everything that is good and beautiful and noble and develop it in accordance with their own gifts.'[18] However, the Institute of Christian National Education was not given to such flamboyant euphemisms. It states bluntly:

> Native education should be based on the principles of trusteeship, non-equality, and segregation; its aim to inculcate the white man's point of view of life, especially that of the Boer nation, which is the senior trustee.[19]

To the extent that the new custodians of Black education sought to 'civilize and Christianize the native', they were passing on a tradition which they received from a plethora of coterminous forces which ensured the subjugation of the Blacks by the settler race.

The Eiselen Commission duly recommended that all education should be in the medium of the mother-tongue for the first eight years. It was envisaged that this would be extended to secondary level. The official languages were also to be taught 'in such a way that the Bantu child will be able to find his way in European communities, to follow oral or written instruction and to "conduct" a simple conversation with Europeans about his work and other subjects of common interest'.[20] However, the most important recommendation was the reorganization of all education for the Bantu under a government department to be 'integrated organically with all other state efforts'.[21]

In the heat of the Parliamentary debate, the Minister of Native Affairs, Dr Hendrik Verwoerd, introducing the Bantu Education Bill was more than candid when he stated:

> Education must train and teach people in accordance with their opportunities in life according to the sphere in which they live ... Native education should be in accordance with the policy of the state ....[22]

We have seen that this policy was enshrined in the principles of Christian National Education. It must also be remembered that the Nationalists came to power on a ticket of *swart gevaar* [23] whereby the Whites were warned about the impending dangers inherent in the previous government 'native policy'. The Smuts regime was not firm 'enough', there was a danger of integration with the resultant threat to race purity. Therefore Verwoerd stated:

> I will reform it [education for the Africans] so that natives will be taught from childhood to realize that equality with Europeans is not for them ....[24]

Later he said:

> 'it is of no avail for him to receive a training which has as its aim absorption in the European community.[25]

To Verwoerd, the White society (he calls them Europeans) were 'green pastures ... in which [the Native] is not allowed to graze'.[26] It was not that Verwoerd was himself leading Blacks to any pastures that were greener than those of the Whites. He was to commit Blacks to an intellectual aridity that would set them on the road to retardation. Their growth as individuals and as a community was to be stunted effectively by the deliberate policies of the government.

This system of apartheid in education was to be extended to the universities. The University College of Fort Hare[27] was the only institution of higher learning that was specifically set aside for Blacks. Fort Hare has often been lauded by the supporters of what is called universal or liberal education. Yet in his research J. Hunt Davis found that Fort Hare was established in reaction to the alleged bad influences brought back home by Blacks who had gone to the United States for university education.[28] It was an experiment in the control of Blacks by providing education merely for utilitarian purposes. Side by side with Fort Hare, there were Black students at the so-called 'open' universities of Cape Town and Witwatersrand where separate social and cultural facilities were provided for Blacks though they sat in the same lecture rooms as the Whites. In his critique of this system Willie A. Maree, then Minister of Bantu Education, felt that this made 'second-class students' of non-Whites.[29] He feared that it would create hatred towards the Whites. It seems fair to state clearly from the very outset that no Black could be deluded into thinking that the prevailing system was perfect. It reflected a great deal on the hypocrisy of the White liberal university establishments. In fact Dr. T. Alty, Chancellor of Rhodes University, which conferred degrees on Fort Hare graduates, stated:

> At present each and every university in South Africa has the right to say which students will be admitted. We hold it as a right. We are jealous of our rights and of the fact that we have a few Non-European students.[30]

It is quite clear that they used this right to shut out many Black students and to pride themselves on having admitted 'a few Non-European students'.[31] In the light of this, Dr Verwoerd's fears of mixed universities were unfounded:

> If they got their way and the mixed universities emerged, leaders among both white and non-white students would arise who would favour a mixed society, and there would be no opportunity at a later stage to bring about separation.[32]

There was to be no integration under any circumstances. Verwoerd actually expressed the fear that if integration were allowed where 'white and non-white sat together ... it followed inevitably that South Africa would become a mixed society in which the "Black masses" would rule'.[33] One suspects, however, that this prescription was shared by many university administrators, because they accepted too few Black students to their universities, as most of the places were reserved for Whites who were in any case in a privileged position. There would necessarily have been few Blacks who qualified for university entrance because the school system was loaded against aspiring Black university material. In fact, in the same debate Sir de Villiers Graaff stated that

> Whereas the universities had in the past co-operated to uphold the country's social conventions, they would in future be compelled to do as they were told.[34]

Insisting that the government policy was justified Maree stated that

> The government could not and would not allow the retention of institutions which not only refused to practise this policy (i.e. separate development) but directly opposed it, and it was therefore necessary for the government to have control of Fort Hare.[35]

He went on to say that at Fort Hare representation on the governing bodies was on the basis of equality and therefore:

> These practices must arouse the 'futile expectation' that academic status would enable the non-white to overcome discrimination and would make him an agitator against South Africa's racial pattern instead of a valuable member of his own community.[36]

Mrs Margaret Ballinger in the same debate decried the fact that

> a white council nominated by a white Minister would say who the university would teach and how, what and by whom the students would be taught. The only people who would have no say in the development of African culture would be the African.[37]

In the wake of the controversy over government moves to control university education according to its policy of separate development, Dr Verwoerd, then Prime Minister, delivered a significant speech at the Afrikaner University of Stellenbosch. He stated that universities had played an invaluable part in developing the Afrikaner people. If 'Natives studied at White universities, they might not want to return to their own people who would thus lose potential leaders'.[38] This does not necessary follow. Verwoerd could not produce evidence that African leaders who had forsaken their people had done so because of the education they received. Many were in the leadership of political organizations that sought to represent the will of their people. What Verwoerd's otherwise laudable assertion hid, however, was the hideous idea that Blacks had to be tailor-made to fit into the style of government policy.

The Afrikaners Dr Verwoerd refers to were able to rise to a position of dominance because they received very favourable terms after they had been defeated in the Anglo-Boer War in terms of the Treaty of Vereeniging in 1902 and they were grafted into the scheme that was intended to ensure that Blacks would have no stake in the new political order created by the South Africa Act 1910. They used to great effect a favourable political climate, built a sound political base by using the constitution that gave them a foothold and protected their rights. The Afrikaner had power. For Blacks it was a totally different story. They had no power. The Whites had consistently manipulated the Westminster constitution and nudged out, first the few Cape Africans who were on the Common Voters' Roll by qualified franchise, and then, in 1956, by unconstitutional trickery eventually removed the Coloureds.

Article 26 (2) of the Universal Declaration of Human Rights states that

> Education shall be directed to the full development of the human personality and to the strengthening of respect for human rights and fundamental freedoms. It shall promote understanding, tolerance and friendship among all nations, racial or religious groups ...[39]

Article 1 of the Unesco Convention against Discrimination in Education defines discrimination as including

> any distinction, exclusion, limitation or preference which, being based on race, colour, sex, language, religion, political or other opinion, national or social origin, economic condition or birth, has the purpose or effect of nullifying or impairing equality of treatment in education and in particular:
> (a) Of depriving any person or group of persons of access to education of any type or at any level;
> (b) Of limiting any person or group of persons to education of an inferior standard'...[40]

It is necessary to point out that South Africa is not a signatory to this convention. It certainly does not adhere to the notions of human Rights proposed by international organizations. Verwoerd himself greatly opposed all universalism in education and detested what in his view amounted to instructions by the international community which he regarded as interference in domestic affairs of South Africa. It will be remembered that it was General Smuts, then Prime Minister of South Africa, who was instrumental in the insertion of a clause in the Charter of the United Nations Organization declaring the domestic policies of Member States to be sacrosanct. Yet the declaration and the Unesco convention provide a basis, at least a starting-point, for a critique of education policies adopted by successive White minority governments of South Africa.

During the debate of the Separate Universities Bill and the Fort Hare Transfer Act, Maree, the Minister of Bantu Education, chided the opposition for not knowing Bantu leaders. When they referred to these they meant the African National Congress, yet he had received a cable from Bantu Chief Sigcau extolling the virtues of the Fort Hare Bill and the right of Xhosas, I presume, to have their own universities. The African National Congress organized a boycott of schools in protest against Bantu education on 12 April 1955. By so doing ANC was expressing Black opposition to Bantu education and rejected the right of the Nationalist Government to hold the monopoly of total policy in the education of the African child. It was feared by Black people that Bantu education would lead to the lowering of standards. As Dr Verwoerd insisted on the value of African leaders remaining in their community to lead them at Stellenbosch in 1959, two leaders of the African National Congress, Chief Albert J. Lutuli and Oliver R. Tambo, received banning orders preventing them from attending any gatherings. The ANC-led boycott certainly did not achieve what it set out to establish—an alternative system of education, but it had clearly managed to sow seeds not only of suspicion about the real motives of the government but, also, of rejection by Black people of the system of Bantu education that came into the open in 1976.

In its protest against the Fort Hare Bill the Governing Council and Senate of the University College of Fort Hare protested that 'a compulsory rigid division between Europeans and non-Europeans is neither necessary nor desirable nor is it practicable.'[41] The protest note further stated that

> there can be no objection to separate non-compulsory non-European colleges, but there can be no justification for the proposed compulsory ethnic division advocated for a college of intellectual Bantu.[42]

A note that was to be the guiding light for generations of Fort Hare students was struck by SRC President, J. M. Majola: 'We will fight on until we have attained our rights.'[43] He went on to say:

> Only one brick need fall to send the whole pillar of apartheid crashing to the ground ... On this earth where we now stand, our freedom was taken away. On this very earth we can gain the knowledge to free ourselves again.[44]

In the light of the events of 1976 J. M. Majola's statement had a prophetic ring about it. It is he who put the whole protest movement unashamedly in the context of a people struggling for political rights. The struggle for liberation indeed was to be learnt and enacted, ironically, in the very colleges which were designed to control the mental processes of Black people.

Dr T. Alty, in his protest address at Rhodes University stated that

> Universities are very specialized institutions, with very special rights and privileges developed during the past. They carry with them the right to stand aloof from the stress and strain of everyday politics.[45]

For Black students and members of the academic community, nothing could be further from the truth as SASO was to demonstrate decades later. The academic community cannot divorce itself from the concerns of the community. Mr Majola stated that much to the students at Fort Hare and to the world at large. For Blacks, education must be an instrument of liberation.

The Right Reverend Ambrose Reeves, then Bishop of Johannesburg,[46] stated that an open university was

> a university in which the members of staff who do not accept a particular line, even a Christian line, are not outlawed; a university in which no views will be suppressed as dangerous.

What was being imposed upon universities, he said, was

> a particular pattern which would conform to the theory of apartheid, a pattern which down the years might well make it impossible for them to exercise those functions for which universities properly existed.

Internationally, 1968 was generally regarded as the year of the student. There were protests in the Federal Republic of Germany, France and the United States of America against the prevailing status quo. Young people rejected the norms of society and sought to inject new values into their communities. In South Africa, protest was sparked off by the refusal of the government to allow the appointment of a Black academic to the staff of the University of Cape Town. The whole principle of academic freedom was revived. At Fort Hare[47] the issue took on other dimensions. The students protested against the inferior quality and incompatibility of the lecturing staff, most of whom were drawn from Afrikaner universities for purposes of indoctrination. Many were barely able to speak English, let alone to teach in the language. The lecture room became the battleground for ideological conflicts between lecturer and student and it was no longer the arena for the common pursuit of knowledge. Students were concerned about discrepancies in salaries and authority between White and Black lecturing staff. No Black lecturer could be senior to a White one, however highly qualified he might be in comparison with his White colleague. All these sentiments were expressed by the students in the only manner that was open to them.

What exacerbated student feelings was the appearance on the campus of one Blaar Coetzee[48] till then Deputy Minister of Bantu Education. He became notorious for his avowal that he would be able to stem and later reverse the flow of Bantu to the urban areas by 1978. Students duly demonstrated against his presence on the campus and that of the new rector who was to be instituted. This was a great embarrassment to the Nationalist establishment at Fort Hare.

The Fort Hare episode provided various lessons for Black students. It hastened the most pressing need for an organization that would not only demonstrate the solidarity of the Black students, but which would also formulate Black student opinion on the education they were receiving and the institutions at which they were learning. There was minimal contact between the students at Turfloop[49] and Ngoye[50] let alone at the Western Cape[51] and Durban-Westville.[52] The first meeting of Black students held at Marianhill in December 1968 expressed itself purely in terms which sought to promote solidarity between Black students. In time SASO was to move from student power to Black power.

In remote Turfloop in the Transvaal Highveld, Onkgopotse R. Tiro[53] was to shock the gathering of academics and White patrons of Bantu education. Tiro was a gifted orator. He devoted his speech to an attack on discrimination even within Bantu education. He attacked the government for failing to abide by its own policies of giving control of Black universities to the Blacks. All opportunity and privilege was still reserved for Whites. 'My dear people,' he said, 'shall we ever get a fair deal in this land? The land of our fathers.'[54] He noted:

> The system is failing because even those who recommend it strongly, as the only solution to racial problems in South Africa, fail to adhere to the letter and spirit of the policy . . .[55]

> The fault of all wrongful actions in South Africa ... rests on all those who do not actively dissociate themselves from and work for the eradication of the system breeding such evils. [56]

The reaction of the university authorities to Tiro's speech was swift. During that same week-end Tiro was summoned before the disciplinary committee and summarily dismissed from the university. He was given no opportunity to defend himself. The SRC quickly responded by calling upon all students to boycott the lectures and demanded the reinstatement of their fellow student. The authorities suspended the SRC and the entire student body was suspended, lectures terminated and police called in 'to restore order'.

Even before SASO could issue a directive, various campuses staged protests against the expulsion of the students of Turfloop. By then, in addition to Tiro, the entire SRC and the campus leadership of SASO were expelled. The University of the Western Cape in Bellville was immersed in very determined student action that defied both the rector and the police. Again SASO was blamed. Stiffer regulations on student activities were formulated. The South African Students' Organization assembled student leaders at the Federal Theological Seminary at Alice where a Declaration was passed whereby all Black students were called upon not only to boycott classes, but to work actively for the eradication of Bantu education. The following weeks were to see a massive demonstration of student power and Black solidarity. All Black campuses were declared battlegrounds against racist education. The parents were also involved in all activities in support of the students. Commenting on the May/June strikes the pamphlet *SASO on the Attack* commented:

> Basically, Tiro's speech constructively opened the eyes of the people to the flaws and evils of the racist educational structure. But this Black truth was turned into a white lie by the authorities at [the university of] 'the North'.[57]

The occasion of the strikes provided Black students with the opportunity to examine their own theories of education. The question constantly on the lips of students was that 'We shall close down these universities permanently and what do we put in their place?' The result was a complete re-evaluation of all the hallowed notions about the universal, liberal education leading to education as an expression of a people's quest for liberation and a grappling with their common destiny.

Dr D. G. S. Mtimkulu represents the conception of education in the mind of the African as a quest

> for integration into the democratic structure and institutions of the country. To them one of the most effective ways of achieving this is by education—an education essentially in no way different from or inferior to that of other sections of the community.[58]

I find it very difficult to accept this thesis. It seems to me that he fails to understand, in the first place, that there are no democratic institutions in South Africa. An awareness of that fact on the part of Blacks will lead them to the political aspirations to which education must lead them. In whatever way one looks at it, education is a tool in the hands of the user. For the ruling class, it is an institution that must be captured in order to control the minds of the subjects and to lead them to an understanding and acceptance of their place in society. For the oppressed, it must open horizons to an understanding of the truth about the world and to the search for a means of breaking through the mental and physical stranglehold of the oppressor. One seeks to use education to ensure perpetual domination and the other is determined to use it for liberation within the shortest possible time. Dr Mtimkulu's understanding of education is exactly what leads to élitism in the Black community and those who have the means and manage to reach the mountain-top seek only individual salvation and ignore their wider commitment to the oppressed community.

Richard Shaull states this view very clearly when he writes:

> In fact those who, in learning to read and write, come to a new awareness of selfhood and begin to look critically at the social situation in which they find themselves, often take the initiative in acting to transform the society that has denied them this opportunity of participation. Education is once again a subversive force.[59]

Shaull here obviously talks about the training of illiterates but the same principle applies to any who are deprived of an education that is fulfilling and ensures human dignity. Paulo Freire makes the valid point that the oppressed must indeed take charge of their own education:

> Who are better prepared than the oppressed to understand the terrible significance of an oppressed society? Who suffer the effects of oppression more than the oppressed? Who can better understand the necessity of liberation? It will not be defined by chance but through the praxis of their quest for it, through recognizing the necessity to fight for it.[60]

The danger in Dr Mtimkulu's idea is that those educated in that colourless world of the oppressor fall into the trap of the structure of their thought, becoming conditioned by the 'contradictions of the concrete, existential situation by which they were shaped'.[61] Their model of humanity is the White man, who is privileged, educated, does not work hard and lives in luxury and comfort. He becomes divorced from the concerns of his people and is so many removes from them as to become a pale reflection of the oppressor himself.

> Their vision of the new man is individualistic; because of their identification with the oppressor they have no consciousness of themselves as persons or as members of the oppressed class.[62]

Such people merely want to mimic the oppressive class, in fact, to become better oppressors of the less privileged.

On this understanding of education, therefore, men are brought to a critical recognition of the causes of their oppression so that through revolutionary action they can create a new situation, one which makes possible the pursuit of full humanity. Paulo Freire defines the pedagogy of the oppressed as an instrument for their critical discovery that both they and their oppressors are manifestations of dehumanization. In his introduction Richard Shaull sums up the position of the radical in this way:

> The radical committed to a human liberation, does not become the prisoner of a 'circle of certainty' within which he also imprisons reality. On the contrary the more radical he is, the more fully he enters into reality so that, knowing it better, he can better transform it.[63]

This understanding of education for liberation eschews notions that Blacks want the same education that is provided for Whites by the same government that oppresses them. The fundamental objection of the new radicals of the Black Consciousness movement was the realization that even if Blacks went to the same schools and were taught by the same teachers as those who teach Whites, while the entire system of oppression and White privilege existed, they would still be obliged to agitate for total control of the education of the Black child. Yet one understands quite well that it would be impossible to have this control as long as the instruments of power were still in the hands of the oppressor.

Another aspect of education is one which the emergent African states have been articulating. H. F. Makulu documents the development of the aims of education in Africa from the spreading of European civilization during the colonial era to that of preparing the African child to use the best elements of his tribal environment and to transform it by bringing into it what he had received from Western education. This may sound dangerously close to Dr Verwoerd's policy but Makulu points out that 'there was a definite shift from the idea of mere assimilation of western ideas to that of development from within'.[64] Though education was to broaden one's horizons, it had to be rooted in one's life experience, history and customs, if it was to be translated into a means for development and advancement. As an instrument for power, education was the key to privilege. It was seen as the door to the European's technological mysteries.

In the new Africa, education stands at the very centre of nation-building 'in its economic development, in the business of social planning and in the development of political institutions'[65]. According to this view, therefore, instead of education being seen as for the good of the individual so that he can make a contribution to the community, it is seen as a means to enable the individual to develop for the good of the community. Another aspect in which philosophy of education in independent Africa approximated that of the gurus of Bantu education was in the role of culture. Makulu states that the African leaders wished to give proper stress in education at all levels and by all possible means to their own culture. 'As the students of Africa are exposed to the scientific and cultural influences of the outside world', he says, 'they need to be grounded in the knowledge of their own cultural heritage.'[66] He diagnoses the defect of colonial education as caused by the fact that 'people from outside their culture have been judges of what is good and what is bad in African culture. This may well be the root of the prevalent misunderstanding and disrespect for the cultures of Africa.'[67] If nation-building is to be one of the most important objectives of educational policy in Africa, it not only needs to recognize the discordant elements in the various peoples but has to weld the various groups together by cultural, social and political linkages and bring them to an appreciation of their common destiny. However, Makulu again warns that the renewed call by Africans themselves for the establishment of a cultural basis to education is different from that of previous decades of educational non-development. Africans are not interested in a 'mere adaptation of a few elements from African life', he says, 'but in the whole orientation of education in relation to intrinsic African values to make it African and not merely a useful instrument of power borrowed from Europeans'.[68] Steve Biko also echoed these sentiments when he stated that the government's obsession with culture is to project an arrested image of culture.[69] The culture of the oppressed in South Africa is the one that brings together the tribal past of the various oppressed people into their present life-style under an oppressive system that enriches their human experience. In this way the oppressed are bonded by a national consciousness and a common aspiration. A syllabus designed by the oppressor merely presents the oppressor's view of our culture. His view is, of course, coloured by the oppressor's dominant self-interest. What the Whites call 'culture' in South Africa is a mere preservation of the species or specimen of the African past in the zoo of Afrikaner ideology.

'Education fails when it does not make the child understand himself and his social and cultural past and the life of the society of which he is a member.'[70] This leads one to the ideas of African personality which have done so much in instilling true patriotism. It was felt that the content and methods of education in Africa must be in line with the political will of the nation, must relate to the realities of the technological coming-of-age of the new African industrial societies as well as the imperative process of economic development. There must be a clear understanding of the common national goals in any effective educational system in Africa today.

Indeed these and similar views were debated by the South African Parliament which consists of only White people, when the controversial education measures of the Nationalists were being piloted through Parliament: the Bantu Education Bill, the University College of Fort Hare Transfer Bill and the Separate Universities Bill. The Minister of Bantu Education, W. A. Maree, went on to state that Fort Hare was nothing more than an English university for non-Whites.[71]

He promised that Fort Hare would be given a Xhosa character. He also spoke of the importance of preserving the culture of the Xhosa. The minister in charge of White education emphasized during the same debate that one of the purposes of the Bill was to induce non-Whites to be bearers of their own culture, which they must transmit to their own group. He went on to affirm that:

> They [the non-Whites] must get the opportunity to develop to the full on the basis of their identity as a people.[72]

In his Stellenbosch speech Dr Verwoerd said the following:

> They [the universities] not only train people for the professions, they also train leaders of the people, safeguard and spread knowledge, and lead the search for further knowledge.[73]

This speech led the Native Representative for Transkei, W. P. Stanford, to state that it would lead to a development of anti-European African leaders. It is necessary at this point to stress that though Verwoerd and his ministers were putting forward ideas that were in principle in keeping with a great deal of progressive thinking in education, Verwoerd still maintained a stranglehold on education of the Blacks to ensure political control. His words about culture and the nations must be seen against the background of the divide and rule policies of his government. What was good for the Bantu, according to the Nationalists, was less than what was good for the Whites. The rationale behind this attitude is well captured by Makulu when he says:

> The fear of competition for jobs and demands for equal rights pushed some White settlers to extremes and they asserted that education of the native should not be of the kind that would make him forsake his place in the tribal community. If he must be educated, his education should not encourage him to be anything beyond a good servant.[74]

The demands of the student activists of May/June 1972 imposed upon SASO the duty to convene a National Formation School. This was a method of training whereby a group of students would stay in a residential centre where they discuss matters of common interest in a seminar or in groups. At the end of it, findings are presented as the common idea of the seminar on a matter of topical interest. This event took place at the Edendale Lay Ecumenical Centre in December 1972. Prominent Black educationists, representatives from a variety of Black community organizations and students attended. The theme was 'Towards Black Education'. This was in recognition of the fact that Bantu education was not Black education. It was designed by the oppressor according to his oppressive, prejudicial and discriminatory policies. Any Blacks who were involved in that system were merely carrying out government policy. There was now a demand by Black students for a truly Black system of education that took decisive account of the needs and aspirations of Black people. The priorities of political self-determination, national consciousness and nation-building, a design to help Blacks break out of the confines of psychological enslavement imposed by the system and that education should reflect the spirit of the community in all ways, were all set out clearly in the discussions that followed. SASO's policy on education was based on:

(i) the rejection of the concept of Black universities according to the model of government policy. It asserts that the aims of the establishment of ethnic institutions was to control the education of Blacks in South Africa.

(ii) the belief that the education provided by the state for Blacks was irrelevant to the pressing needs of the Black Community as it is derived 'from a model that is not in keeping with the cultural and historical ethos of Black people'.[75]

A Charter for a Black University adopted by the Formation School was seen as laying the foundation of 'education for liberation, self-reliance and development aimed at a communalistic and egalitarian society'.[76] The charter further sets out the aims and objectives of Black education.

(a) Black education must be aimed at actualizing our aspirations for an egalitarian and communalistic society;
(b) Black education must act as a catalyst for political, social and economic change;
(c) Black education shall serve to unite Black people and promote community endeavour and foster a spirit of Black communalism;
(d) Black education should at all times inculcate into the Blackman a sense of initiative enquiry, creativity and self-reliance that will equip him with the tools to make him a meaningful member of his society. [77]

The charter ends by stating that:

> an aspect of the above endeavour would be to discourage élitism and intellectual arrogance which promotes alienation, acquisitiveness and class structure. [78]

According to SASO, therefore, Black students had to involve themselves in the community and subject their own egos to the needs of society. The alienation referred to may not be one of classical socialism, but it is a warning against the development of a mentality among the students that drove them to set themselves apart from those forces that nurtured them. Again Black Consciousness, though founded on the assumption of identity of aspirations by all Black people, still had to guard against the development within the Black community of a *petite bourgeoisie* alienated from the grass-roots of the suffering people.

But who are the Black students? Black students felt it was necessary to ask themselves this question, if they were not to drift away into a malaise of intellectualism and irrelevance.

They were first and foremost Black people—oppressed, enslaved by the strictures of the White minority regime, mentally and physically. This first realization was to help students reject an apparently privileged position in the community and the lure of being sucked into a position of relative privilege.

The students asserted that 'education in South Africa was unashamedly political'[79] and therefore believed that Black education was tied to the liberation of the Black people.

These were clear definitions that Black students were examining in South Africa through SASO and other Black Consciousness organizations. This enabled Black students in Soweto, the Cape Flats and Chatsworth to realize that the ideal of a true and meaningful education was difficult if not impossible to conceive as long as the social forces that hampered intellectual development were at play. Indeed, how can a student in Soweto see it otherwise. The school is understaffed and under-equipped with educational material. Homes are overcrowded. There is nowhere to read, and no incentive for schooling. These are the *prima facie* issues that made the students realize that they had 'a moral obligation to articulate the needs of the Black Community'.[80] Those needs could be summed up by the word 'liberation'. It was liberation that went to the root of the problems in South Africa. A wholesale removal of the status quo by revolutionary means. That was the call Black students made to the Black community. This is the message Henry Isaacs as Vice President of SASO addressed to his constituency: 'To be creators of history implies being masters of your circumstances.'[81] He went on to assert that: 'We cannot shirk the responsibility to transform this society for fear of offending the entrenched White racist political interests. Now is the time to stand up and be counted.' [82]

As a result of the demands imposed upon it by the mass exodus of students from Black university campuses between May/June 1977 and June 1973, SASO initiated the Free University Scheme. This was a partnership programme that was designed to put into practice the philosophy for Black education set out in the Charter for a Black University. Students would enrol with the University of South Africa or the University of London which offered tuition by correspondence. Seminars would be arranged to help students with their studies and also to relate these to the ideas that were enshrined in the charter. Students were also expected to take part in community development projects. Expert lecturers from among Black academics and practitioners were recruited and the scheme was launched with great hope in 1973.

A circular issued by SASO on the scheme in 1973 stated:

> Our aim is to make students become part of their oppressed communities and work meaningfully towards changing the status quo, and thereby ridding the community of the many ills that afflict it . . . Therefore, the students that will be in the Free University Scheme will be required to contribute and make available their skills for the benefit [of] and use by the Black community.

This shows a great concern by SASO not only to provide an alternative means of education to students but to stem the tide towards élitism and involve the student in the concerns of the community. It was necessary for students to be made to see that they were 'part of their oppressed community' because very often, after acquiring education, the élite seek to identify with the oppressor against their lessfortunate compatriots.

However, the Free University Scheme was never a great success. Financial considerations meant that no full-time staff could be found for it. It continued to be administered by SASO full-time staff who were involved in crisis after crisis after 1973. Many SASO leaders were banned during this time which meant that new personnel took over a project with which they were not familiar. There was no incentive for science students in the scheme because facilities for laboratory work were very difficult to organize. Besides, many of the initial intake of students had to find full-time employment. As a result, they were not able to attend seminars and to devote themselves to community development as initially envisaged. What the scheme did establish, however, was that Blacks could organize themselves to carry out their own political programme.

SASO, which was the first organization to popularize the philosophy of Black Consciousness in South Africa, soon spread these ideas through the length and breadth of Black South Africa. Its reports were widely circulated and discussion groups were formed on many campuses and schools and in the ghettos. The *SASO Newsletter* was widely read. Very soon many other organizations were founded which based themselves on the philosophy of Black Consciousness. The South Africa Students' Movement was founded in Soweto in 1970. It saw itself as a sister-organization of SASO with schools as its operational base. It published a newsletter *Thrust* which, according to *Black Review* reflected SASM's 'vigour, enthusiasm and determination'.[87] SASM soon established branches in Indian and Coloured schools in Johannesburg, the rest of the Transvaal and the Cape. In 1973, the National Youth Organization was formed. It committed itself to 'project the Black consciousness image . . .' and to work for the elimination of psychological and physical oppression of Black people.[84] These organizations were at the forefront of the activities of 1973. On the face of it the reason behind the Soweto uprisings in 1976 was the language question. Though it remains government policy that mother-tongue instruction be extended to post-primary schools, the government has decreed that 'in all secondary schools half the subjects be taught through the medium of Afrikaans and half through the medium of English'.[85] Many teachers have always resisted this on the basis that there are no suitably qualified teachers to teach in the medium of Afrikaans. This, in fact, was not a new instruction in 1976.

The Afrikaner Nationalist Government enforced the use of Afrikaans as a medium of instruction in order to assert its political supremacy. It was part of their stock-in-trade designed to conquer the minds of the Blacks and to ensure their total subjugation. Blacks did not reject Afrikaans because the Afrikaners were allies of the English. They reject Afrikaans because it represents all that Blacks over the years have been struggling against. For the Afrikaner believes that 'his adherence to and insistence upon the use of Afrikaans wherever possible have been the chief means by which Afrikaner national self-realization has been achieved and maintained'.[86] A widespread use of Afrikaans would demonstrate the Afrikaner's unchallenged dominance of the country. One can read this in Dr Andries Treurnicht's statement after the riots had erupted:

> In the white area of South Africa where the government provides the buildings, gives subsidies and pays the teachers, it is surely our right to determine the language divisions. Why are pupils sent to schools if they don't like the language divisions?[87]

To this simple mind the issue was cut and dried. Afrikaans was congruent with the government and therefore there had to be a *quid pro quo* from those who are at the receiving end. This is the notion that Blacks reject. They do not live by the grace of the government, but the taxes they pay which are disproportionate to their real income, and are used to boost Nationalist policies.

> For the year 1974-75 R131m was spent on the education of the Africans, R435m on the education of whites. In 1976 per capita expenditure was $696 for whites, $45 for Africans; teacher: pupil ratio 1:22 for whites, 1:60 for Africans... Schooling for whites is free and compulsory; for Africans it is not compulsory and African parents must find money for fees, uniforms and books. [88]

In May 1976, the General Students' Council of SASM passed a resolution 'totally rejecting the policy of Bantu Education, and especially the use of Afrikaans as a medium of instruction.'[89] The Soweto Students' Representative Council was formed as an Action Committee of SASM with regional responsibility. It was charged

> to coordinate and arrange meetings and demonstrations in support of SASM's policy on Bantu Education and Africaans medium in schools. [90]

During the trial of eleven leaders of SASM and SSRC a Dr A. B. Fourie of the Bantu education Department told the court that Bantu education was in no way inferior to the education offered to Whites. He did not believe that Bantu education was designed to keep Blacks in an inferior position. Even the judge had to remind Fourie of the words of Verwoerd to that effect. Fourie had to concur with defence counsel's suggestion that 'after June 1976, 503 out of 700 teachers in Soweto resigned, and of 27'000 pupils only 14'000 were left', and this was 'one of the greatest tragedies in the history of this country'.[91] Testifying at the same trial the Right Reverend Dr Manas Buthelezi, Chairman of the Black Parents' Association, stated that Black education was of great importance and that the differences between it and White education had been of great concern to the Black community. 'Education was an important liberating factor which created hope,'[92] he said. The disparities in education and the discrimination that the above figures lay bare testifies to the root of the problem.

The events of 1976 were a trial not only of Bantu education as such but also of the political system. The students of Soweto were under no illusion about the nature of the struggle.

Soon after the Soweto revolts, Justice Minister J. Kruger appointed a one-man Commission of Inquiry into the cause of the student uprisings. The commission immediately heard a succession of White 'experts' on Blacks. It was scorned by Blacks as being inconsequential, proving nothing and solving nothing. In many ways the Nationalists have pre-empted the findings of the commission in declaring certain anti-government organizations illegal, banning activists and detaining and charging others for criminal offences.

In their concern with agitators they are ignoring the real problems. Two statements in this regard are worth noting. A Soweto teacher told the court recently: 'Black children were aware of the differences in education and did not need inciting.'[93]

The Right Reverend Desmond Tutu, now General Secretary of the South African Council of Churches, puts it even more clearly when he says:

> I do not need agitators to tell me that this system is oppressive and unjust. I don't have to be told by agitators that I am getting a raw deal in my own country.[94]

He speaks for many in Soweto when he speaks thus. Trial upon trial took place with indecent haste. The leaders of Black Consciousness were the prime targets of detention, arrest and banning.

Soweto presents a microcosm of the feelings of revolutionary zeal in the hearts of many young Blacks. Black Consciousness was soon noticed as the driving force behind much of the thinking that is going on in the townships. Judge Snyman, who was appointed Commissioner on the 1974 strikes at Turfloop, blamed SASO largely for spreading subversive ideas. He said that

> it is not a true student's organization, and membership is not limited to students. Its policy cannot be distinguished from that of a political party. The organization has a comprehensive political policy embracing virtually every facet of South Africa and South Africa's international politics . . . So, the aim of Black consciousness, and therefore, of SASO is the overthrow of the present system in South Africa.[95]

In his reply the then SASO president, Diliza Mji, was very emphatic:

> Because these ills are anchored in the whole apartheid structure it is not possible to separate the educational system from apartheid, not possible to hit at the educational system without hitting at apartheid.[96]

Kruger blamed the Black Consciousness movement, the African National Congress and the Pan Africanist Congress for the student uprisings. The Black Peoples' Convention chose to observe ruefully:

> It is high time that the government accepted once and for all that what they regard as being good for Blacks is often rightly seen as poison by Blacks.[97]

Soweto, therefore, saw the emergence of the new brand of the Black man. The *Survey of Race Relations in South Africa, 1976*, comments as follows:

> The authentic student leaders appeared to be dedicated, intelligent, militant young activists, fearless people with no family responsibilities owning no property . . .[98]

Though the South African Institute of Race Relations in this view is expressing the opinion of the Progressive Reform Party in prescribing bourgeois capitalist solutions, they accurately portray the calibre of the student militants. South Africa was to see the appearance of unashamedly independent people dedicated to the restoration of their birthright. Fear was banished for ever in the minds of the people. Passive resistance was a thing of the past.

The Times of India commenting on the Soweto revolts observed: 'This psychological revolution cannot be undone, whatever else happens in South Africa in the short run.'[99]

The young Black people have altered the face of apartheid in South Africa. Though many suffered, are in gaol or are harrassed and victimized, yet their sense of self-respect has been buoyed. Bantu Education has undergone cosmetic changes. Soweto shook the moral foundations of Afrikaner ideology. The greatest impact of the student uprisings was in the radicalization of the Black community. There is now a renewed invigorated community spirit. Black solidarity has become a fact and is here to stay. The students established their right to intellectual independence as a prelude to social and political emancipation.

But what are the implications for social research in South Africa? In the last decade or so, South Africa has been bombarded with a huge volume of critical thinking on the ordering of its society. The mind of man was to break through all artificial strictures that imprison the mind. South Africa is a state whose totalitarian nature is complete. Through the student initiative the veil was lifted and the state laid bare to a critical evaluation. The claims to peace and democracy could no longer be sustained as the people themselves exposed the lie.

Notes

1. The South African Students' Organization was inaugurated at a conference of representatives from Black universities, colleges and seminaries at the University of the North, Turfloop, near Pietersburg, Transvaal, in July 1969. Steve Biko, who died in the custody of the security police on 12 September 1977, was elected President. Membership of SASO was open only to African, Coloured and Indian students.
2. SASO Policy Manifesto, Article 4(b)(i).
3. Ibid., Article 4(b)(iv).
4. Ibid., Article 2.
5. Ibid.
6. 'Aims and Objects', SASO Constitution.
7. G. W. Sneesby, *The Education of the Bantu in South Africa*, Britain and South Africa Forum, 1974. Mr Sneesby was an Inspector of Schools in the Bantu Education Department.
8. Ibid., p. 3. In saying this Sneesby seeks to justify Bantu education in the eyes of his British readers by alleging that it was a continuation of British colonial policy.
9. Ibid.
10. M. D. C. de Wet Nel was a member of the Nationalist (Opposition) Party during General Smuts' post-war government. He later became minister responsible for the application of Nationalist race policies. When he retired from that position he became Commissioner-General of the Venda National Unit.
11. Quoted in *Apartheid: Its Effects on Education, Science, Culture and Information*, p. 33, Paris, Unesco, 1972.
12. J. N. le Roux later became a prominent member of successive Nationalist Governments.

14. Freda Troup, *Forbidden Pastures: Education under Apartheid,* London, International Defence and Aid Fund for Southern Africa, 1976. This book, published in April, a few months before the outbreak in Soweto, could not have been more timely. It focuses on a matter that was topical after Soweto.
15. Dr W. M. M. Eiselen was Chairman of the Commission of Inquiry that led to the Bantu education system. He later became Commissioner-General of the North Sotho ethnic group and first Chancellor of the University of the North.
16. Quoted in Troup, op. cit., p. 18.
17. Ibid.
18. Quoted in Troup, op. cit., p. 21. On the significance of Christian National Education and the Institute of Christian National Education see Troup, op. cit., pp. 18-21 and *Apartheid . . .,* op. cit., pp. 33-5.
19. Quoted in Troup, op. cit., p. 20.
20. Quoted in Troup, op. cit., p. 21. G. W. Sneesby does not mention that this is the motivation for the teaching of official languages. He writes: 'There has been a great deal of misrepresentation of the present situation regarding medium of instruction in schools . . . it has been stated that English is forbidden as a medium of instruction. . . . Such a statement gives a distorted picture of the actual position.' One immediately notices Sneesby's own distortion when he does not state that only as much English was to be taught as would enable the child to be a good servant.
21. Ibid.
22. Quoted in *Apartheid . . .,* op. cit., p. 37.
23. Black danger or menace.
24. Quoted in Troup, op. cit., p. 22.
25. Ibid.
26. Ibid.
27. Founded in 1916 as a college for higher learning for Africans. However, by 1959 there were also Coloured and Indian students. During the debate on the University College of Fort Hare Transfer Bill, the Opposition constantly referred to this institution as one of the last vestiges of the English heritage left in South Africa.
28. Hunt Davis Jr is First Vice-President in the Centre for African Studies in the University of Florida.
29. *Keesings Contemporary Archives,* 30 May to 6 June 1959, p. 16843.
30. *Eastern Province Herald,* 6 April 1959.
31. Ibid.
32. *Keesings Contemporary Archives,* op. cit., p. 16843.
33. Ibid.
34. Ibid.
35. Ibid.
36. Ibid.
37. *Keesing's Contemporary Archives,* op. cit., p. 16844.
38. *Eastern Province Herald,* 26 February 1959.
39. Quoted in *Apartheid . . .,* op. cit., p. 30, and Leslie Rubin, *Universal Declaration of Human Rights in South Africa,* p. 43, South Africa Information Programme of the International University Exchange Fund.
40. Ibid.
41. *Eastern Province Herald,* 14 February 1959.
42. Ibid.
43. *Eastern Province Herald,* 29 October 1959.
44. Ibid.
45. *Eastern Province Herald,* 6 April 1959.
46. Bishop Ambrose Reeves was deported from South Africa after the Sharpeville massacres of 1961.
47. The writer was a student at the University College of Fort Hare from 1966 to 1968. He was expelled with twenty-one others after the strikes in September 1968.
48. He was appointed Minister for Community Development, a portfolio that carries out the Group Areas Act.
49. The University College of the North, later the University of the North, is located at Turfloop near Pietersburg. It is set aside only for the Sotho-, Tswana-, Pedi-, Venda- and Shangaan-speaking students.
50. Ngoye, the University College of Zululand, later called the University of Zululand, located at Empangeni, accepts only Zulu- and Swazi-speaking students.

51. The University College of the Western Cape was later called the University of the Western Cape. It is at Bellville, Cape, and is open only to Coloured students.
52. The University College of Durban-Westville became the University of Durban-Westville for Indians only.
53. O. R. Tiro was immediate past President of the Students' Representative Council at Turfloop. In 1973, he escaped to Botswana where he was killed by a parcel bomb in 1974.
54. Quoted from Denis Herbstein, *White Man We Want to Talk to You,* pp. 72-73, London, Penguin Books, 1978.
55. Ibid.
56. Ibid.
57. *SASO on the Attack: An Introduction to the South African Students' Organisation,* p. 6, 1973.
58. Quoted in *Apartheid . . .,* op. cit., p. 35.
59. Introduction by Richard Shaull in Paulo Freire, *Pedagogy of the Oppressed,* p. 9, Penguin Books, 1972. Paulo Freire's works, particularly the psycho-social method of literacy training, were widely used by Black Consciousness groups.
60. Freire, op. cit., p. 22.
61. Ibid.
62. Ibid.
63. Ibid.
64. H. F. Makulu, *Education, Development and Nationbuilding in Independent Africa,* p. 18, London, SCM Press, 1971. In his Foreword to this work President Kenneth Kaunda of Zambia says of the role of education in confronting the problems facing Africa: 'This is the collective challenge facing today's young Africans, and posterity stands to condemn them if they fail to live up to their responsibilities by assuming an insular approach to the role of education, and failing to take up as their mission the educational upgrading of all those capable of this in the societies in which they live. . . .'
65. Makulu, op. cit., p. 31.
66. Ibid.
67. Ibid.
68. Ibid., p. 34.
69. Steve Biko, *I Write What I Like,* pp. 40-7, London, Bowerdean Press, 1978.
70. Makulu, op. cit., p. 35.
71. *Eastern Province Herald,* 23 April 1959.
72. *Eastern Province Herald,* 9 April 1959. The minister went on to say: 'We want to make provision for them in separate institutions so that they can develop autonomy on their own basis.' The United [Opposition] Party spokesman, M. P. Bowker retorted: 'The government is demonstrating to the world its incapability and immaturity to govern the Native people of this country. You [the Minister] talk of Xhosa culture. I wonder what a Bushman university would look like? Bushmen would probably not be allowed to paint on white canvas. You would keep them in the rocks—and that is just where you are putting Fort Hare.'
73. *Eastern Province Herald,* 26 February 1959. The Nationalists made effective use of overseas authorities to establish the validity of their course of action. For instance, the Minister of Education, Arts and Science, J. J. Serfontein quoted Ortega Y. Gasset, the Spanish philosopher-statesman and Thomas Hodgkin. All parties in that Parliament were committed to the suppression of Black people but they differed in the methods to be used.
74. Makulu, op. cit., p. 18.
75. *SASO on the Attack . . .,* op. cit., p. 6.
76. Ibid.
77. Ibid.
78. Ibid.
79. Ibid.
80. Ibid.
81. Ibid.
82. Ibid.
83. P. M. Gwala (ed.), *Black Review, 1973,* p. 63, Durban, Black Community Programmes, 1974.
84. Gwala (ed.), op. cit., p. 64.
85. Sneesby, op. cit., p. 9.
86. Ibid., p. 11.

87. *The Star* (Johannesburg).
88. Rubin, op. cit., p. 44.
89. From transcripts of the matter, State V. Twala and ten others (unreported), popularly known as the 'trial of the Sowetoll'.
90. The defence at the trial denied that the Action Committee was the predecessor or had anything to do with SASM.
91. *Rand Daily Mail*, 28 November 1978.
92. *Post*, 27 February 1979.
93. *Rand Daily Mail*, 14 November 1978.
94. *The Star* (Johannesburg).
95. Thoko Mbanjwa (ed.), *Black Review, 1975/6*, p. 155.
96. Ibid., p. 156.
97. Ibid., p. 103.
98. *A Survey of Race Relations in South Africa, 1976*, p. 69, Johannesburg, Institute of Race Relations, 1976.
99. Mbanjwa, op. cit., p. 104.
100. *Post*, 9 June 1979.

10 Structural and cultural factors in a liberated South Africa

John Rex

The society which was brought into being in the Union of South Africa as a result of European imperialism and colonialism is one which involves in a unique way class formations and ethnic formations, a form of class struggle and, also, processes generated by ethnic pluralism. It is obviously a matter of argument as to how exactly these processes intersect and overlap at the present time. Some see the situation as one of relatively straight forward class struggle under capitalist conditions. Others speak of a class struggle involving two separate working classes. Some speak of a single capitalist economy, others of a dual economy and society. Some see the polity and ruling ideologies as being at odds with the imperatives of capitalism. Others see these as serving capitalism's basic needs. Finally, some see the conflicts within the society as exhaustively explained in terms of class struggle, while others suggest that there is an irreducible pluralist element involved in the society's political make-up.[1]

This article is not in the main an attempt to enter these debates about the sociology of South Africa's present. Its central aim is the speculative one of considering what elements will confront one another if, as seems likely during the next few years, a combination of pressures including those of external guerrilla pressure, internal disturbances in both rural and urban areas, and Big Power competition for influence, lead to the overthrow of White political dominance. In such a situation the various social segments which have been constituted under present conditions and whose present *raison d'être* arises from those conditions, will confront one another anew and will develop new relations with one another and so constitute a new social formation. As M. G. Smith has pointed out in his *The Plural Society in the British West Indies,* the various segments of a plural society are held together by the political dominance of one of them, with the consequence that the very existence of the society is threatened when this domination ends.[2] In these circumstances, it is necessary to look at the nature of the segments, the circumstances of the overthrow of the existing order, and the possibility of new relationships arising.

I have attempted elsewhere[3] to outline the elements involved in a general typology of colonial societies. It is not possible to repeat this here in full, but since the placement of the South African social type within such a typology is essential to the transcendence of the class versus pluralism debate, it is necessary to indicate its main lines here.

Colonial societies, I see to be constituted, through the penetration of societies of varying degrees of complexity by the advanced commercial and industrial nations (usually capitalist ones)[4] either through trade and tax-farming, through the forcible expropriation of goods and of labour, or through the forcing of indigenous rulers into a subordinate tributary feudal status. Consequent upon this, new societies are also constituted through the forced transplantation of populations.

The types of the colonial societies which there can be depend, I have suggested, upon three constitutive and five process variables. The constitutive variables are the type of colonial society in existence prior to imperial penetration, the mode of production and exploitation established by the imperialists and the overall stratification of social groups and categories in the society. The process variables involve: the process of 'liberalization' involved in the transition from forcible exploitation to more normal peaceful capitalist economic forms, the process of political independence, the development of race relations and ethnic relations, the further incorporation of the colonial economy into world capitalism, and the process of political and economic revolution within this system.

First, then, in placing South African society, we should look at its constitution in terms of the three constitutive variables.

The pre-colonial societies which settlers encountered were intermediate in structure and complexity between those which were found amongst small bands and tribes of hunters and those which existed in the complex Asian empires. Thus a powerful chieftainship had developed amongst the Nguni-speaking and Soto/Tswana-speaking tribes and with this a standing army. An intertribal order under Zulu hegemony appeared to be developing as a result of military conflict. At the same time the south-western part of the country was occupied by nomadic bands of hunting and gathering peoples, known to the White settlers as Bushmen and Hottentots and now recognized as San and Khoi-Khoi.

The basic modes of production established by the settlers were: first of all, large farms or latifundia established by trekking White farmers, at the outset for their own subsistence, but later for production for the market; secondly, a small-scale development of plantation agriculture with indentured labour in the sugar areas; thirdly, the development of large-scale mining of diamonds and gold using 'compound' labour; and finally, the development of 'secondary' industry using native labour suffering various degrees of lack of freedom. Characteristic of the mode of production and the mode of exploitation was the 'compound' which, as I have suggested elsewhere,[5] was the central institution of South African society.

The subsequent stratification of colonial society turned on the types of coloured groups which emerged, upon the kinds of secondary colonialists who were present, upon the emergence of a settler world including farmers, workers and urban capitalists, upon missionaries of metropolitan religions, and upon an originally imperial administration. It is in relation to this stratification system that the roles of the principal ethnic groups in South Africa are to be understood.

The Bantu-speaking peoples form the overwhelming majority and are primarily peasants, workers, migrant labourers, or low-level professionals and traders serving their own community. Compared with other societies in Africa the actual numbers who can be called bourgeois or *petit bourgeois* in class terms is infinitesimal and those who do exist form a tiny tip of a separate black pyramid within the society. These Black Bantu-speakers are separated by a rigid caste-like barrier from White society and though the barrier may tilt it is not breached.[6] The archetypal Bantu-speaker is a migrant labourer and it is around his class interest, which unites in one person the interests of peasants and workers, that the whole political culture and organization of the African peoples of South Africa revolves.

The Cape Coloureds are the offspring of mixed unions between Dutch settlers, Khoi-Khoi and imported Black African and Malay slaves. After the early East India Company period in the Cape, they were marginal to the country's main productive institutions though they played a special role in the Cape vineyards, in various skilled and semi-skilled occupations connected with the building trade and eventually in factory work. Like the North American and Caribbean slaves they lost their indigenous language and culture, but helped to creolize Dutch into Afrikaans. They were classified as neither Black nor White, and yet not simply categorized as in, say, Barbados, in terms of a colour/status continuum. They became, in effect, a separate legal estate enjoying fewer rights than the White man, but more than the Black. This separate status of 'Coloured' people makes the total racial classification system of South Africa unique.

The South African Indians include two interrelated groups. On the one hand there are the indentured plantation workers' descendants who could be said to have the same relation to the *Coloured*[7] population as to the descendants of Indian plantation workers in Guyana to the African-descended Black and Coloured populations of that country. On the other there were the so-called 'passenger' Indians who came at their own expense to seize such trading opportunities as the South African colonial system threw up. Historically, the product of these two related immigrations were, on the one hand, a group of secondary colonialists engaging in trade and competing with settler and metropolitan enterprise and, on the other, a stratum of factory workers, privileged, like the Coloureds, in comparison with the Blacks, but underprivileged compared with the Whites. Both before and after the indenture period, cultural and organizational bonds appear to have existed between these two kinds of Indians.

In the plantation societies, it is usual to distinguish between the 'plantocracy' on the one hand and settlers ranging from urban capitalists, through workers and farmers to poor Whites. A similar distinction can be made, although it is sometimes obscured, in South Africa. On the one hand, there were the large-scale capitalists, particularly in the mining industry, who, together with their metropolitan allies, represented colonial capitalism and who exercised a great deal of political power, particularly in the days of Cecil Rhodes when the mines were developing and settler independence in the Transvaal was overthrown. On the other, were the highly privileged and protected workers and farmers, who formed an aristocracy of labour in industry, a large landholding, if inefficient, group of farmers in the countryside, as well as the local capitalists who were able to benefit from the economic take-off provided by the mines. The 'mining plantocracy' lived off cheap unskilled labour, but it resisted the political pressure of 'White settlerdom' as much as it could. It even tried from time to time to move with the times, if only to try to benefit from the untapped skills of the African population. Inevitably what emerged was a struggle in politics within the overall White group between the two interests. The mining industry appeared to win under Smuts in the 1920s but suffered a setback when Smuts joined forces with Hertzog. Its influence was probably cast in favour of liberalization of the race laws in 1946, but almost immediately White settlerdom reasserted itself with the Nationalist victory of 1946. Finally, under the Nationalists, capitalist pressure reasserted itself and the governments of Verwoerd and Vorster partially adapted to capitalism's demands. The outcome, politically, was the resultant of two opposing forces and was bound to be so until African power asserted itself.

The suggestion which is made here is that the most important class distinction was between the 'mining plantocracy' and its allies and the rest of White settlerdom. This involves asserting that many lesser White capitalists threw in their lot with the settler, and, therefore, the farmer and worker interest, and that the White working class had privileges which kept them closer to small and medium capitalists and farmers in their interests, than it did to non-White workers. This, of course, is an over-statement and underplays the class differences between workers, farmers and industrial capitalists. It is also the case that many settler capitalists and, indeed, White workers and farmers supported political initiatives coming from the Chamber of Mines. None the less, I would maintain that an important distinction is to be drawn between large-scale mining and other capitalist interests which are not constrained solely by settler electoral pressure and the settler interest which has to fight against both alien expatriate capital and the rising pressure of the Black population.

All of this is further complicated by the division of White settlerdom into two ethnicities: Afrikaans and English. Such sheer ethnic difference does exist, but it also reflects the class division between the mining plantocracy and the settler interest as such, and the distinction between settler farmer-workers on the one hand and settler capitalists on the other. Generally English is the language of capitalism, and even the attempt to create a specific Afrikaner capitalism has led to Afrikaans firms moving into an English-speaking world and their members speaking English. None the less the political success of Afrikaner Nationalism has meant the survival of the Afrikaans language and, sometimes, its dominance over English, at least in the civil service. Afrikaans as a language has become the focus for settler organization and culture against the cosmopolitan language and culture of the English.

In other colonial situations, missionaries and administrators have formed something of a third force between settlers and natives. They did also in the Cape in the 1830s, and again shortly before Union. But already by 1900 the Cape government represented and was controlled by capitalist rather than imperial forces, and after Union the only third party left was that of a few expatriate churchmen who were readily gaoled or deported by the Nationalist Government.

In fact, in the absence of this third party, the struggle for control of government has been between two groups of settlers implanted by two conquering powers. The nearest parallel is Quebec. But, whereas Quebec as a concentrated French state under an English government could aim at secession, the Afrikaners, having seen their Dutch ancestors displaced by the British and being dispersed geographically could only go for domination. In the long run they succeeded, making the South African polity one which was subject to Afrikaner settler rule.

Turning to the variables which refer to processes of change, we notice that South Africa has, as its dominant institution, the gold mine and that, far from the institution of unfree labour being simply a survival from an earlier mode of production, the South African economy as such has been built around this institution. As Legassick has pointed out, in the specific situation in which economic development occurred the duality of what he calls 'contradictions' which functioned as a means to primitive capitalist accumulation continues into the present and is functional for the purposes of contemporary capitalism. Moreover, although secondary industry has now outstripped the mines in the contribution it makes to the economy, its growth has been in large measure dependent on the mines and its style of labour exploitation, while not as closely regulated as that of the compound, is none the less marked by strong extra-economic coercion. Only recently has trade-unionism among industrial workers made much headway and then partially as a form of social control of workers by employers and the government.[8] On the question of liberalization, which is usually represented by labour emancipation and land reform in colonial situations, one cannot but note the resistance of South Africa's labour system to these processes. True, slaves were emancipated and land tenure in the African areas was somewhat individualized. True, also, there are now some firms which could operate and would prefer to operate with free labour and free trade unions. But overall, as will be pointed out below, the compound, the reserve, and the native location are still the essential institutions of the South African system of labour exploitation. From the point of view of profitability too, they are efficient and attract capital. Apartheid, white domination and forced labour all pay dividends.

The process of political independence is a matter to which we have already made implicit reference in discussing the role of administrators and missionaries in the stratification system. In the case of South Africa, two British provinces had already moved towards settler government by the time of Union, and the Union itself was formed by coming to terms with two Boer republics which had established themselves when trekking farmers, moving beyond the range of any central or metropolitan government, had conquered the native peoples and established their own racial supremacy. The completion of the process of independence saw the transfer of virtually complete sovereignty to the settlers as such and within the settler group to the politics, culture and traditions of the Afrikaans section. In government, however, it was necessary for the Afrikaner settlers either to overthrow or to come to terms with colonial capitalism. They did come to terms, though this was a two-way transaction in which colonial and settler capitalism had to modify their ways to fit in with an Afrikaner government.

The race relations situation which emerged had a twofold origin which had been negotiated between 1886 and 1910. On the one hand the principle of 'no equality in church or State', which had been the maxim in terms of which the Transvaal was governed, remained unchallenged in the Transvaal and Orange Free State, while the Cape and Natal permitted integration or assimilation only to a token African, Coloured and Indian élite. On the other hand, after an initial period in which there was a free market in labour, and with Blacks and Whites competing, Black wages rose, a dual labour market was established in the mines with highly protected and well-paid White labour in skilled work and near-slave labour drawn from the reserves doing the unskilled jobs. Both of these systems were rationalized in terms of racial beliefs at systematic level in terms of theology, but at a much more unsystematic level in the belief systems of the White population. On the one hand God was believed not to wish the Blacks to be like White men, since they had their own destiny. On the other hand 'everyone knew' that Africans could not draw a straight line, were idle, irresponsible, kleptomaniac and so on. Moreover, Myrdal's cumulative principle also operated. Being discriminated against, Blacks were diseased and ignorant, and being diseased and ignorant, it seemed that discrimination against them was justified. Miscegenation became the unspeakable sin, the sin against the Holy Ghost, and South Africa's Whites came to erect colour bars more unscalable than any previously known to man.

No capitalist society is static and as Marx saw, all capitalist societies were bound to generate class conflict between wage-workers and their employers.

In this case, however, there were two distinct groups of wage-workers, and a 'social formation' which generated 'class' differences through several interlocking modes of production and a political system in dominance. The question, however, was, whether the revolution which began to take shape was one which was explicable in Marxist terms or whether a far more comprehensive theory of revolutionary dynamics was needed. In fact, African leadership moved from élite accommodation to an attempt at a class alliance and, alternatively to the notion of Black revolution. The South African Communist Party tried to rationalize this in terms of a theory of 'internal colonialism', but the Black, Coloured and Indian leadership divided between Marxist (principally Moscow-oriented) and nationalist theories. Change of a revolutionary sort was more and more in the offing by 1978, but it was still unclear as to whether this would be led by Marxists aiming at the overthrow of capitalism, Marxists envisaging a temporary accommodation with capitalism, anti-capitalist or pro-capitalist Black Nationalists, or populist leaders able to act decisively because they had been able, at a political price, to buy the military hardware or economic influence necessary for effective political action.

We are thus able to place South African society, speculatively at least, in terms of a typology of colonial societies. Alternatively we may look at it as one of the sub-species of settler societies, or in terms of the specificity of its mode of production.

Settler societies are those societies in which metropolitan settlers engaged in farming, in colonially situated capitalist enterprises, or in free and usually unionized wage-labour, form a large part of the population and have been sufficiently strong to establish that political independence will mean *their* hegemony in the new independent society. Apart from South Africa, the other societies in which such settler dominance has been evident are Chile, Argentina, Uruguay, Brazil, Mexico, the United States, Canada, Australia, New Zealand, Algeria and the British territories of East and Central Africa. South Africa, however, is unique amongst these as can be seen from reviewing the other cases.

In the Spanish South American territories mentioned, as in Australia and New Zealand, what were established from the first were New Spains and New Englands. Although there were in all cases indigenous native minorities, the main structures of the new societies rested upon purely settler enterprises with the indigenous people being pushed back into territorial reserves. In Mexico the new society was less of a settler society and involved much greater merging of Spanish settlers and Amerindians, while Brazil involved the merging of the Portuguese and the African populations. In the United States, again one had an original plantocracy and settler capitalism together with imported African slaves, later poorer European settlers, Spanish-speaking Latin Americans, immigrants and the indigenous populations. In the United States and in Brazil an original colonial economy based on plantations was superseded by an urban-based settler one with the main labour force being provided by an ever-filling melting pot of new poor European immigrants, so that the indigenous population was pushed back into reserves and the descendants of the slaves into urban ghettos and slums.

Canada provides an example of another society which exploits the labour of poor European immigrants, which has a significant problem of indigenous reserves, but no significant slave-descended population. New Zealand is a society of settlers and a small indigenous group, benefiting from peculiarly favourable resources and markets and not dependent upon the recruitment of large masses of cheap labour. Australia, of recent years, has moved toward the Canadian type with the immigration of large numbers of 'new Australians' from Europe. Finally the North, East and Central African territories all present us with cases in which the settler bid for power failed and, at most, settler interests have been able to find protection only through alliance with new élites.

Against this background the uniqueness of the South African case is easy to see. This is one territory in which there was a settler minority large enough to take political power *and* in which the main source of labour was found within the colonial territory itself—amongst the indigenous people.

The mode of production in South Africa is one in which capitalism is able, if one may put it that way, to capitalize upon an unfree labour supply. The essential institutions of this system are, as I have already indicated, the mining labour compound, the rural reserve and the urban 'location'.

Compound labour is the central institution for the organization and exploitation of labour in South Africa. The Rhodesian variant of this basic social form has been excellently described in Charles van Onselen's study *Chibaro* and it is to be hoped that in the future similar studies of the main South African form will be made. What can be said here is that the compound provides a form of labour exploitation, which from an employer's point of view has all of the advantages and none of the disadvantages of slavery and indentured labour. The worker is kept under something approaching prison conditions in a total institution, having neither the benefits of trade unions, nor the protection of family life. On the other hand, unlike the plantation owner, the employer has no obligation to care for him beyond the period of his nine-month labour contract. As the Marxists put it, the cost of the reproduction of labour does not fall on the employer.

The essential support for this system of labour is, of course, the rural native reserve, which is not so much an area reserved for native agriculture as a place where a reserve army of labour is kept. Forms of taxation and landholding are imposed on the reserve which do sufficient to provide a homeland, and guarantee the reproduction of the labour force, but at the same time make it essential that able-bodied males should supplement their income by wage-earning. It need hardly be pointed out that the sufficiency of subsistence which it is necessary for the reserves to provide is compatible with a fairly low life-expectancy for the inhabitants.

The stick of harsh economic conditions and the carrot of what may appear as attractive money incomes, however, are by no means sufficient to ensure a continuing labour supply for the mines from the reserves, even with the aid of special recruiting companies. Consequently it has been necessary to turn to surrounding territories such as Botswana, Lesotho, Swaziland and Mozambique as well as to the British territories in Central Africa to supplement the supply. The 'independence' of these territories *vis-à-vis* South Africa has in no way prevented their acting as additional 'reserves' for the mines. It is not surprising, therefore, that the South African Government has now seen fit to put its own native reserves on an equal footing with surrounding territories. Political independence and economic dependency is the future which South Africa envisages alike for the Transkei, Kwazulu, Botswana and Mozambique. The question, however, is now whether, with the existence of guerrilla forces on her border, South Africa can continue to treat her neighbours in this way. At this moment, the question is whether genuine economic development in Mozambique and Botswana can break the yoke of dependency. If they can, the crucial supporting institutions of the mining industry will be broken.

The third essential institution of South African society, however, has still to be discussed. This is the native location in the towns and cities. In principle one would be inclined to suggest that the growth in factory labour outside of the migrant compound system would lead to the emergence of a free Black working class, permanently settled with their wives and children. Moreover, such a working class without the support of the reserves would be bound in the long run to fight for higher wages. The location, however, ensures that the circumstances of urban residence are such that no such working class can emerge. The condition of tolerating migration to the towns is that the workers should not become organized in their own self-defence. If they do it is easy enough for the government to get rid of them. The whole location system with its special police and its special system of administration and finance (through the beer-halls) combines with the attempt to attach urban Africans to their homelands to ensure that no permanent African proletariat emerges.

We have looked at South Africa as a type of colonial society, as a type of settler society, and a society with a particular pattern of social relations of production. In each case we are brought back to a recognition that the understanding of the structure and dynamics of such a society can only be understood in terms of a class analysis. Oddly enough, however, it is just this kind of class analysis that contemporary Marxism in its dominant form does not provide.

Certainly I would agree with the point made, not only by Marxists as well as by non-Marxists like Adam, that there is no conflict of principle between the South African polity and the economy. The labour system which is permitted by the apartheid system is highly efficient from a capitalist point of view. The sociological function of the ideology and practice of apartheid is not to exclude Blacks entirely from the White areas but to have them there on such terms as will allow for the maximization of their exploitation.

The kind of Marxism to which I am sympathetic is one which does not merely stop at showing that certain imperatives follow from the laws of capitalist development, but rather one which shows how various collective actors (classes) emerge and act in history. What writers like Legassick call class analysis, on the other hand, is merely an analysis which rejects as unsatisfactory or even unreal, any change which does not lead to the overthrow of the capitalist system, and, since it is believed organized labour must bring about this change, all group formation and action which is not led by the unionized settler workers tends to be dismissed as no change at all.

In fact, very great changes are likely to occur in South Africa over the next fifty years for several obvious and interconnected reasons. These include (a) the fact that South Africa has an economic system highly dependent upon and capable of being wrecked by the United States and Europe; (b) the fact that South Africa is even more important to the West strategically than it is economically or ideologically; and (c) the fact that with the collapse of Rhodesian and Portuguese power, guerrillas bearing Soviet arms and able to call on Cuban advisers are already at the gates. African leaders therefore have the chance to set their own objectives for the medium-term future. They have many potential allies in their fight against White supremacy. They may aim at overthrowing the labour system and at modernizing colonial capitalism. Finally they may be able to consider overthrowing capitalism itself.

Rightly or wrongly the first priority for most African leaders is the overthrow of White supremacy and White government. But in so far as they do this their critics suggest two reasons why this is insufficient. Marxists would say that it makes no difference who governs if the mode of production and the social relations of production remain the same, while pluralists of M. G. Smith's type would envisage anarchy.

My reply to the Marxists would be that they are curiously blinkered if they cannot see the difference in sociological and political terms between capitalism operating under conditions of White supremacy and a non-racial capitalism. If, as Legassick and Innes admit, the per capita income of Africans in 1974/75 was only 9.3 per cent of that of Whites, then it must make a difference to the social structure if Africans were able to enter the better-paid jobs. There would then be class divisions of a new kind amongst the Blacks and the Whites. There really would be an African bourgeoisie and an African aristocracy of labour to a degree which is nowhere evident under the present system. And there would be poor Whitism on a scale which Afrikaners have always feared but never envisaged as likely. It might be possible, under such circumstances, to envisage class struggle as superseding race conflict and it is hard, therefore, to see why Marxists should not welcome it.

But suppose that African nationalism remained strong and that the new African government had to contend with the other segments and ethnic classes. Suppose too that it came to some kind of accommodation with foreign capitalism akin to that reached by the United National Independence Party in Zambia. What kind of political and cultural hegemony would this African ruling group exercise?

The main African political theorists who have suggested answers to these questions are Fanon and Cabral. Fanon, from experience, has little truck with the idea of an international- and European-led Marxist revolution. As Fanon's teacher Aimee Casaire once said: 'The main aim of the people of Martinique is not the liberation of the French proletariat.' The colonial peoples must liberate themselves through a national revolution. It is only once that revolution has been accomplished that class struggle begins and then opposes the new native bourgeoisie, not so much because it is bourgeois but because it is neo-colonial and allied with imperial economic interests. The new society must be one which, while it is socialist is also national and anti-colonialist and anti-imperialist. The question of minority rights then has to be settled under the hegemony of the liberated majority.

The Fanonist view thus places a high value on the liberated national culture. Indeed, it is of the essence of Fanonism that it sees the colonial period as one in which men have been trained to see themselves as inferior and every suggestion that the pre-colonial culture is different has to be critically examined. Applied in the South African case this would mean that priority would be given to a restoration and development of African culture and institutions. Under this dispensation, moreover, each minority culture would have to be examined and judged according to the degree to which it was tainted by colonialism.

Necessarily the position of the White man in this society would be drastically changed. Indeed it would be expected that a majority would leave.

Those who remained would do so on the understanding that their rewards would be in proportion to their contribution. In the case of technical experts such rewards might be considerable, but the expertise would itself have to cease being a matter of privilege and the expert would soon have to face new competition. Equally the Asian settler population would be subject to scrutiny. Where some of its members enjoyed special privileges in trade they would lose them, and they too might find it unrewarding to live in South Africa. But some traders would remain as would the majority of the Indian population, who are actually industrial workers. Sharing something of the Black man's experience of exploitation, some Indians would no doubt stay and would be encouraged to reconstitute and develop their own ethnic identity.

Cape Coloured people would present a very special problem in this situation. Like the Indians and the Whites, they would lose their special privileges, although they would be upgraded *vis-à-vis* the Whites. But Coloureds suffer a disability which no other group suffers so completely. They have lost their language and their culture and they clearly face problems of identity and self-esteem. The cultural programme of Fanonism is peculiarly apposite to them because they above all have been victims of colonialism in South Africa in the same way as the people of Fanon's native Martinique. They do not merely have to return to their cultural origins. They have to create a new culture. Probably participating in the new national one would not answer their problem, for this would still mean dancing to someone else's tune.

The Black majority would not itself suffer the problems of the Coloureds in the same degree. Bantu languages, culture and social organization have survived and would take on a new lease of life that they never could in the White-sponsored Bantustans. But it remains open to question whether English as a national language, Christianity as a religion, or the existing pattern of education would survive. Immediately it certainly would, for there are limits to the extent to which the institutions of any one Bantu nation could meet this need. What is likely, however, is a gradual replacement of aspects of the inherited traditions by elements of African culture which colonialism repressed.

Of course it should be remembered that what we are talking about are political ideals only and that political reality would be shaped by power struggles and interests as much or more than it would by such ideals. But it is interesting to notice that the ideals mentioned here are specifically rejected in the social philosophy of Cabral which guides post-liberation cultural policy in neighbouring Mozambique.

According to the philosophy of Cabral, which is a form of African Leninism, the culture of pre-colonial times is likely to be nationalist, racist and regressive. This culture has to be developed in a progressive way by those sections of the *petite bourgeoisie* who have not been corrupted either by colonialism or regressive nationalism. Moreover, this progressive leadership is international in outlook and oriented to the international socialist revolution. Black hegemony and the cultivation of a specific Black Consciousness are to be rejected. They are seen as dangerous because they represent a possible guise for the restoration of the old bourgeois pattern of social relations.[9]

Of course the validity or relevance of these two doctrines depends in part on what happens to capitalism. So far we have been discussing political abstractions only. In fact it is likely that the issues posed theoretically above will be posed in history either by a new Black capitalist or pro-capitalist élite, or by Black anti-capitalist revolutionaries. The strength of Fanonism lies in the fact that it goes on having dealt with the issues of national and cultural liberation to talk about class struggle against a compromised Black capitalist élite.

Prima facie the alternative doctrine, that of Cabral, would appear to be socialist from the outset. But in rejecting national culture and consciousness and insisting with Lenin that a socialist consciousness should come to the people from outside, it makes the forces of revolution themselves subject to outside and possibly to a new colonialist control. Surely there is a problem here in that those who purport to lead the revolution may well come to claim the right to control its fruits.

One thing which should be clear, however, is this: those who manage the capitalist system will still wish to survive and will not give up and leave because a Black national political revolution has occurred. The question is, how could they accommodate themselves to the new regime.

Clearly the first resort will be to offer rewards to a governing élite and to subvert the idea of a really popular national government, but sooner or later such tactics will not work. Those who have helped to make the early revolution (of whom the children of Soweto are perhaps the early forerunners) will not let the revolution be betrayed in this way. The people will demand and fight for social and economic as well as political change and at this point industries such as mining will have to address themselves to the problem of the cheap labour system.

I fully expect that the mines and other industries will be found to have some leeway in this matter. Cheap labour is a bad habit which will not be abandoned unless political circumstances dry up the supply. But when this happens wages will be increased *for a smaller number of workers*. Cheap labour will be abolished at the cost of increasing unemployment. To some extent this is happening already, long before liberation. It will be the natural response of the system to the circumstances which liberation creates.

In the long run, then, it seems unlikely that the older types of colonial capitalism will survive the national revolution and it may prove to be the case that newer types of capitalism which flourish on cheap labour now would not be competitive if they ceased to do so. But if in the long run many men die and change becomes inevitable, in the short run many compromises may be possible. That is to say, if a transition to some sort of post-colonial and post-capitalist society is inevitable in the long run the substance of immediate post-liberation history will consist of these compromises and adjustments.

One should not, however, suggest that the future of South Africa will be either with Black nationalism or with socialism. Both items are on the agenda. What South African history will be about will be the ending of capitalist exploitation in its peculiar colonial form. The task of the sociologist is to envisage the kinds of structural change which revolution and liberation will bring, both in terms of the restructuring of industry and the economy and in terms of a new cultural and political dispensation.

It might be objected that the whole of the last part of this chapter is fundamentally idealist and that actual history will be marked by brutal conflicts of interest. The assumption, here, however, is that in the long run such solutions, as for instance the massive disemployment of the population in order to solve the problem of recalcitrant cheap labour, will not work, and that at some point the economic and political restructuring of South African society must begin.

Notes

1. I will not attempt to review here the whole literature which analyses South African society from these polarized perspectives and from many intermediate points. As I pointed out in a review article on 'The Sociology of South Africa' however, there have been few strictly sociological studies of the whole South African social system. One which emphasizes and elucidates the pluralist as well as the class aspect of social differentiation is Pierre Van den Berghe's *South Africa: A Study of Conflict,* while Heribert Adam's *Modernizing Racial Domination* shows that the impact of the polity and the Nationalist Party has not simply been to retard capitalist development, but in its modern form under Verwoerd and Vorster to make racial domination and capitalist development compatible with one another. Three articles by Harold Wolpe, 'Industrialization and Race in South Africa', in Zubaida (ed.), *Race and Racialism;* 'Capitalism and Cheap Labour Power in South Africa: From Segregation to Apartheid', *Economy and Society,* Vol. I No. 4, and 'White Working class in South African', *Economy and Society,* Vol. V, No. 5, represent formulations of the problem by a White Marxist sociologist, and finally my own 'The Plural Society—the South African Case' *Race,* Vol. XII, No. 4, shows how the pluralist perspective should be revised in terms of class analysis.

    Apart from the sociological debate, there has been a debate amongst Marxists about the specificity of class struggle in South Africa. A good example of this is provided in Slovo's 'South Africa—No Middle Road' in Davidson, Slovo and Wilkinson's *Southern Africa. The New Politics of Revolution.* This debate turns, as did an earlier debate amongst American Communists, on whether alongside its modern capitalist economy, South Africa still contained an internal colony and what the relationship was between the struggle against colonialism and the class struggle within and against capitalism.

    Finally, a related debate has broken out amongst historians following the publication of the second volume of *Oxford History of South Africa.* Here a number of Marxist historians have joined issue with the liberal tradition in South African historiography, which they see as explaining South African racism as an archaic survival of the frontier, while they themselves maintain that it is functional to, if not actually the product of the capitalist mode of production. The argument takes many forms and covers many aspects of social history and the so-called neo-Marxists are far from being a single monolithic group. The literature on both sides of this debate has been listed in Harrison M. Wright's *The Burden of the Present: Liberal-Radical Controversy over Southern African History.* The writings of M. Legassick listed in that book are of especial importance to sociologists as is the specific study of the White gold-miner's *Class, Race and Gold,* by Frederick Johnstone. Legassick has moved towards giving a generalized Marxist account of the dynamics of South African society especially in his article 'South Africa, Capital Accumulation and Violence', *Economy and Society,* Vol. III, 1974.

2. To refer to Smith's perceptive understanding of the importance of the political structure of colonial society here is by no means to accept his 'culturalist' account of pluralism. What we can surely accept is that in a plural colonial society the state is a structure in dominance in the Althusserian sense and that this dominance may continue in the post-colonial period, even though the inhabitants of the political structure have changed.
3. Most explicitly in my essay 'New Nations and Ethnic Minorities: Comparative and Theoretical Questions', *Race and Class in Post-Colonial Society* (produced for Unesco) and in more general terms in my book *Race Relations in Sociological Theory*.
4. Whether history will eventually show that there are communist colonial forms is a question which I leave open at this stage. I think that there may be, but that their structures will be significantly different from those arising from capitalist exploitation.
5. 'The Compound, the Reserve and the Location—The Essential Institutions of South African Labour Exploitation', *South African Labour Bulletin,* Vol. I, No. 4, April 1971. See also in the same journal 'The Plural Society, the South African Case'.
6. Lloyd Warner's concept is suggested here, but it needs to be pointed out that if the term 'caste' is used it is used only to emphasize the unbreakability of the barrier, not to imply other parallels with the Indian caste system. (See his 'American Class and Caste' *American Journal of Sociology,* vol. XLII, 1936.)
7. Not, it should be noted, the same relation to the African population. The difference between South Africa and Guyana is that the indigenous population of South Africa remained demographically and, in a sense, politically strong.
8. See Legassick, 'South Africa, Capital Accumulation and Violence', op. cit, and also M. Legassick and D. Innes, 'Capital Restructuring and Apartheid: A Critique of Constructive Engagement', *African Affairs,* Vol. 76, No. 305, 1977, pp. 437-87.
9. This reflection on the relative meanings and significance of Fanon and Cabral's writing is prompted by discussions which I had with Frelimo intellectuals and cultural advisers during a visit to Mozambique in 1976.

Bibliography

ADAM, Heribert. *Modernizing Racial Domination: The Dynamics of South African Politics.* Berkeley, University of California Press, 1971.

CABRAL, Amilcar. *The Role of Culture in the Struggle for Independence.* Paper presented to the Unesco Meeting of Experts on the Concept of Race, Identity and Dignity, Paris 3-7 July 1972.

DAVIDSON, B.; SLOVO, J.; WILKINSON A. *Southern Africa: The New Politics of Revolution.* Harmondsworth, Penguin Books, 1976.

FANON, Franz. *Black Skin, White Masks,* London, Paladin, 1970.

——. *A Dying Colonialism.* Harmondsworth, Pelican, 1970.

——. *Towards the African Revolution.* Harmondsworth, Penguin, 1970.

——. *The Wretched of the Earth.* London, McGibbon & Kee, 1965.

JOHNSTONE, Frederick. *Class, Race and Gold.* London, Routledge & Kegan Paul, 1976.

LEGASSICK, Martin. South Africa: Capital Accumulation and Violence, *Economy and Society,* Vol. III, 1974.

LEGASSICK, Martin; INNES, Duncan. Capital Restructuring and Apartheid: A Critique of Constructive Engagement, *African Affairs,* Vol. 76, No. 305, 1977.

REX, John. The Compound, the Reserve and the Location: The Essential Institutions of South African Labour Exploitation. *South African Labour Bulletin,* Vol. 1, No. 4, April 1971.

——. New Nations and Ethnic Minorities: Comparative and Theoretical Questions. *Race and Class in Post-Colonial Society,* Paris, Unesco, 1978.

——. The Plural Society: The South African Case. *Race,* Vol. XII, No. 4, 1971.

———. *Race Relations in Sociological Theory*. Weidenfeld & Nicolson, 1970.
———. The Sociology of South Africa. *Journal of South African Studies,* Vol. 1, No. 2, April 1975.
SLOVO, Joe. South Africa No Middle Road. In: B. Davidson, J. Slovo and A. Wilkinson (eds.), *Southern Africa: The New Politics of Revolution.* Harmondsworth, Penguin, 1976.
SMITH, M. G. *The Plural Society in the British West Indies*. Berkeley, University of California Press, 1965.
UNESCO. *Race and Class in Post-Colonial Society*. Paris, Unesco. 1978.
VAN DEN BERGHE, Pierre. *South Africa: A Study of Conflict*. Berkeley, University of California Press, 1967.
VAN ONSELEN. *Chibaro, African Mine Labour in Rhodesia 1900-1933*. London, Pluto Press, 1976.
WARNER, W. Lloyd. American Class and Caste. *American Journal of Sociology,* Vol. XLII, 1936.
WILSON, Monica; THOMPSON, Leonard (eds.). *The Oxford History of South Africa*. London. Vol. 1, 1969, Vol. 2, 1971, London.
WRIGHT, Harrison M. *The Burden of the Present: Liberal-Radical Controversy over Southern African History*. London, Rex Collings, 1977.
WOLPE, Harold. Capitalism and Cheap Labour Power in South Africa: From Segregation to Apartheid. *Economy and Society*. Vol. 1, No 4, 1972.
———. Industrialization and Race in South Africa. In: Sami Zubaida (ed.), *Race and Racialism*. London, Tavistock, 1970.
———. The White Working Class in South Africa. *Economy and Society,* Vol. 5, 1976.
ZUBAIDA, Sami (ed.). *Race and Racialism*. London, Tavistock, 1970.

[I. 52] SS. 80/D. 135/A